IMAGES
of America

JAMESTOWN AND WESTERN TUOLUMNE COUNTY

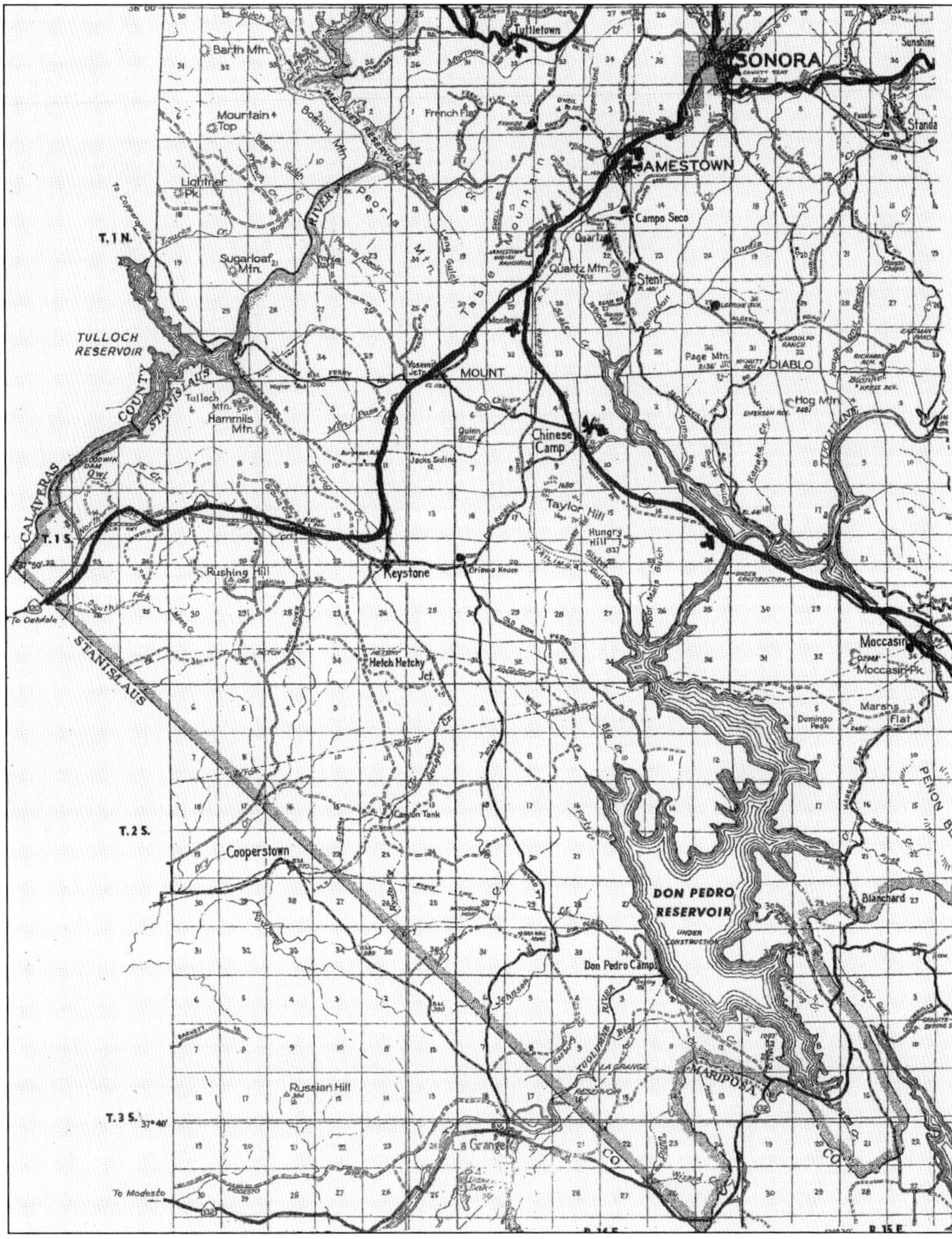

This 1930s map shows the location of Jamestown and the many camps and communities of western Tuolumne County, many of which have passed from the scene. (Courtesy Harry Freese.)

On the Cover: A Jamestown Fourth of July parade makes its way down Main Street. (Courtesy Donn Blount.)

IMAGES
of America

JAMESTOWN AND WESTERN TUOLUMNE COUNTY

Judith Marvin and Terry Brejla

ARCADIA
PUBLISHING

ISBN 978-0-7385-8171-2

Published by Arcadia Publishing
Charleston, South Carolina

Printed in the United States of America

Library of Congress Control Number: 2010934149

For all general information, please contact Arcadia Publishing:
Telephone 843-853-2070
Fax 843-853-0044
E-mail sales@arcadiapublishing.com
For customer service and orders:
Toll-Free 1-888-313-2665

Visit us on the Internet at www.arcadiapublishing.com

Contents

Acknowledgments

This volume was made possible by several individuals who generously provided information or loaned the photographs and images that appear here, many of which have never before been published. They include Paul Barendregt, Donn Blount, Julia Costello, county historian Carlo De Ferrari, Lori East, Charla Francis, Ron Gianelli, Joan Gorsuch, Lewis "Butch" Marliani, Sharon Marovich, Wally Motloch, Thomas Sayer, Daniel and Georgia Vuyovich, Scott Weber, Stephen Willey, Gary Wilson, and Jim Yeisley.

Of great assistance were the previously compiled *Historic Resources Inventories of Jamestown*, which provided contextual histories of Jamestown as well as information on individual properties, and the *Contextual History of Tuolumne County* (Shelly Davis-King and Judith Marvin). The Far Western Anthropological Research Group, Inc., provided its research on prehistoric peoples and the Me-Wuk. In addition, the authors are indebted to those early diarists and journalists who wrote so descriptively on their experiences in Jamestown, Tuolumne County, and the Mother Lode, including *3 Years in California* (J. D. Borthwick); *William Perkins' Journal of Life at Sonora, 1849–1852*; *Hutchings' California Magazine* (James Mason Hutchings 1856–1861); *We Were 49ers! Chilean Accounts of the California Gold Rush* (Edwin A. Beilharz and Carlos U. Lopez); *Miners & Business Men's Directory* (John Heckendorn and W. A. Wilson); *Bright Gem of the Western Seas, California 1846–1852* (James H. Carson); *Adventures of Charles L. Scott, Esq.* (Kathy McCoy, editor); *The Gold Rush Diary of Ramón Gil Navarro* (Ramón Gil Navarro); and the *Annals of Tuolumne County* (Thomas Robertson Stoddart; Carlo M. De Ferrari, editor).

More recent publications provided invaluable information on specific aspects of history: *Gold Districts of California* (William B. Clark); *Sierra Railway* (Dorothy Newell Dean); *California Gold Camps* (Erwin and Elisabeth Gudde); *The Saga of Old Tuolumne* (Edna Bryan Buckbee); *Tuolumne County, California* (Progressive Association); *Tuolumne County, California* (*Union Democrat*); *Mother Lode Album* (Otheto Weston); *Wet Plates and Dry Gulches* (Gilbert L. Campbell); *Growing Up in Jamestown* and *Jamestown as I Remember It* (Doris Fletcher Mills); *The Greening of Paradise Valley* (Dwight H. Barnes); *Early Day Tuolumne County Cattlemen* (Otis Rosasco); *Hotel Willow* (Sally Hamilton); various editions of *Chispa*, the quarterly bulletins of the Tuolumne County Historical Society; and the Official Records of Tuolumne County in the offices of the Tuolumne County Recorder, Surveyor, and Carlo M. De Ferrari Archive.

INTRODUCTION

Located about 4 miles southwest of Sonora, Jamestown was one of the earliest important mining communities along the east side of Table Mountain. Situated in western Tuolumne County, on State Routes 49 and 108, it straddles Wood's Creek, which has its headwaters above Sawmill Flat near Columbia and is fed by Sonora, Curtis, and Sullivan Creeks. Wood's Creek then flows into the Tuolumne River at the historical site of Jacksonville, now beneath the waters of New Don Pedro Reservoir.

For the purposes of this publication, Western Tuolumne County is defined as bounded on the north by Jamestown and Rawhide, west by the Stanislaus River, south by the Stanislaus County line, and east by the Tuolumne River. Located in between were numerous Native American villages, placer mining camps, hard rock mining communities, and the outlying farms and ranches of the agriculturalists. The majority of these sites have been obliterated by more recent mining activity, inundated with the waters of dam and reservoir projects, or simply lost to the vicissitudes of time and weather. They remain, however, in the collective memory of a few; on historical maps; in the diaries and reminiscences of those early-day prospectors, miners, and settlers; and as places that once mattered.

Geographically, western Tuolumne County is dominated by Table Mountain, where molten lava flowed down the ancient Tertiary rivers long before the uplift of the Sierra Nevada. When the Sierra was uplifted, the new rivers turned westward, slicing into the ancient riverbeds, exposing them when the softer sedimentary beds on either side were eroded away, and leaving behind the long prominent flat-topped ridges of volcanic debris to the west and south of Jamestown.

The history of Jamestown is like that of many other such Gold Rush–era communities in the California foothills: first occupied by Native Americans, then traversed by explorers and trappers, settled by Euro-American placer miners during the Gold Rush, later becoming a commercial and trading center, expanded during the 1880s to early 1900s hard rock mining boom, found new prosperity based upon the construction of the railroad and as the hub of railroad transportation and its associated industries in the late 1890s, slumbered during the World War I era, boomed again with the reopening of the hard rock mines in the 1930s, only to be shut down again in World War II. Since that time, a brief resurgence in mining at the Sonora Mine (Jamestown) in the late 1980s and early 1990s provided some steady income, but has since shut down.

The long and important history of Native American use of the land is represented by the group most closely associated with Jamestown, the Me-Wuk, and as elsewhere in California, diseases spread by the newcomers rapidly decimated the indigenous population, beginning with the smallpox epidemic of 1837, so that only a remnant few were left to greet the newcomers. The first Euro-Americans in Jamestown bought gold dust from these natives, trading beads, raisins, and other commodities in equal weight, and became quite rich as a result. The descendants of those Me-Wuk reside here today, working in a variety of occupations and living throughout the county, including at Chicken Ranch Rancheria near Jamestown.

Shortly after gold was discovered on the American River in January 1848, prospectors and miners made their way to the Stanislaus and Tuolumne Rivers, and their tributaries, in search of the precious metal. Initial mining activity and settlement was centered around what came to be known as the Jamestown Mining District, consisting of that portion of the Mother Lode belt that extends from French Flat southeast through Rawhide, Jamestown, Quartz Mountain, and the town of Stent to the vicinity of the Belcher Mine, a distance of about 8 miles.

Placer gold was first found in the rivers, streams, and drainages, with the mining laws of the Jamestown District enacted in November 1853, stating, "Each miner shall be entitled to one claim of 100 square feet, and no more." The laws went on to state that it was unlawful for "anyone to dig within 12 feet of any building, or in any way, to hinder or obstruct the entrance to said buildings." Interestingly, the community had already become more important than the prospectors and miners. The placers at Jamestown ultimately yielded $3 million, while those at Campo Seco yielded $5.5 million. The total value of the output of gold was estimated at more than $30 million in 1970, with placer gold producing $3.5 million.

The day of the individual miner was over by the mid-1850s, but it was not long before the indefatigable prospectors found their way upstream to the sources of the gold in the auriferous gravels of the Tertiary rivers beneath Table Mountain and in the rich Mother Lode vein. The hard rock mines at Rawhide, Jamestown, Quartz Mountain, and other locations kept the area busy from the 1880s through World War I, and again in the 1930s.

Jamestown prospered not only as a center of mining, but also of trading and transportation. Located equally between the placer mining camps on the Stanislaus and Tuolumne Rivers, it became a center of trade for those small settlements without the population or economy to develop a commercial center. The coming of the railroad in 1897 solidified its position as the transportation center of Tuolumne County, a position it maintained until overtaken by the advent of the automobile. Its economic basis today is centered by tourism, especially Railtown 1897 State Historic Park, and its associated hotels, restaurants, and service industries, as well as residential development.

One

IN THE BEGINNING

Long before Euro-Americans arrived in the area, the land that is now southwest Tuolumne County had been occupied by succeeding waves of Native Americans over thousands of years. Little is known of those early peoples, except through archaeological evidence, which reveals a pattern of seasonal movement, with fall and winter villages below the snow line in the oak-gray pine woodland and summer camps in the higher conifer forests. This pattern continued through the ages, with the acorn becoming the dominant food source by about 600 years ago; clear village sites remain evident, often including house depressions and other structural remains, as well as special-use localities consisting of bedrock milling features.

The ancestors of the Me-Wuk (also spelled Miwok), who continue to reside in Tuolumne County, lived in the area at the time of the Gold Rush. They traditionally occupied a large portion of the central Sierra Nevada, the adjacent foothills, and part of the Central Valley. Linguistic studies suggest that the ancestral Me-Wuk arrived in the Sierran foothills and mountains about 800 years ago.

Regardless of when the Me-Wuk arrived in Tuolumne County, by the time of the Gold Rush they were a well-established society of hunters, fishermen, and plant-food gatherers, consuming all manner of foodstuffs: antelope, elk, rabbit, salmon, waterfowl, deer, quail, blue and live oak acorns, and gray pine nuts. The archaeological record contains remnants of a rich material culture, with flaked stone hunting and butchering tools; plant processing implements; cooking, eating, and storage vessels; and beads and ornaments of shell, animal bone, and stone. Other items made of basketry, cordage, or wood have not survived.

The old Me-Wuk villages were clustered around the Stanislaus and Tuolumne Rivers, and their streams and drainages, with the first large-scale contact between native people and outsiders occurring when Spanish explorers and missionaries arrived looking for new converts. Many Me-Wuk people wound up at Mission San José, while those still living in their traditional territory were overrun by gold seekers and settlers who fenced them off their hunting grounds and limited their access to other resources.

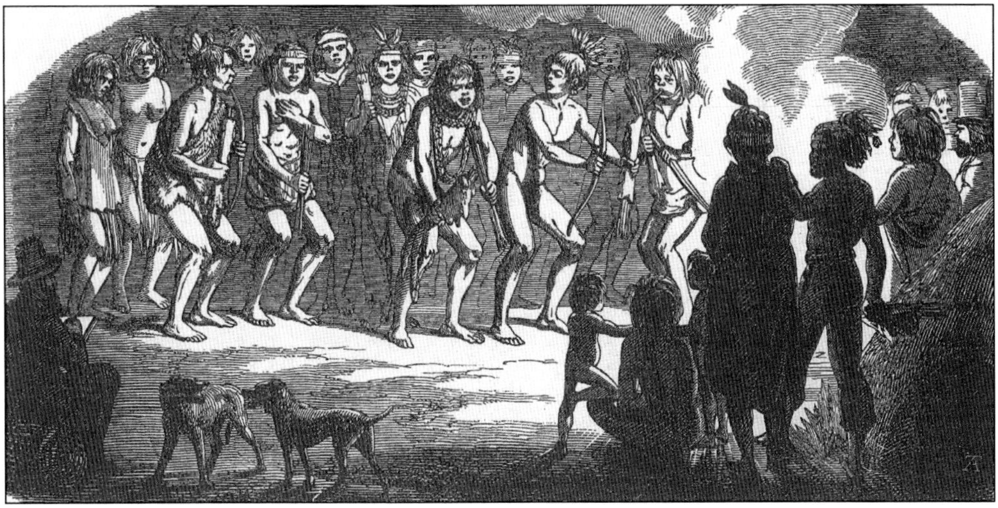

Dances played an important role in Me-Wuk rituals, which were held in a large, semi-subterranean assembly and dance house. In the charge of an official fire tender, the dance house was used for social and ceremonial gatherings, where gambling and dancing were conducted. Around 40 or 50 feet in diameter, it had a fire in the center, smoke hole in the roof, and foot drum for music. (*Hutchings' California Magazine*.)

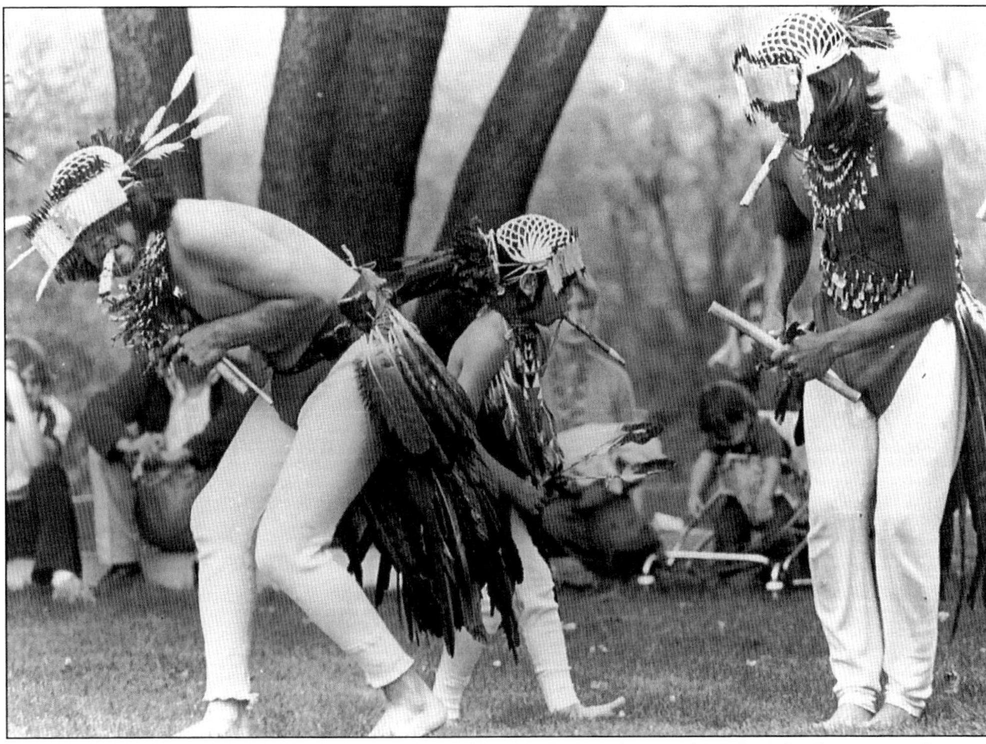

Today the Me-Wuk in Tuolumne County work to preserve their cultural and religious traditions. They have settled at the Tuolumne Rancheria and the Chicken Ranch Rancheria near Jamestown. Here Frank La Pena leads a dance group dressed in traditional headbands of flicker feathers, with turkey-feather skirts, dance plumes, elderberry clapper sticks, and bird-bone whistles. (Courtesy Oakland Museum.)

The acorn was the staple of the Me-Wuk diet. Acorns were gathered into burden baskets and then were cracked with a hammerstone on a flat rock or portable mortar. The shucked meats were ground into meal, usually on a bedrock mortar (a large flat outcropping with cuppings or mortar holes) with cobblestone pestles in a community mill. The meal was then leached of tannins using water in a shallow basin lined with leaves or grass. The leached meal was cooked over heated rocks in a cooking basket and was served as soup, mush, biscuits, or bread and eaten with the hand or the shell of a freshwater mussel. They stored the excess harvest in outdoor granaries or indoor baskets. (Both, *Hutchings' California Magazine*.)

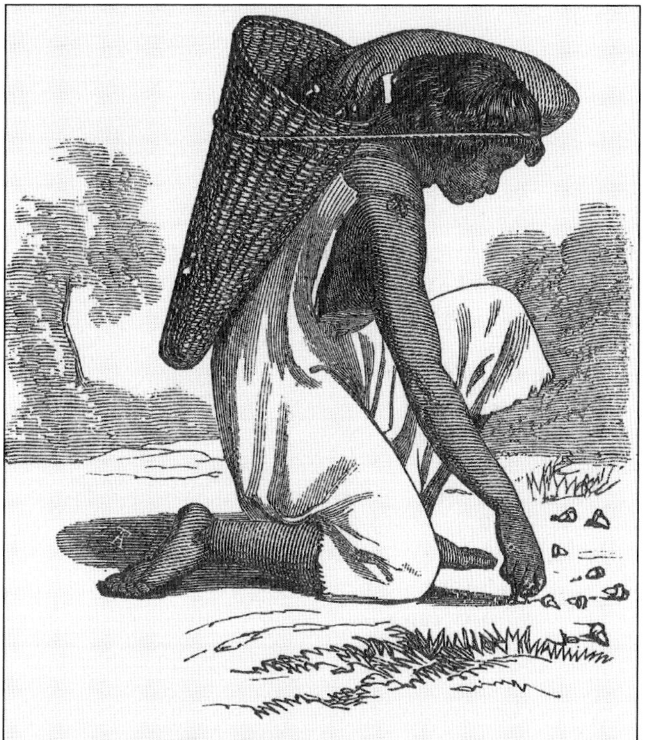

AN INDIAN WOMAN GATHERING ACORNS.

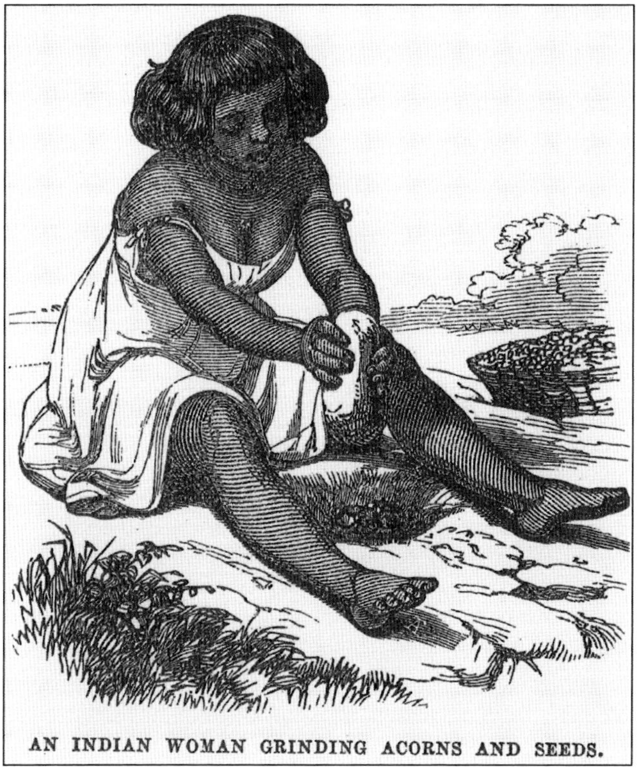

AN INDIAN WOMAN GRINDING ACORNS AND SEEDS.

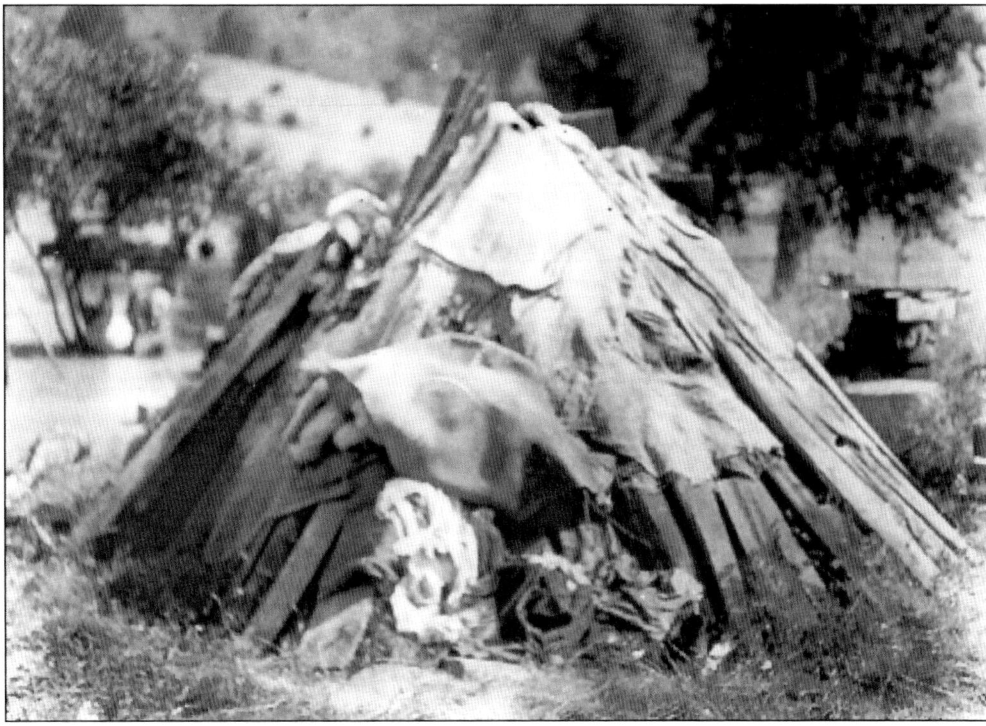

The Me-Wuk constructed a variety of dwellings. In the mountains, the dominant form was a conical bark house (8–15 feet in diameter), which retained heat generated by a central fire that kept out the cold and damp. In lower elevations, the Me-Wuk built a structure with poles arranged in a circle that were thatched with grass, brush, or tules. (Photograph by E. W. Gifford; courtesy Phoebe Hearst Museum of Anthropology.)

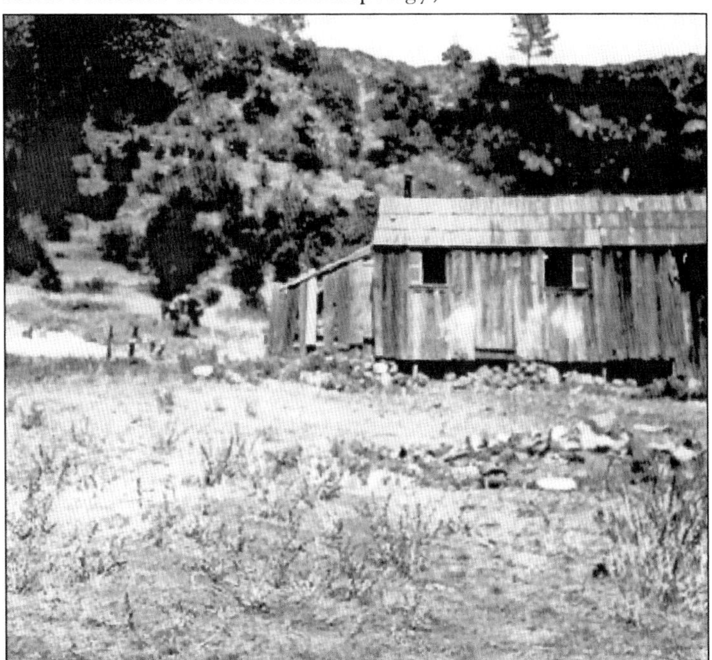

This 1913 view of a Chicken Ranch Rancheria dwelling below Table Mountain was taken by the ethnographer E. W. Gifford. By this time the Me-Wuk resided in typical Euro-American structures, with board-and-batten siding, shake roofs, stone foundations, windows, and an interior stove. Still in use, however, were the sweat lodge and dance house. (Photograph by E. W. Gifford; courtesy Department of Anthropology, UC Berkeley.)

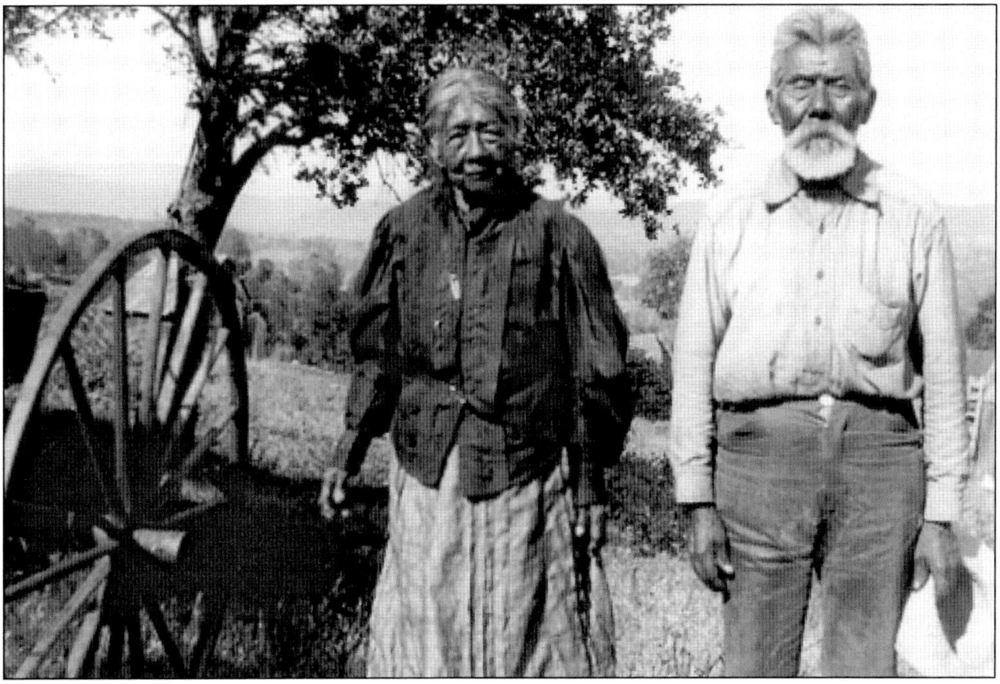

Chicken Ranch Rancheria residents Susie and Tom Williams were photographed near their residence in 1913. Both were full Me-Wuk, born at Wood's Creek, and resided near their aboriginal home throughout their lives. Their buckboard is in the foreground, and a Chicken Ranch Rancheria residence is in the background. (Photograph by E. W. Gifford; courtesy Department of Anthropology, UC Berkeley.)

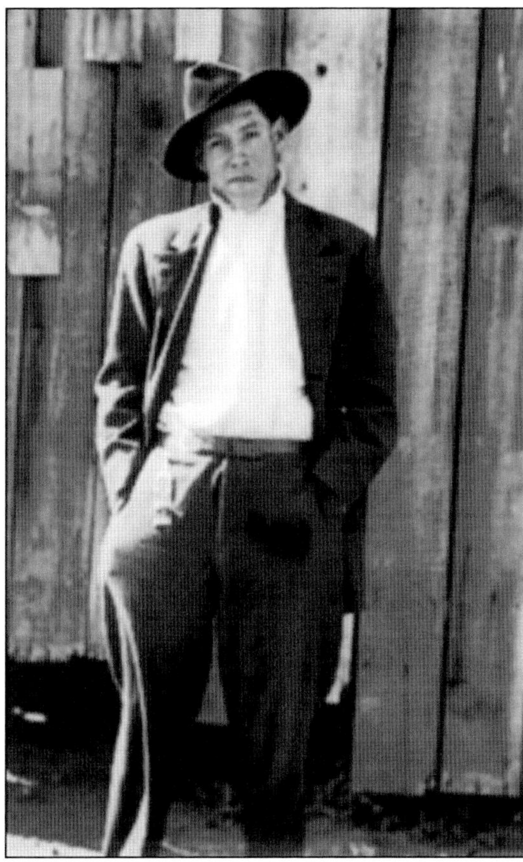

John Kelley, the nephew of Susie and Tom Williams, was half Me-Wuk, with a white father. Born in Sonora, he was residing at Chicken Ranch Rancheria when ethnographer E. W. Gifford, who chronicled Miwok material culture and lifeways in the 1910s–1930s, took this 1914 photograph. (Photograph by E. W. Gifford; courtesy Department of Anthropology, UC Berkeley.)

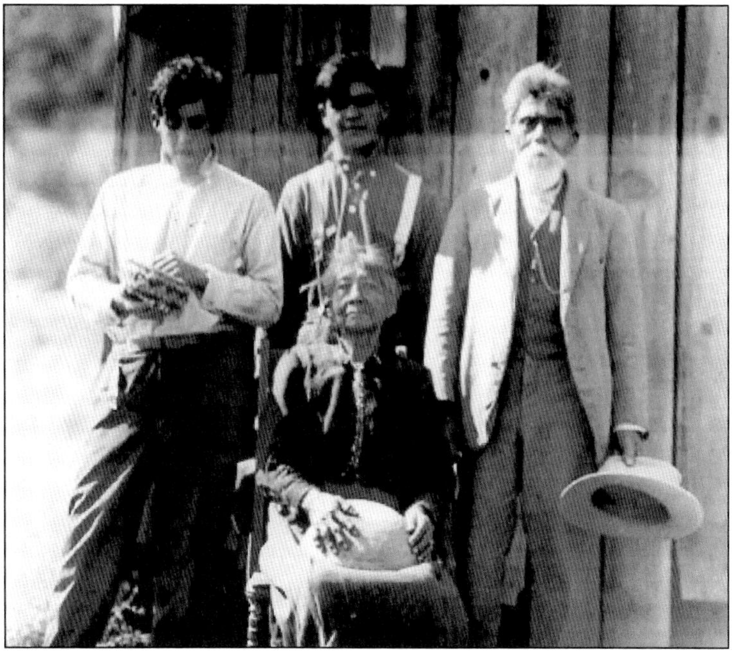

John Kelley (standing, left), John Light (standing, center), and Susie and Tom Williams, shown at their home at Chicken Ranch Rancheria, were one of the 11 Me-Wuk tribes officially recognized by the Bureau of Indian Affairs. John Kelley is holding a traditional Me-Wuk ornamental basket, while Susie is holding a coiled food basket. (Photograph by E. W. Gifford; Courtesy Department of Anthropology, UC Berkeley.)

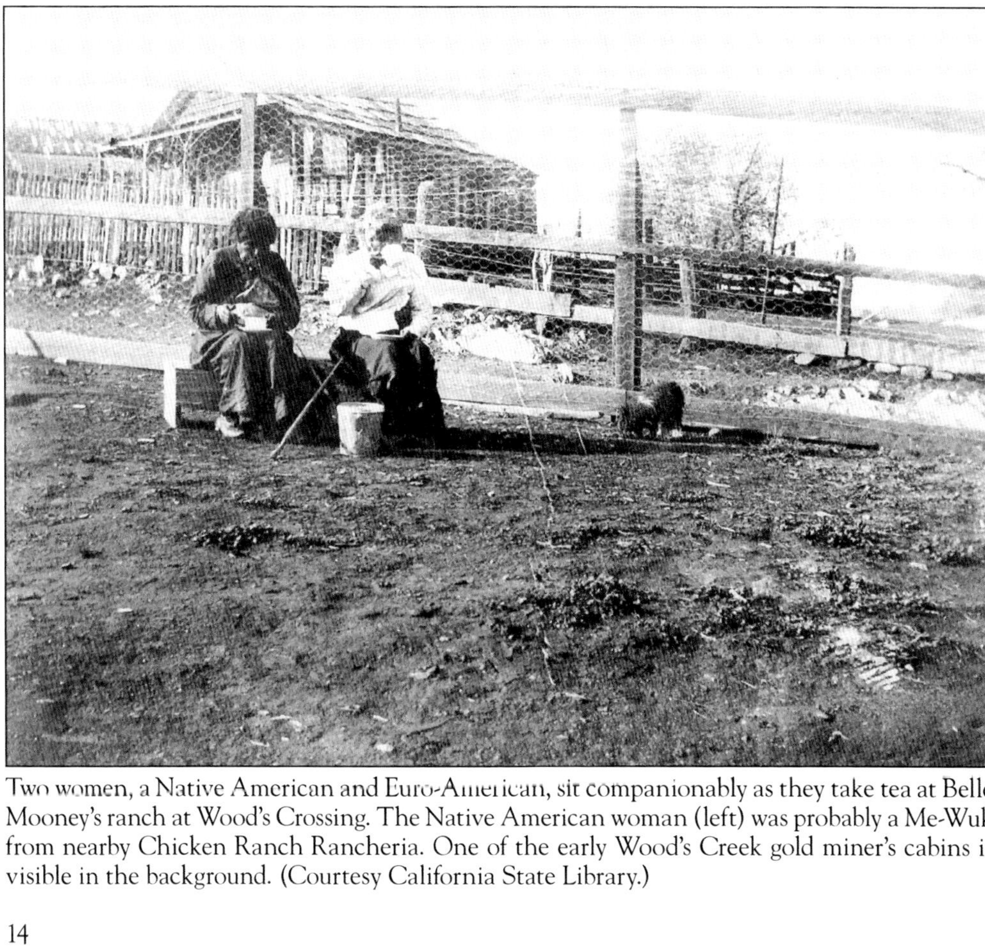

Two women, a Native American and Euro-American, sit companionably as they take tea at Belle Mooney's ranch at Wood's Crossing. The Native American woman (left) was probably a Me-Wuk from nearby Chicken Ranch Rancheria. One of the early Wood's Creek gold miner's cabins is visible in the background. (Courtesy California State Library.)

Two

EUREKA! I HAVE FOUND IT!

The gold discovery at Sutter's Mill on the American River in January 1848 precipitated a worldwide rush of peoples to the Sierra Nevada foothills. Gold was soon found in Tuolumne County along the banks of Wood's, Sullivan, and Sonora Creeks and the Stanislaus and Tuolumne Rivers. By the summer of 1848, Mexican and Californian miners had established themselves on the Stanislaus River and on upper Wood's Creek at the Sonorian Camp. By early autumn, a group of Oregon prospectors, including Benjamin Wood, discovered rich gold deposits several miles downstream from the Mexican diggings. According to another account, gold was discovered near Jamestown by a group of Philadelphians. Following them were the Mexicans, Chileans, and Frenchmen, and later the '49ers from all over America.

Wood's Crossing, settled in August 1848, was reputedly the first mining ground worked in the Southern Mines, with a post office established in 1850. By the spring of 1849, when the easily mined gold had disappeared, the settlement moved about a mile up Wood's Creek to the present site of Jamestown. Among the tents and temporary shelters was the imposing tent of Col. George F. James, a San Francisco attorney who was elected alcalde. His tent had a well-stocked bar, hotel, and trading facilities where, according to legend, he lavished champagne on the miners, in keeping with his pretentious lifestyle. The community honored him by naming the town after him, but soon thereafter, following bankruptcy, James departed the town in the dead of night, and the townspeople renamed the settlement American Camp. Before long, however, the familiar name reappeared, to be made official in 1853.

After slumbering for a bit, Jamestown again became important with the development of the Table Mountain drift workings. By 1855, the community was noted as one of the oldest settlements in Tuolumne County, located midway between the Stanislaus and Tuolumne Rivers in the midst of the auriferous region, which followed the Sierra foothills. The surface diggings were rich, and extensive tunneling operations in the adjacent Table Mountain boded well for it always being a favorite mining locality.

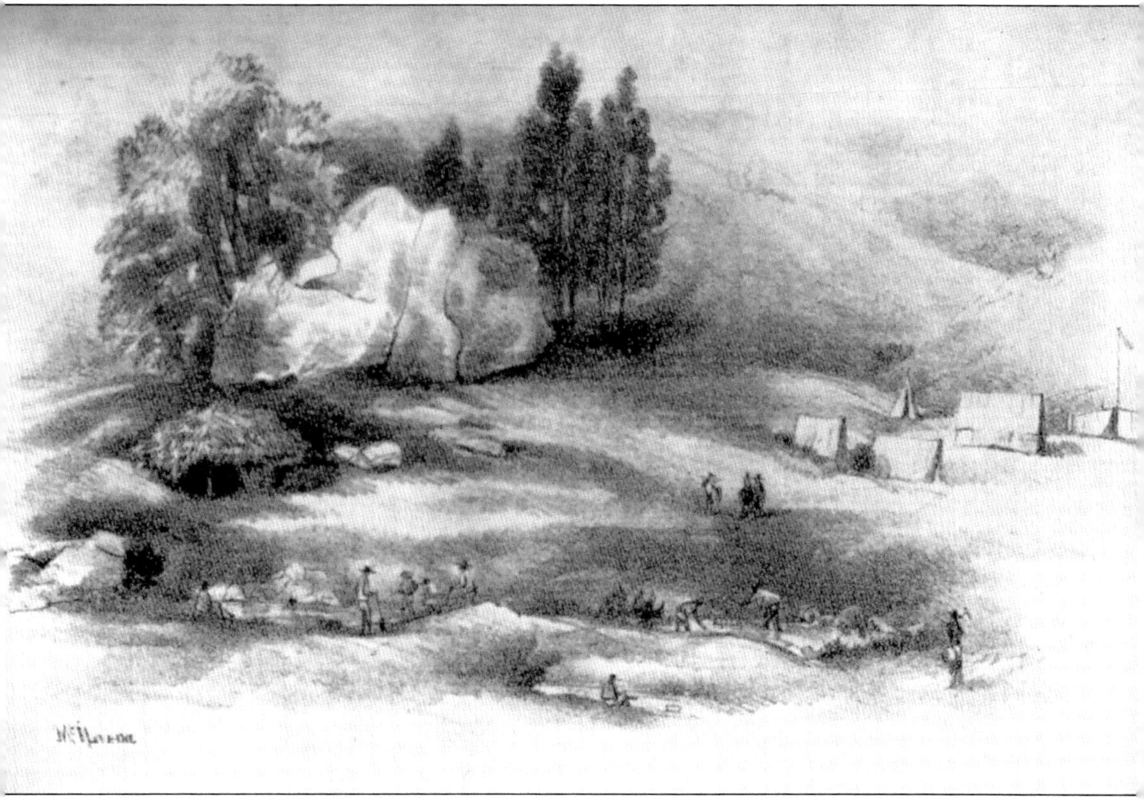

In the summer of 1949, about 400 miners resided in brush huts and canvas tents in Wood's Creek. All claims were occupied. James Carson noted, "In '48 the miners had no division of the ground into claims—they dug where it was richest, and many times four or five could be seen at work in a circle of 6 feet in diameter." In 1853, however, the Jamestown District Mining Laws established that each miner was entitled to one claim (100 feet square) or prove that he paid a valid and legal consideration for each claim. Any claim not worked within six days was to be forfeited, and miners were to be entitled to the priority of water according to the date and situation of the location of their claims. (Lithograph by William McIlvaine Jr.; courtesy Bancroft Library.)

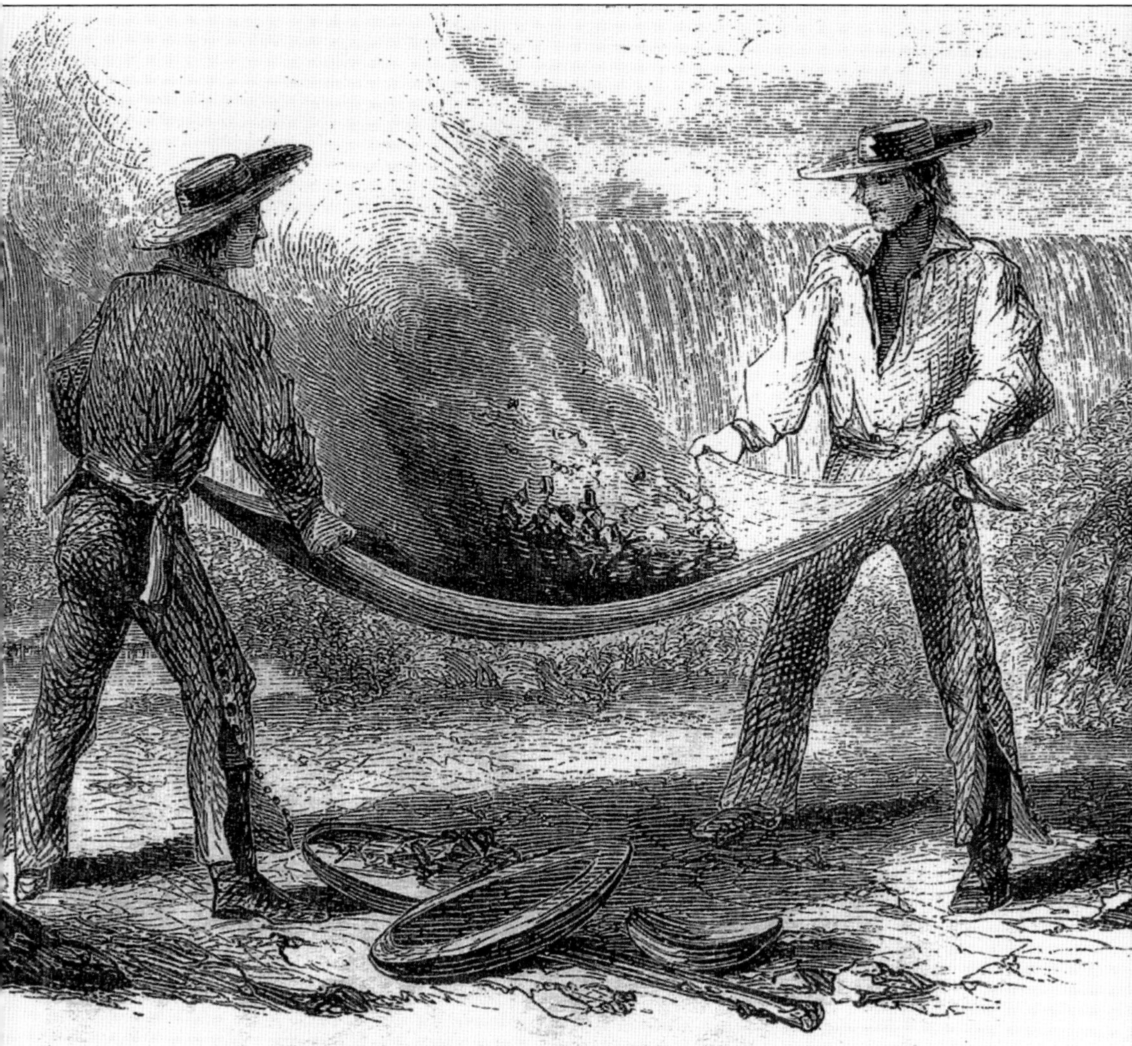

WINNOWING GOLD, NEAR CHINESE CAMP.

If no water was available, gold was concentrated by winnowing on a blanket. Near Chinese Camp, two Mexican men winnow the gold, a common practice in their country. The Mexicans were skilled miners, having a long and prosperous history as gold-hunters, and were the " '48ers," the first, and the most populous, foreign group to reach the California gold region. While they discovered many of the richest diggings in the country, they seldom remained in possession of rich diggings, as they were very soon run off the field. The passage of the Foreign Miner's Tax in 1850, which primarily taxed Mexicans and Central and South Americans, saw them returning home in a steady stream. (*Hutchings' California Magazine.*)

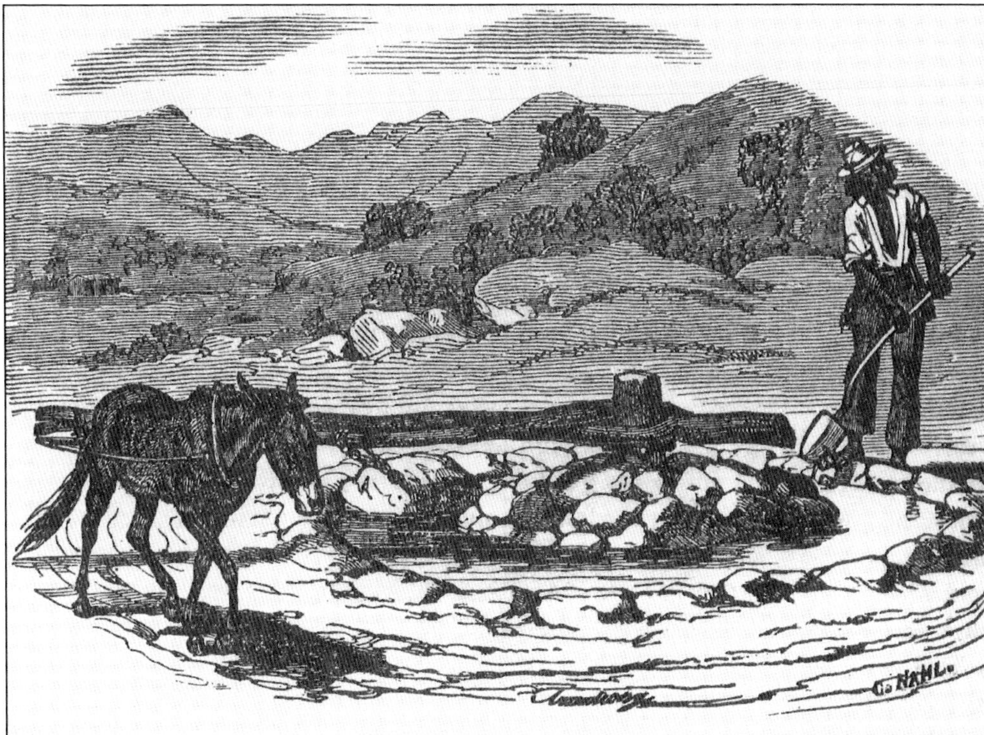

THE MEXICAN RASTRA.

After the pay dirt or quartz was removed from the mine, it was necessary to separate the ore from its matrix. The Mexican *arrastra*, one of the most effective methods of saving the recovered gold, was constructed of a circular track of stone with a low wall around the outside and a center post with a horizontal shaft. Several large stones were then attached to the shaft with chains, which were drawn around by donkey or mule power, grinding the quartz to powder. Gold, being the heaviest, would seek the lowest places; quicksilver was introduced, amalgamated with it, and eventually smelted off. *Arrastras* were also commonly used by miners of other nationalities and later in large numbers by the hard rock miners in the second gold rush, when they were built of concrete. (Above, *Hutchings' California Magazine*; below, courtesy Bancroft Library.)

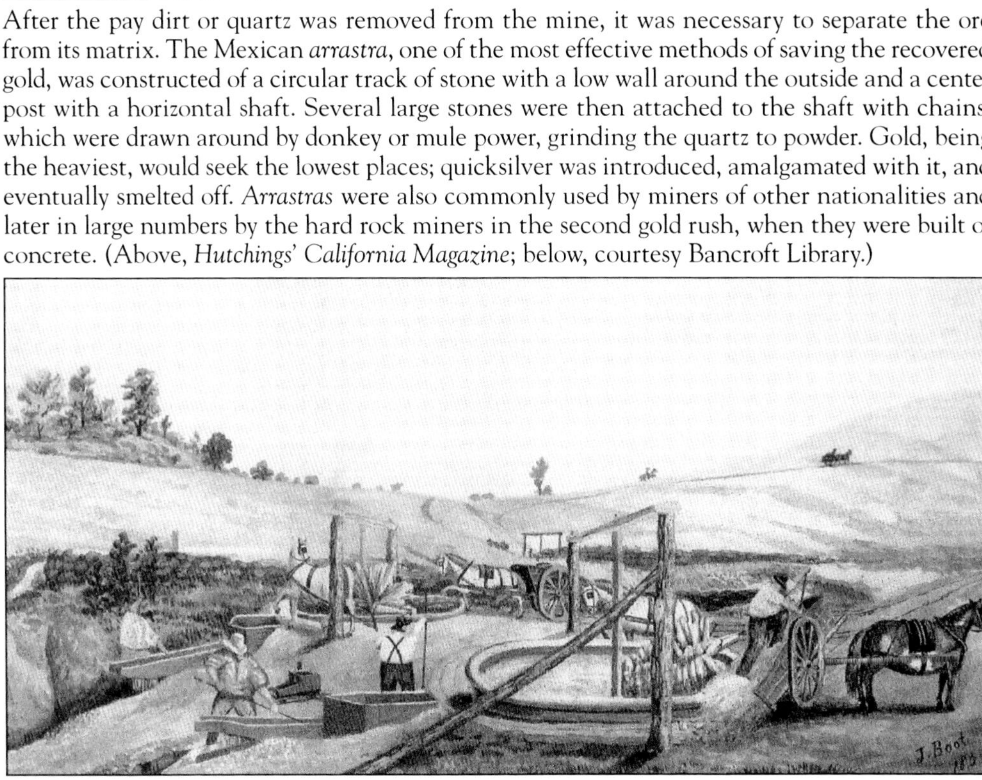

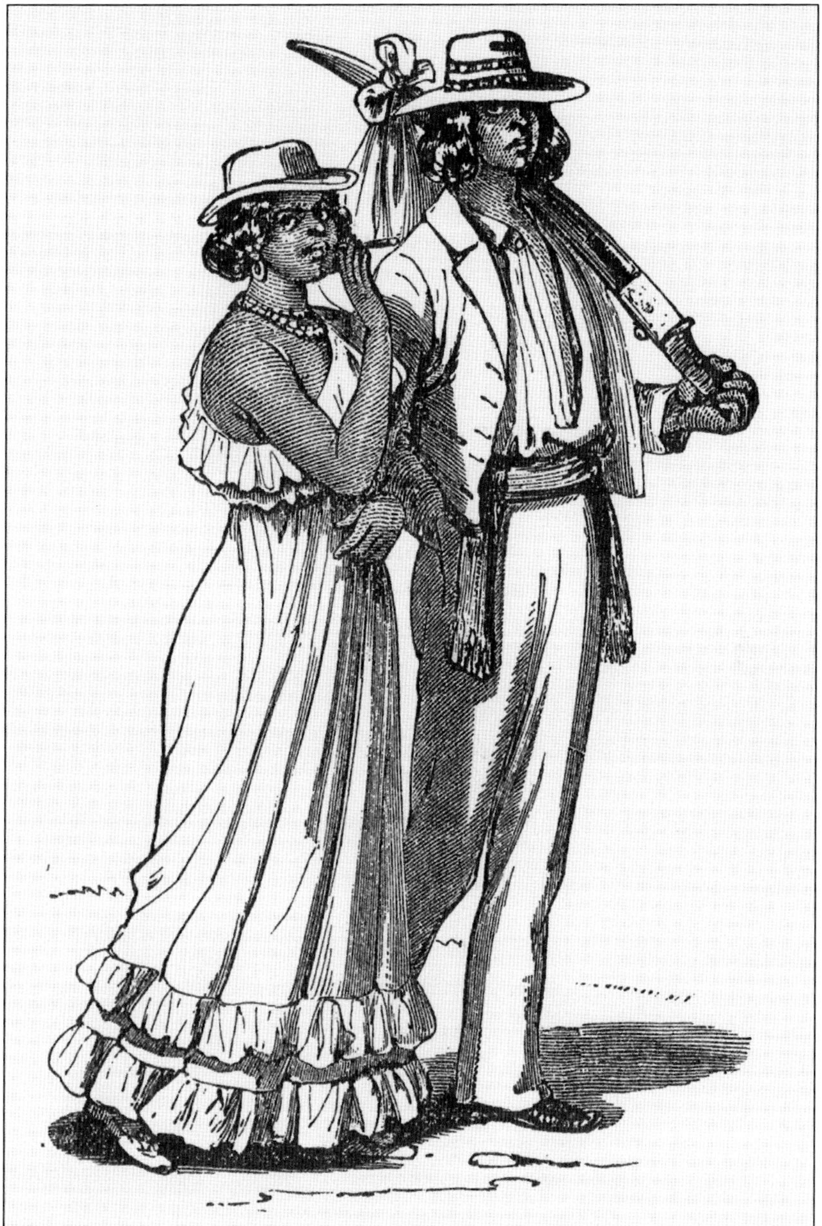

The first report of the gold strike in California reached Chile in August 1848, bringing Chileans to the area, where they eventually played a significant role in local affairs. Their population reached 7,000, the second-largest foreign contingent after the Mexicans from Sonora. Many Chileans brought their wives and families to California. Chile quickly became a major supplier of mining equipment, as well as liquors, foods, apparel, cutlery, building materials, and other supplies. Their dress was similar to that of the Mexicans, but they wore a black wool poncho with red, blue, and yellow bands rather than a *zarape*. They wore heavy leather 6-inch-wide belts divided into various pockets, in which they carried their tobacco, *cigarrito* paper, tinderbox, and money. The belts were fastened with buttons of silver dollars and often of gold ounces. (*Hutchings' California Magazine*.)

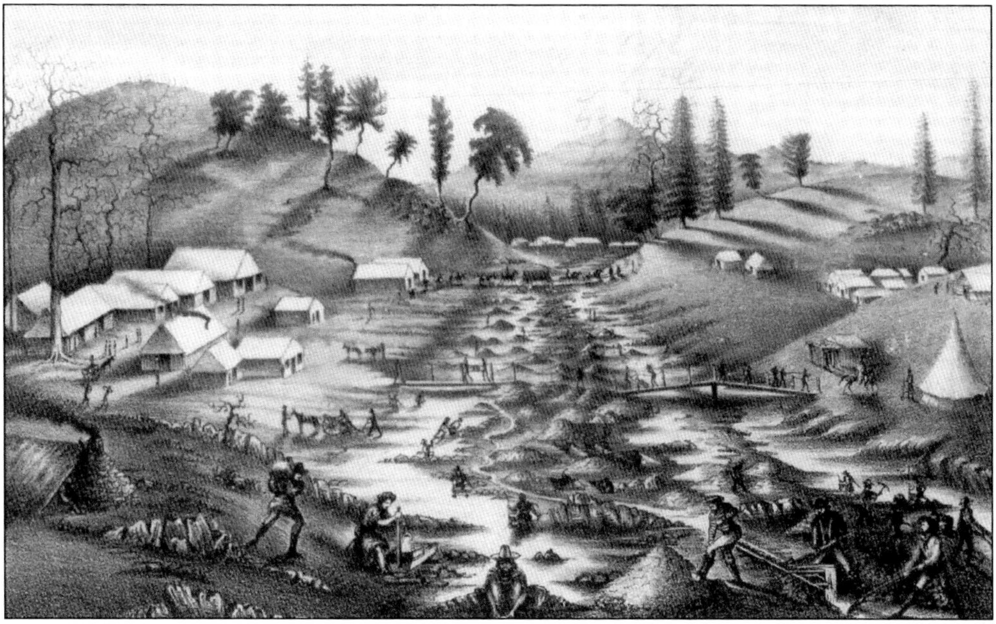

By late 1849, Jamestown was described by James H. Carson as a vast canvas city on a flat, "with a hundred flags flying from restaurants, taverns, rummills, and gaming houses." Claims were now measured off with tape measures, under the direction of the alcaldes, to prevent disputes. By August 1849, however, the diggings were almost exhausted and, in 1854, were noted as "retrograded." (Courtesy Bancroft Library.)

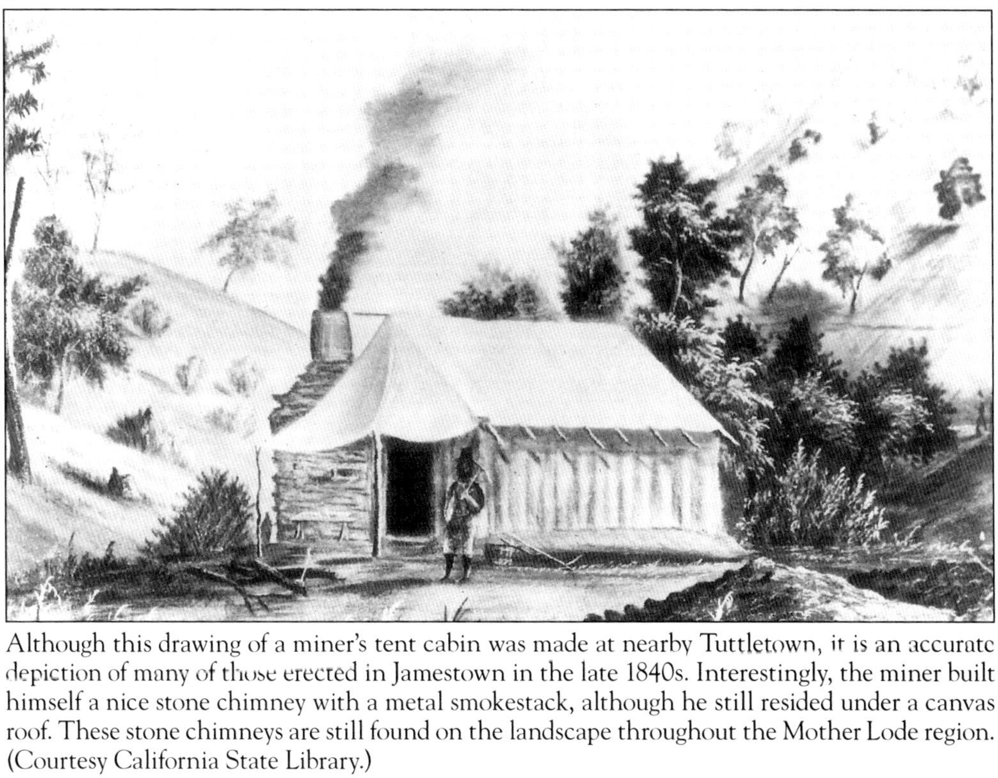

Although this drawing of a miner's tent cabin was made at nearby Tuttletown, it is an accurate depiction of many of those erected in Jamestown in the late 1840s. Interestingly, the miner built himself a nice stone chimney with a metal smokestack, although he still resided under a canvas roof. These stone chimneys are still found on the landscape throughout the Mother Lode region. (Courtesy California State Library.)

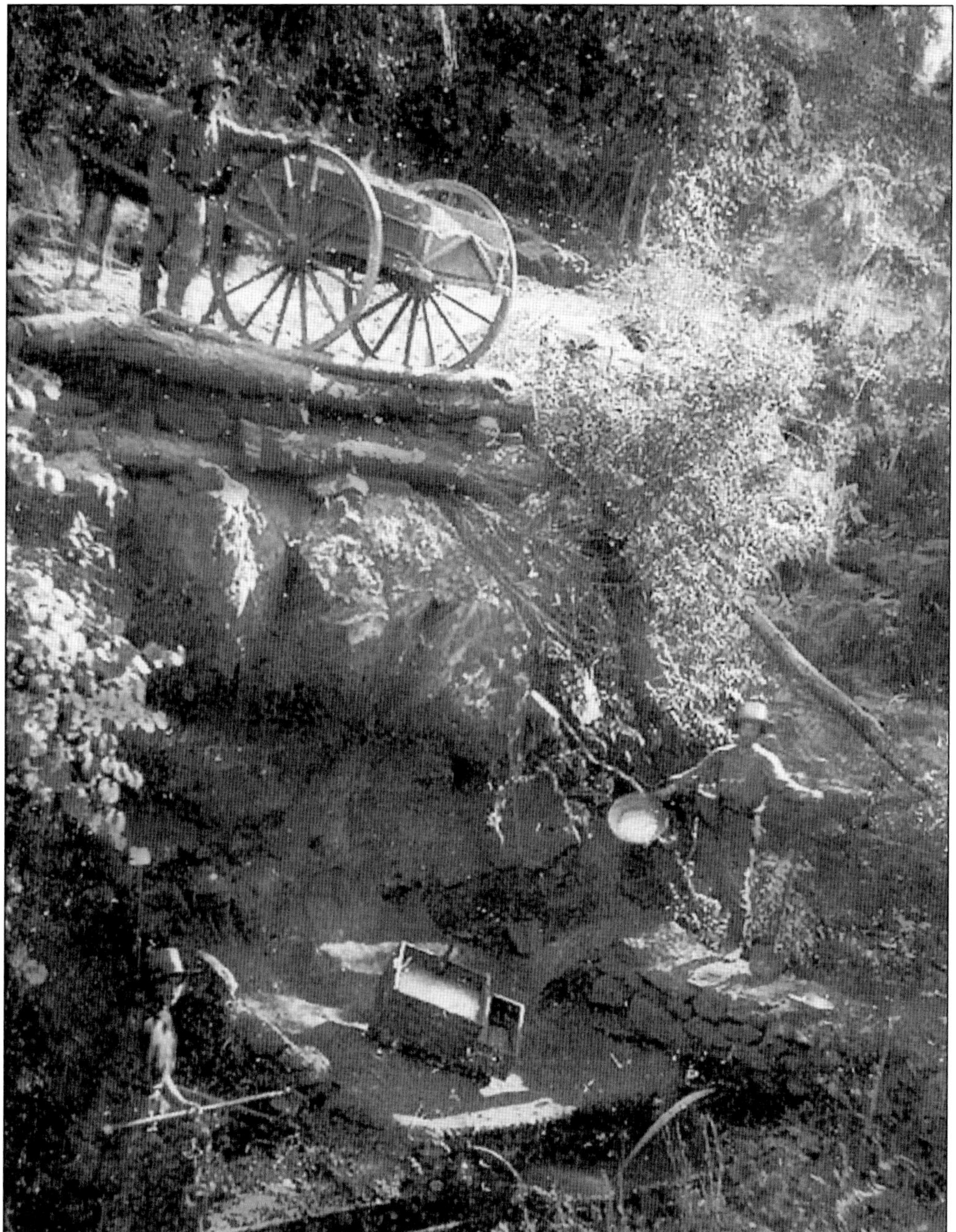

This daguerreotype, one of the earliest of mining in Tuolumne County, was taken in 1854 near Chinese Camp on the Tuolumne River. Harvey Myron Sampson and Jeremiah Sampson, from Upstate New York, and an unidentified companion pose with tools of their trade, the gold pan and rocker box, while they dig out the bank to find the placer gold. Arriving fairly late to the California gold fields, they returned home again and married soon after. Harvey would later move to Iowa and eventually live out his days in Siskiyou County, California. (Courtesy Bancroft Library.)

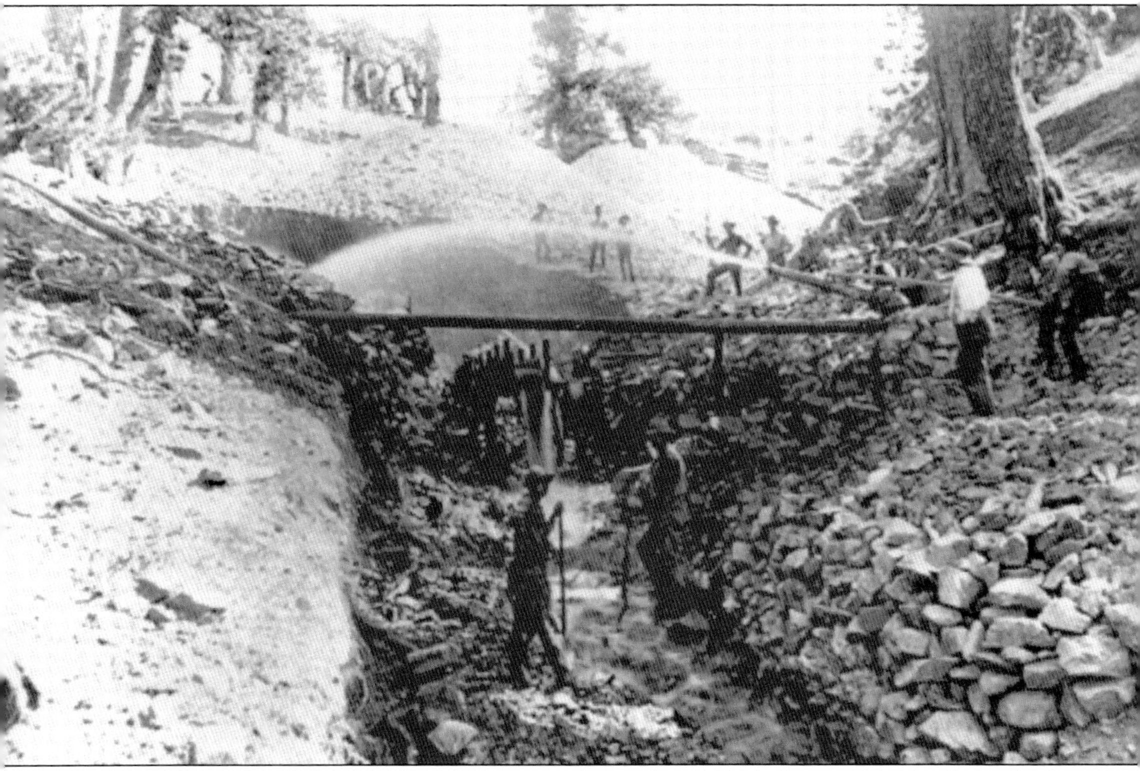

Gold left by water on hillsides or in stream channels is called placer gold, which usually has a higher percentage of gold than vein gold. It accounted for the greatest amount of gold found in the early years of California. In the hydraulic method, water from upstream (in the background) was carried downstream along the hillside in a ditch, then funneled through a hydraulic nozzle to wash the river gravels into their sluice box. The gold collected in the riffles of the sluice box, while the waste piled to the side. In this typical view, the miners are working upstream, with the lower portion of the creek already channelized with hand-stacked rock. Miners would continue working upstream in this fashion, digging more ditches as needed, until there was no more evidence of gold. (Courtesy California Department of Conservation.)

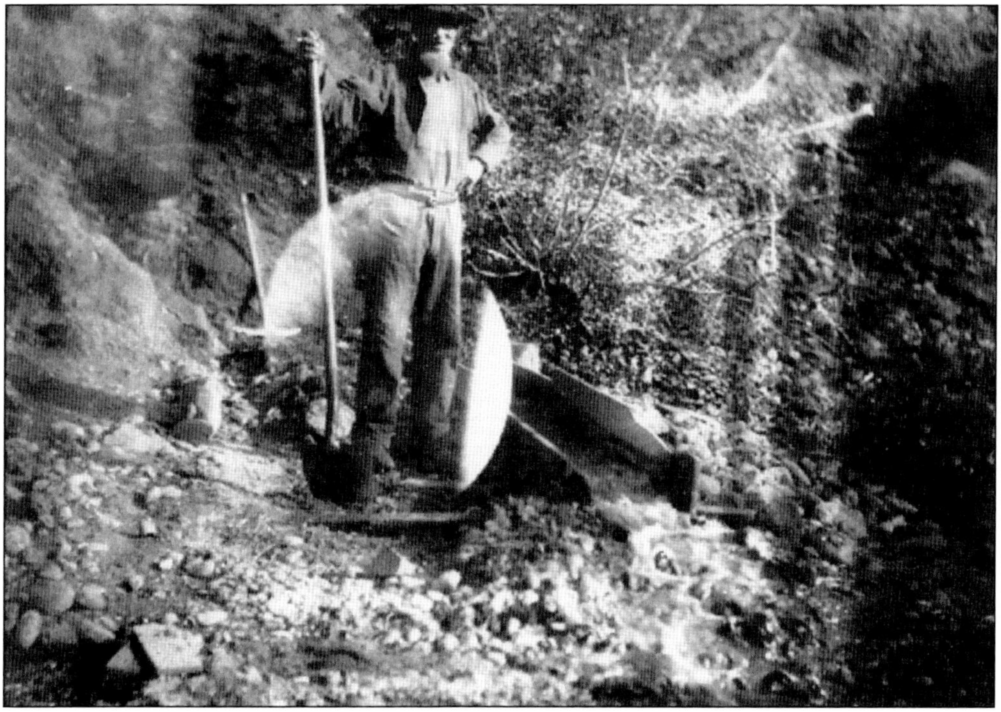

Even though most of the free gold was found in the late 1840s and early 1850s, many individual prospectors continued to work their claims, hoping to score a nugget or just to subsist. The Depression years also saw an influx of men who survived on bacon and beans from a gold pan. This miner is pictured with his sluice box and shovel. (Courtesy California Department of Conservation.)

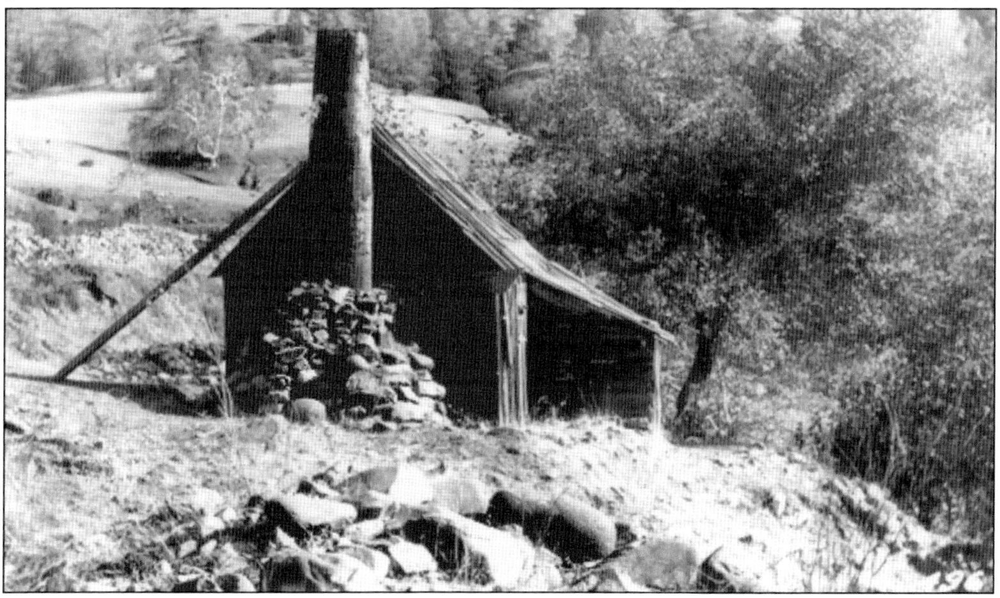

Residing in solitary cabins beside their claims, the prospectors and miners lived with little more than a stone fireplace, single bed, kitchen table and chair, wood countertop with wash pan, dishes and utensils with perhaps a small cupboard, and nails for clothes hooks. (Courtesy California Department of Conservation.)

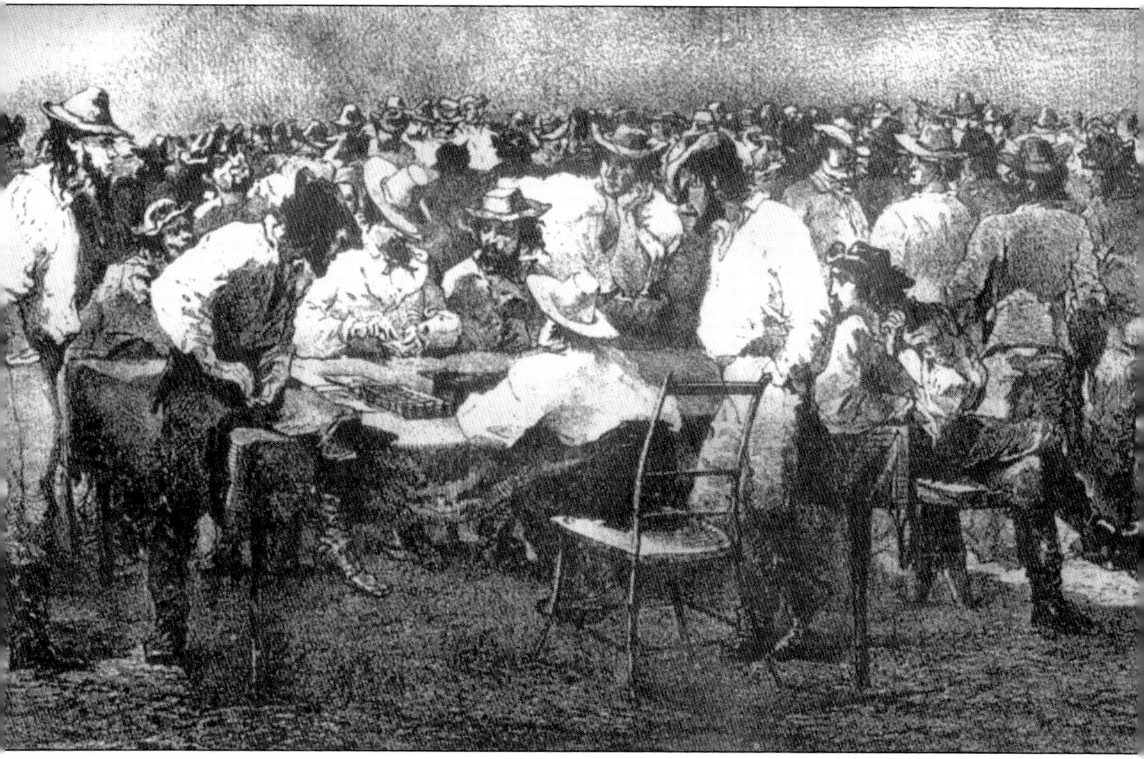

The gambling tables of Jamestown had continuous crowds, so miners quickly disposed of their hard-earned riches. Gold dust was valued as high as $10 per ounce at monte banks, presenting a scene similar to that of San Francisco during the winter of 1848. James H. Carson, visiting Jamestown in May 1849, noted that he had seen Spaniards betting an *arroba* (25 pounds!) of gold at a time and winning or losing as if it had been a bag of dirt. Monte, also known as Three Card Monte in America, was a confidence game played with three face-down cards, the punter hoping to select the Queen of Hearts. Of course, the dealer and the shill had other plans, and the "mark" rarely won. (Courtesy J. D. Borthwick.)

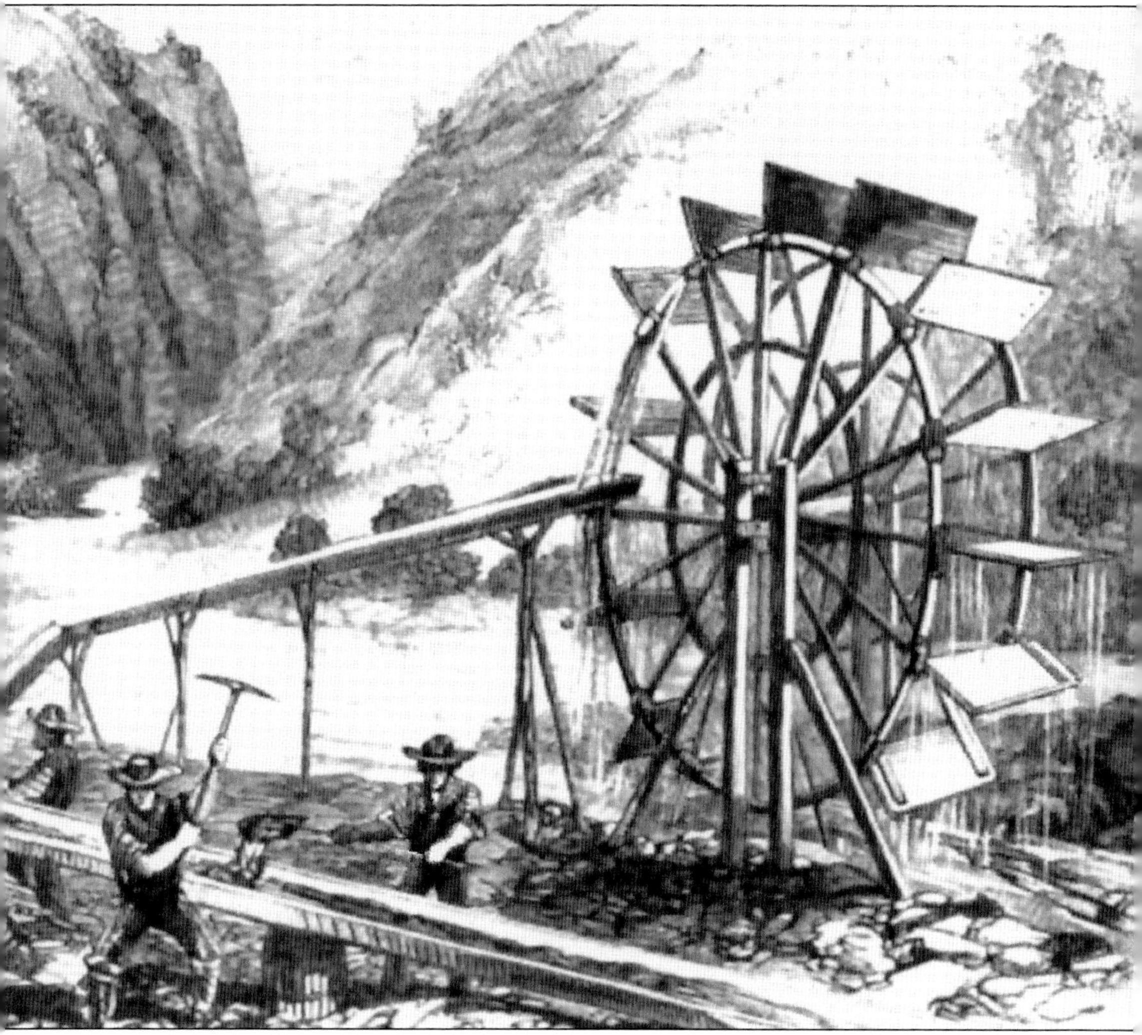

In this period image, miners are hard at work on the upper Tuolumne River, which they dammed to divert the stream so that they could dig clear to bedrock. The men are using a flutter wheel to operate a pump to dry out the workings, raising the river water to run through a flume to their sluice box, where they washed the stream gravels to extract the gold-bearing ore. These enterprises were a considerable investment, but were necessary since easy-to-find gold nuggets were discovered quickly by the first prospectors. A great deal of gold was recovered this way, and shares in these partnerships could be bought and sold for as much as $2,000. (Courtesy Charles Nordhoff.)

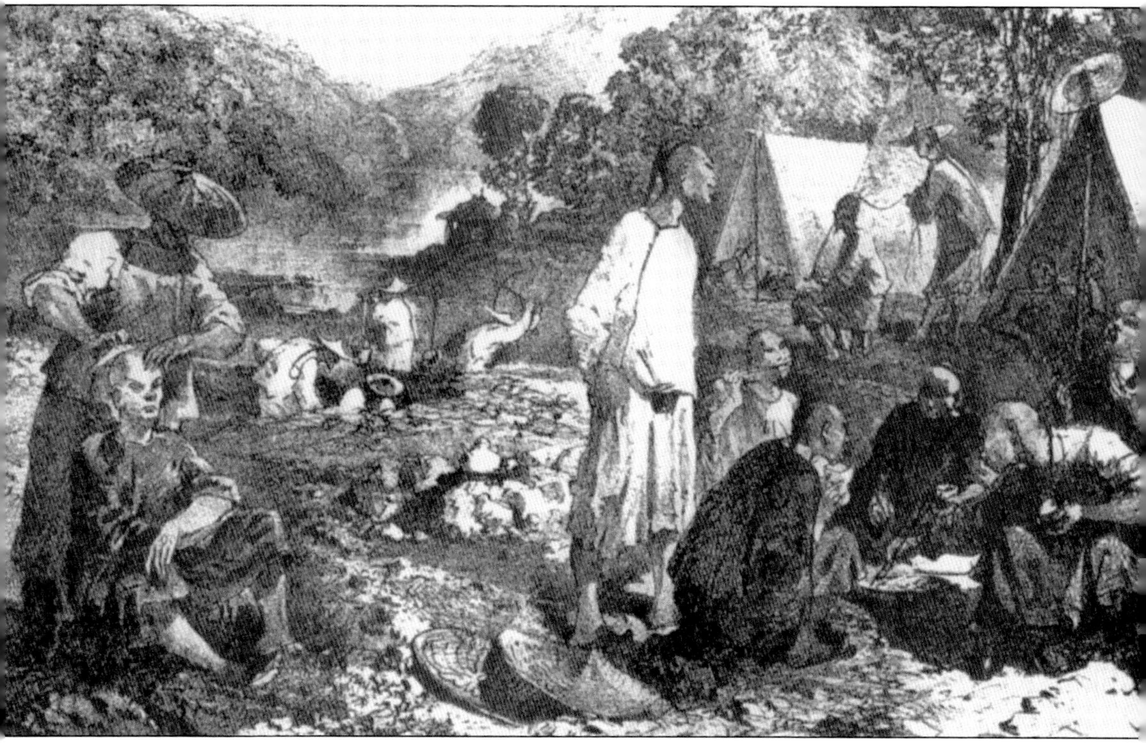

As the easily recovered gold was quickly appropriated, many of the early placer mining areas were reclaimed by Chinese miners from Guandong Province in southeast China. In this scene, some are hard at work mining, while others are occupied with their daily activities. When artist J. D. Borthwick visited the camps, he noted, "The Chinese invariably treated in the same hospitable manner anyone who visited their camps, and seemed rather pleased than otherwise at the interest and curiosity excited by their domestic arrangements." After the gold was exhausted, the ever-declining population pursued non-mining employment, becoming cooks, laundrymen, produce peddlers, domestics, and menial laborers in sawmills and on ranches. Some confined their activities to the various Chinatowns of the county, while others served the needs of local white communities. (Courtesy J. D. Borthwick.)

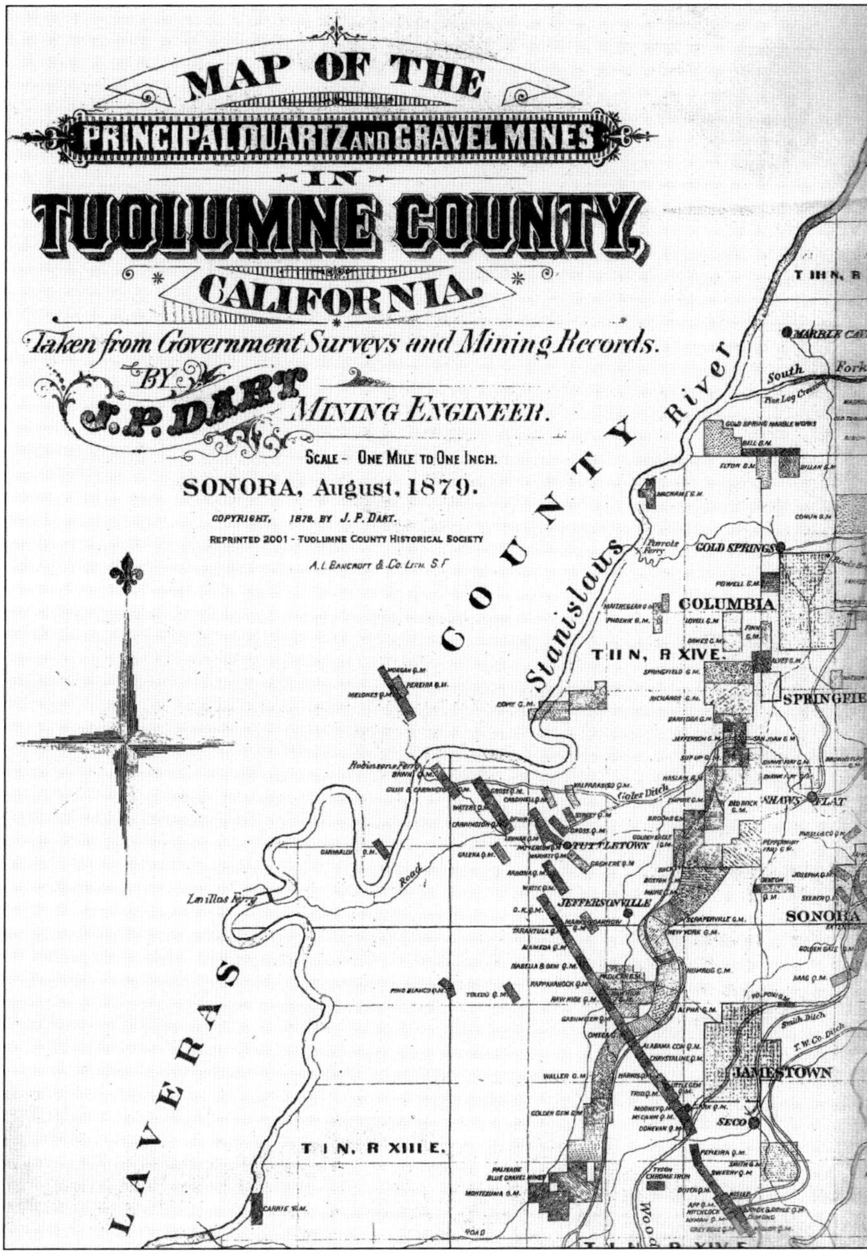

By 1879, when the principal quartz and gravel mines were platted, the mines followed the Mother Lode vein northwest to southeast, with the gravel and drift mines on Table Mountain coursing southwest along the old Tertiary riverbed. The most profitable mine on Table Mountain was the New York Tunnel, where a three-pound lump of gold was discovered in June 1854. Artist J. D. Borthwick described the diggings as very rich, with coarse gold found in large lumps. Most of the gold was found at a depth of 3 or 4 feet from bedrock, which was composed of masses of sandstone full of circular cavities. The hard rock mines, where gold was found deep underground, followed the Mother Lode vein from northwest to southeast, through Jamestown, Quartz Mountain, and Stent, to Jacksonville. A distance of about 8 miles, it has been called the "Jimtown" district. (Map by J. P. Dart.)

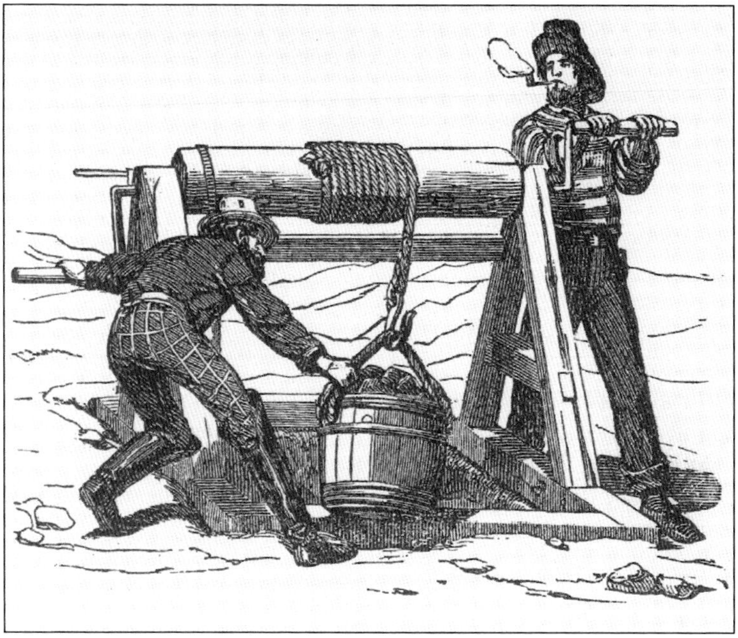

In order to extract the gold from the ancient gravel beds or in the quartz veins, the miners either had to "drift" in to the ancient river bottom beneath the mountain or sink a shaft or run a tunnel. When pay dirt was reached, it was raised to the surface by a windlass and bucket, as seen here. (*Hutchings' California Magazine*.)

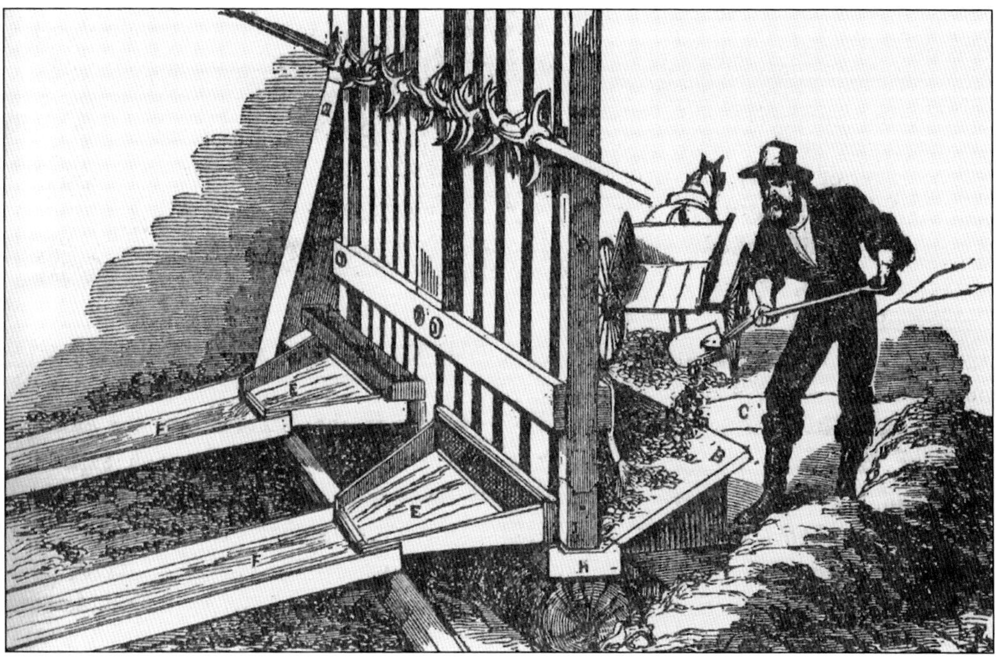

The California Battery, the most popular method of extracting gold, consisted of a hopper, five circular cast-iron stamps, a battery box, and an amalgamating box. The rock was crushed by hand, fed into the hopper, washed down with water, pulverized in the stampers, and passed through discharge screens onto the amalgamating box to be combined with quicksilver and then to an inclined plate or blanket table below. (*Hutchings' California Magazine*.)

Three

Jimtown

By 1855, the era of the individual miner was over, and men formed companies to erect large water wheels, turn the rivers, and extract the gold from the interstices in the bedrock. Others sank shafts and ran drifts into Table Mountain to extract the gold from the ancient Tertiary river below, but these were no longer one- or two-man operations. As companies were formed, some stability was imposed upon the mining scene, and many were determined to settle down. They sent for wives and families, built in wood and stone, and established a community.

At the height of the Gold Rush, the population in and around Jamestown was estimated to be around 6,000, with most hailing from the eastern states. This figure plummeted rapidly with the exhaustion of the easily obtainable gold. Jamestown was not immune to a series of fires that plagued most Gold Rush camps due to overcrowding and flimsy construction. A large fire in 1855, in effect, cleaned up the town, causing more durable structures to be erected, as some early pioneers became permanent residents and families settled in town. With the era of successful placer mining basically over by the 1860s, the town went into a slow decline until being resurrected by the hard rock mining boom of the late 1880s. When the Sierra Railroad reached Jamestown in 1897, it sustained a wave of revival and growth and confirmed the town as a transportation center. Jamestown produced its first newspaper, the *Mother Lode Magnet*, and by the early 1900s, it was again noted as a thriving place, with its proximity to the Mother Lode providing the trade to make it flourish. With the reopening of the mines in the 1930s, another period of prosperity was ushered in, and Main Street Jamestown was again rebuilt, often in concrete, which was readily available due to its use in mill construction and rail shipment. The town today reflects those eras of prosperity, as well as the tourism era that began with the centennial of the Gold Rush in 1948 and continues to this day.

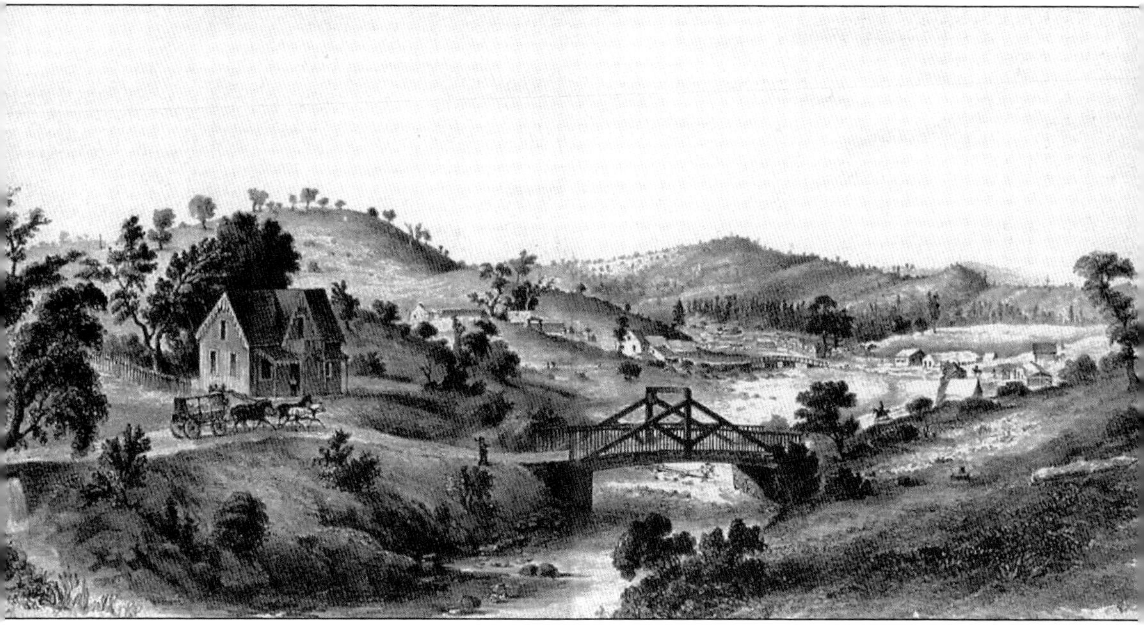

By 1853, Jamestown had developed into the semblance of a real town. Two bridges crossed Wood's Creek, and Main Street was lined with all manner of buildings. Tents and cabins were still in evidence, but the community appeared to be composed of frame buildings, with a large and impressive Gothic Revival home near Wood's Crossing. In 1855, the town boasted about 30 stores and shops, including doctors' offices and a drugstore, bakery, dry goods, and butcher shops. One church, one day and night school, a Masonic Hall, Daguerrean studio, livery stables, hotels, and saloons (many very fine with billiard tables and one with a 10-pin bowling alley) were also there. (Courtesy Bancroft Library.)

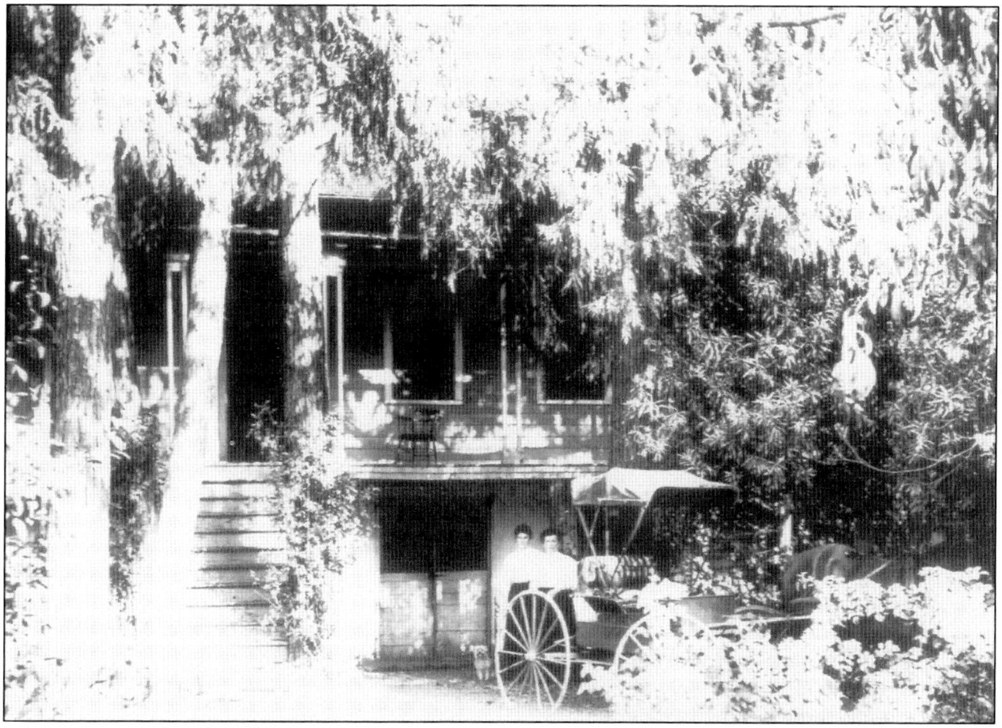

John Pereira, a local orchardist, raised peaches, pears, plums, apples, cherries, figs, and Italian chestnuts on his 360-acre farmstead. He operated a winery, producing 5,000 to 15,000 gallons a year, a precursor of times to come. His Pereira Pavilion, where people danced and drank lemonade into the early hours, was located on Willow Street; he resided on Main Street in this 1850s home reminiscent of Oliver Larkin's Monterey adobe. One of the oldest homes in Jamestown, it was once buffered from Main Street by formal gardens and surrounded by barns, a reservoir, and other facilities. Born in Portugal, Pereira came to Tuolumne County in the early 1850s; married an English woman, Elizabeth; and raised sons James and William. He became one of Jamestown's most important entrepreneurs. He is shown at right in his later years. (Above, courtesy Gary Wilson; right, courtesy Sally Hamilton.)

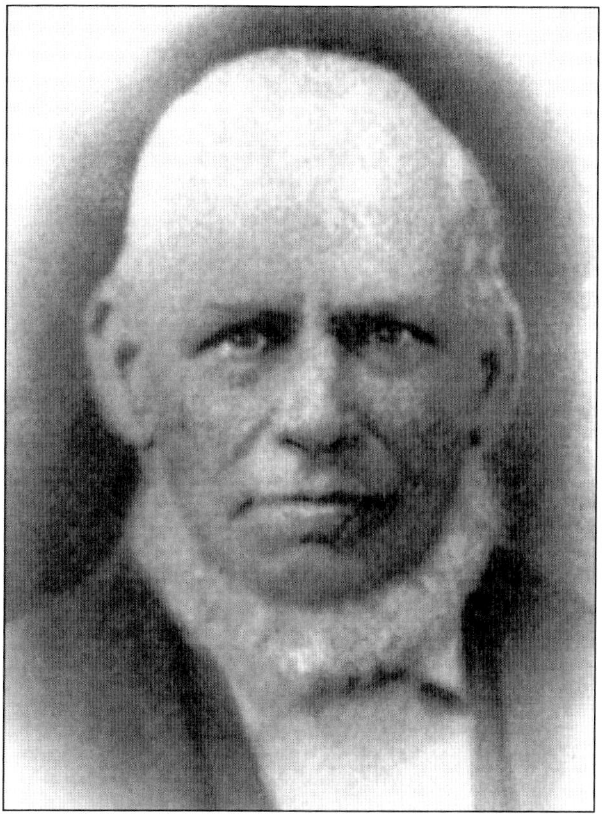

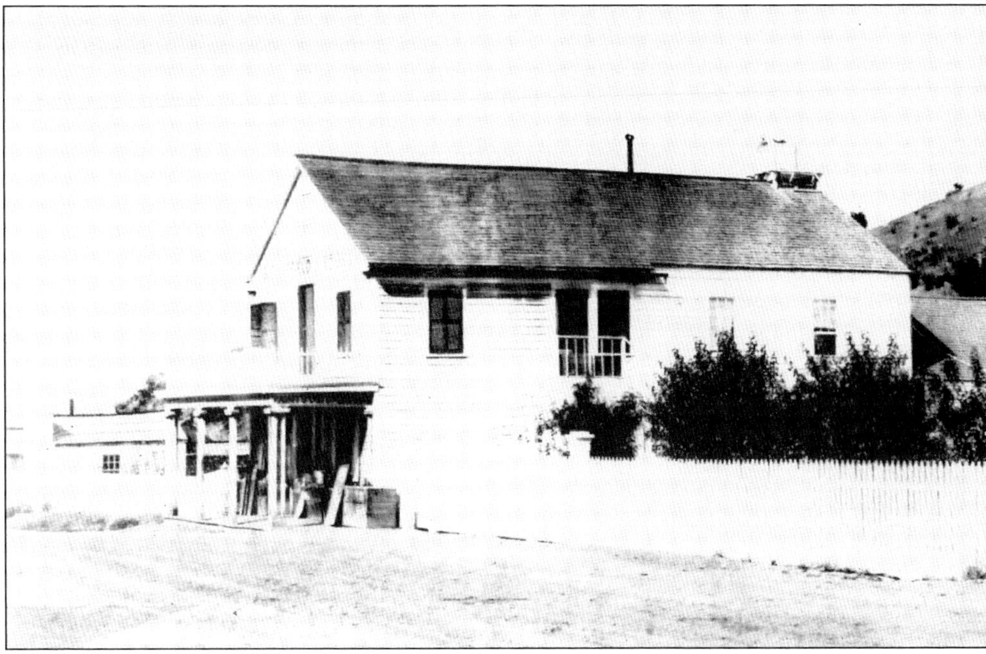

In this earliest known image of the Butterfield General Store, a simple Greek Revival structure built in the 1850s, it faced east toward Main Street. Sometime after 1905, a wing was added to the north elevation, almost doubling it in size, undoubtedly due to the increased patronage engendered by the railroad and the mining boom. (Courtesy Gary Wilson.)

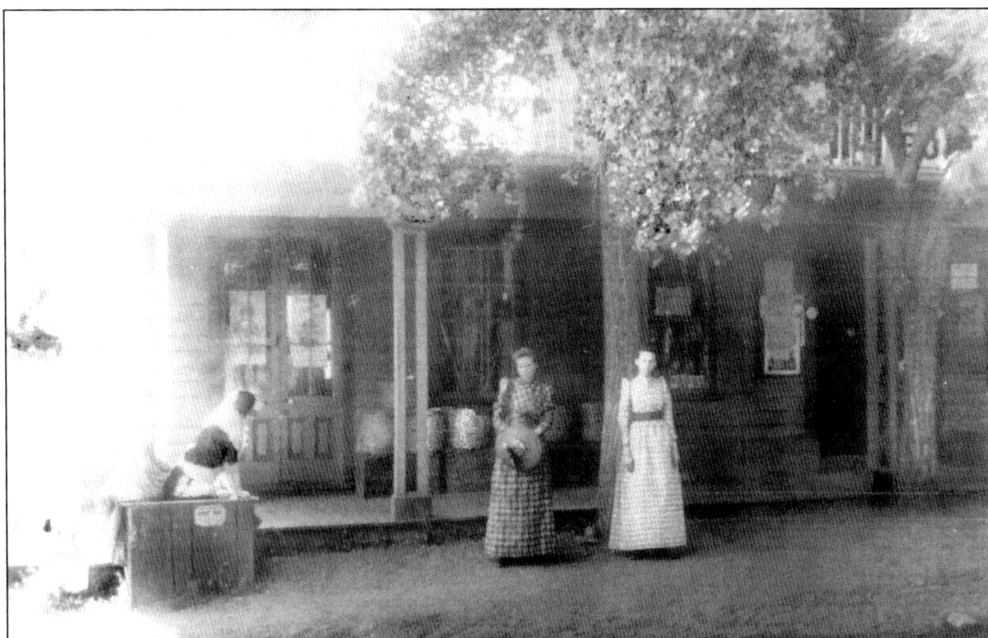

Two ladies, probably Minnie and Gay, the daughters of founder B. F. Butterfield, pose with their attentive dog in front of the oldest continuously operating establishment in Jamestown at that time. In this view of the Butterfield Store, taken around the start of the 19th century, the sisters were operating the business with their brothers: Frank, Rich, and Ben. (Courtesy Gary Wilson.)

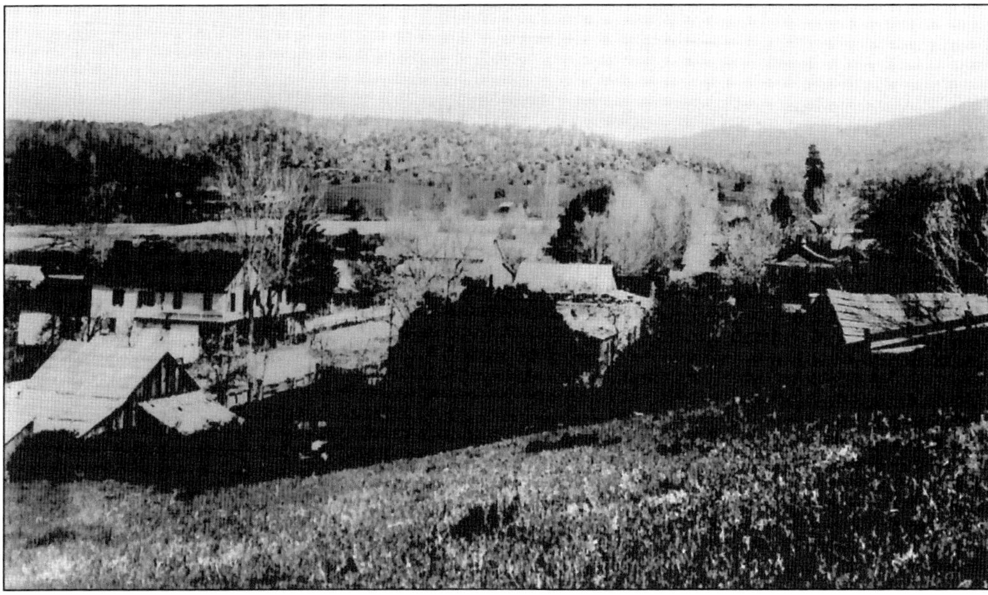

This view from St. James Catholic Cemetery, located on a small hill on the southeast edge of town, was taken between 1884 and 1897. The Butterfield Store is the prominent white building on the left. The church was built here in 1854; the cemetery remains, but the church was relocated in 1915 to the corner of Seco and Donovan Streets and remodeled beyond recognition. The church's bell remains near the cemetery entrance. (Courtesy Tuolumne County Museum.)

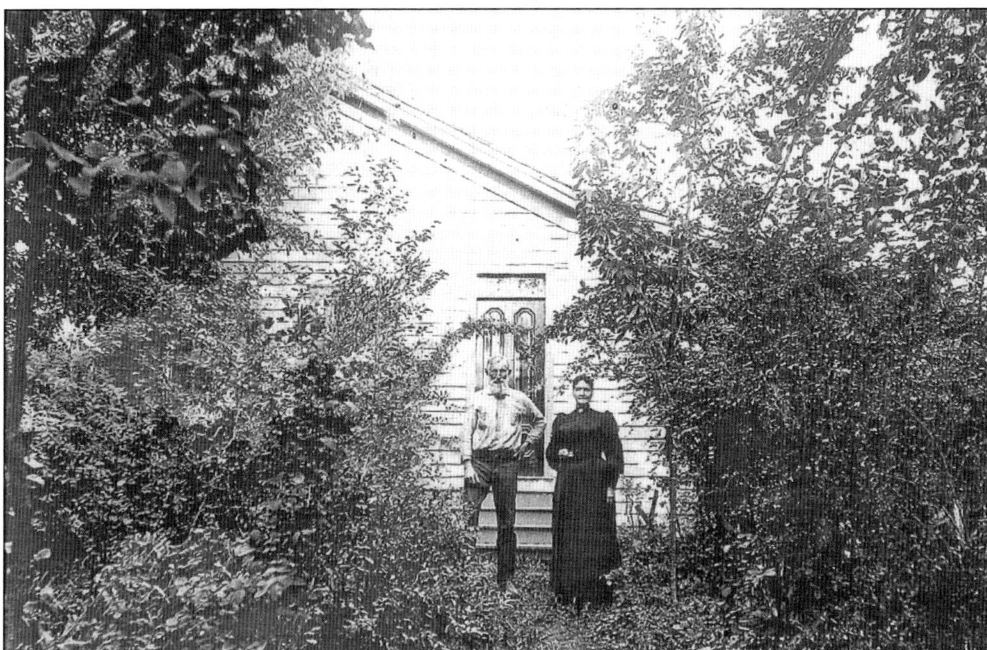

As the camp became a community, the appearance of the town changed. Back streets were lined with one- and two-story frame houses, and picket fences delineated planted yards and gardens, such as the fine frame home and garden of George A. and Frances Leland (pictured here in 1928) built in 1868 on Seco Street. (Photograph by Jesse Brown Cook; courtesy Bancroft Library.)

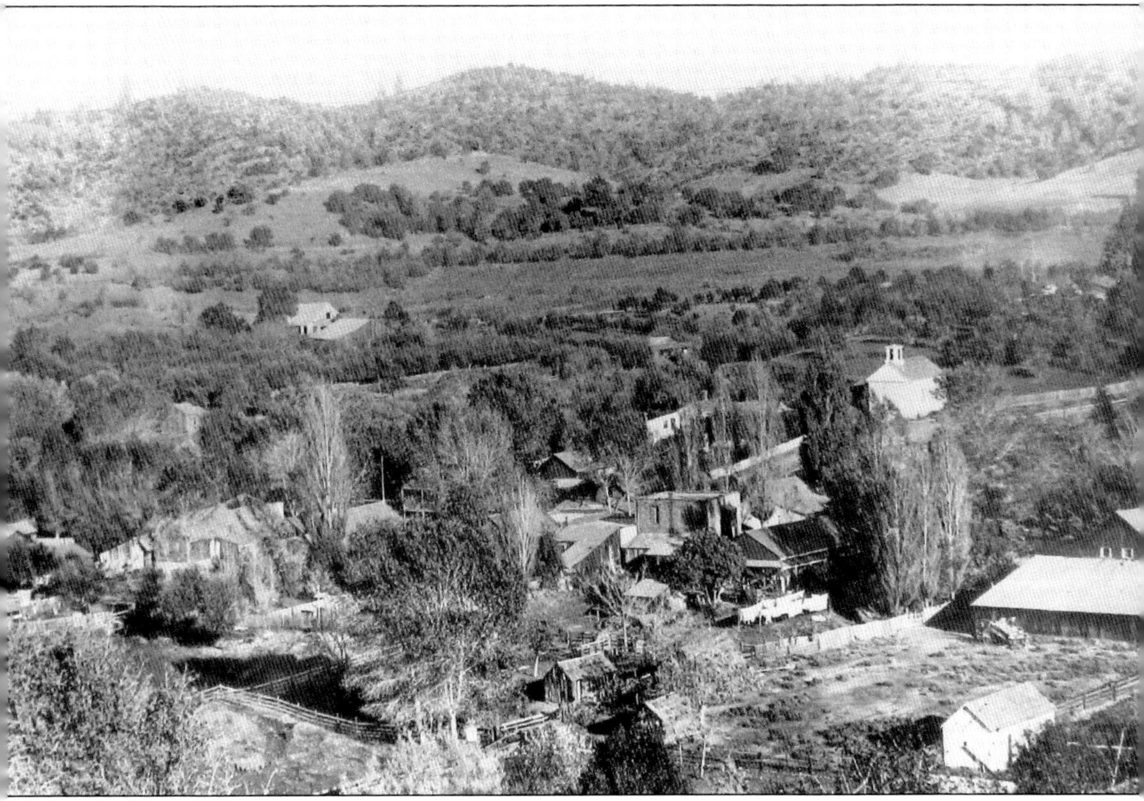

This eastern view of Jamestown was taken before 1897, when the railroad was constructed. Built in 1861, the Greek Revival–style Methodist Church, seen in the background at center right, was remodeled in the Mission Revival style in 1916; the Emporium building was not yet constructed. John Pereira's isolated home, barn, and farmland are near the left center; a large portion would soon be sold to the Jamestown Improvement Company and subdivided for railroad worker housing. The rear of Doña Ramirez's stone building (Masonic Hall) and home are in the center foreground, while the expansive Daigle's Livery Stable is at bottom right. Constructed by Joseph Daigle in 1883 as a stable, the building served as a livery, also known as the "Horse Restaurant," through the early part of the 20th century and became a Texaco station in the 1930s. Although not shown, blacksmiths were important to the community, supplying horseshoing, general blacksmithing, woodworking, and wagon repairing, in association with liveries. (Courtesy Donn Blount.)

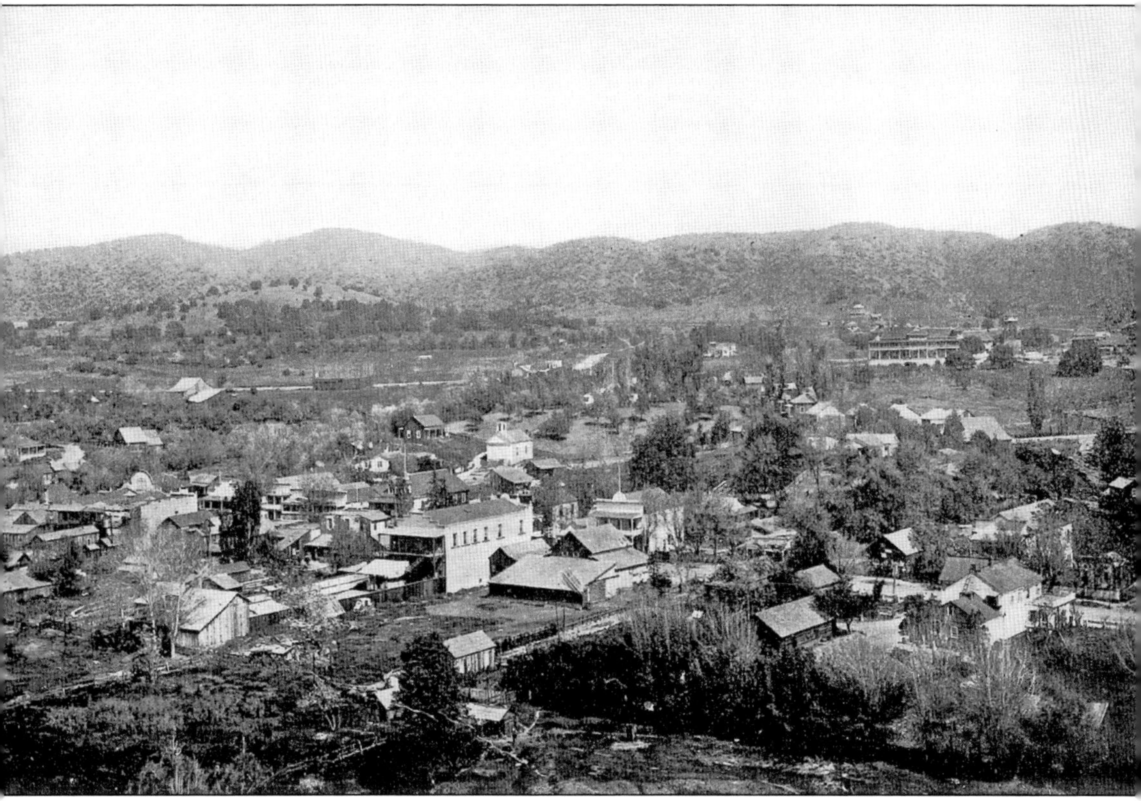

In the early 1900s, the old part of Jamestown (Main Street) was thriving because of its proximity to the Mother Lode. The town boasted well-stocked stores, livery stables, a large and well-equipped foundry, hotels, dry goods emporiums, and drugstores, among other establishments. In this view from the north, taken about 1905, the Methodist Church still anchored the photograph, but two-story buildings with wide porches and verandas line Main Street. With the advent of the railroad, a new neighborhood, visible at the rear of the photograph, sprung up on land acquired from John Pereira, with Hotel Nevills visible on the right, railroad trackage leading past it, and numerous private residences to the rear and sides. Railroad owners Thomas S. Bullock, William H. Crocker, and Prince (descendant of the King of Poland) André Poniatowski, with local partners, formed the Jamestown Improvement Company to develop 120 acres of hillside land as a residential area near the depot, naming it the Pereira Addition. The depot was constructed on land purchased from George Leland. (Courtesy Donn Blount.)

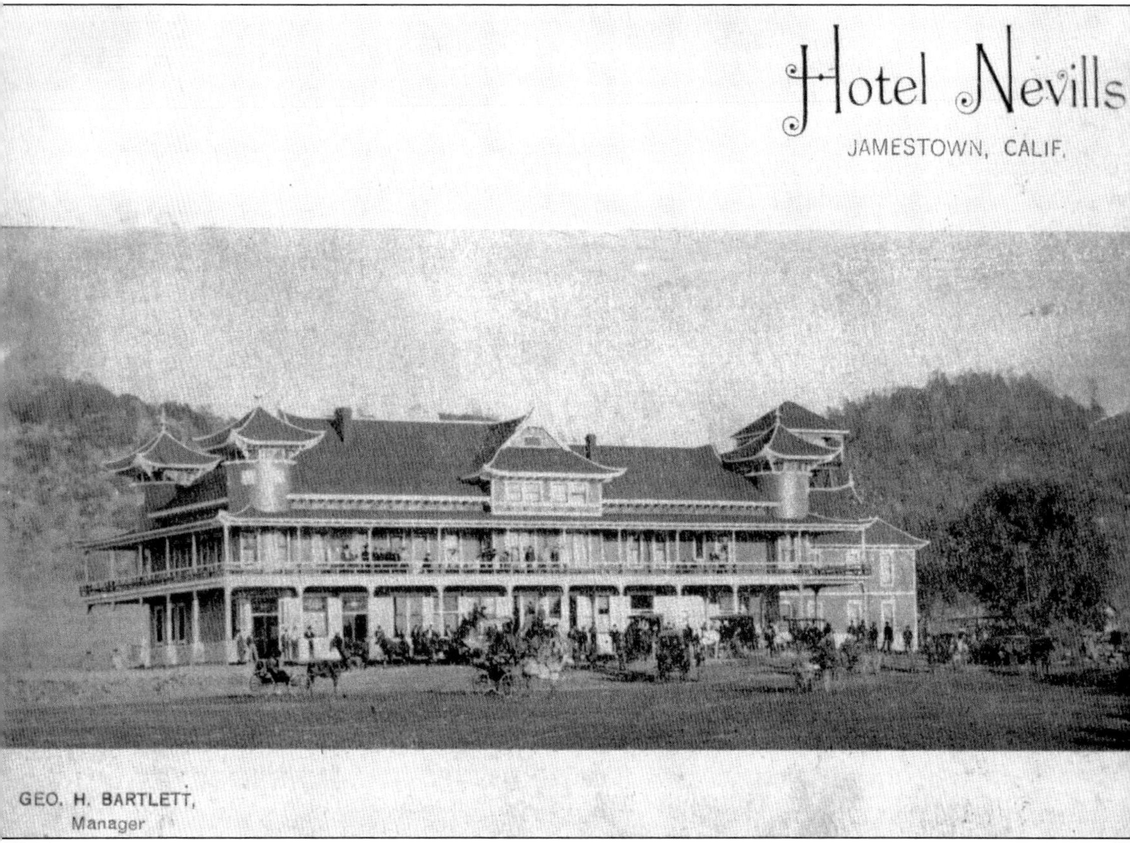

The foundations and ground-floor columns of the Hotel Nevills were local green-streaked quartz, set on a marble porch floor brought from Prince Poniatowski's Columbia marble works. The upper-front balconies and bedrooms, paneled in local Ponderosa pine, overlooked the sweep of Table Mountain, with its jutting Pulpit Rock and Peppermint Falls. The dining room overlooked a garden with palm trees, rose beds, marble walks, and statuary. The large lobby, with a marble fireplace, had leather furniture and fine paintings, while the saloon shone with crystal chandeliers, wide mirrors, and an imported mahogany bar. The dining room had mirrored sideboards, white linen, and silver. A concrete luggage platform, protected from stages and wagons with iron posts and heavy chains, sat between the hotel and depot, while the double-tracked Sierra rails were laid out and abutted just beyond the front of the building so that trains would pull in and out directly before the impressive buildings. (Courtesy Stephen Willey.)

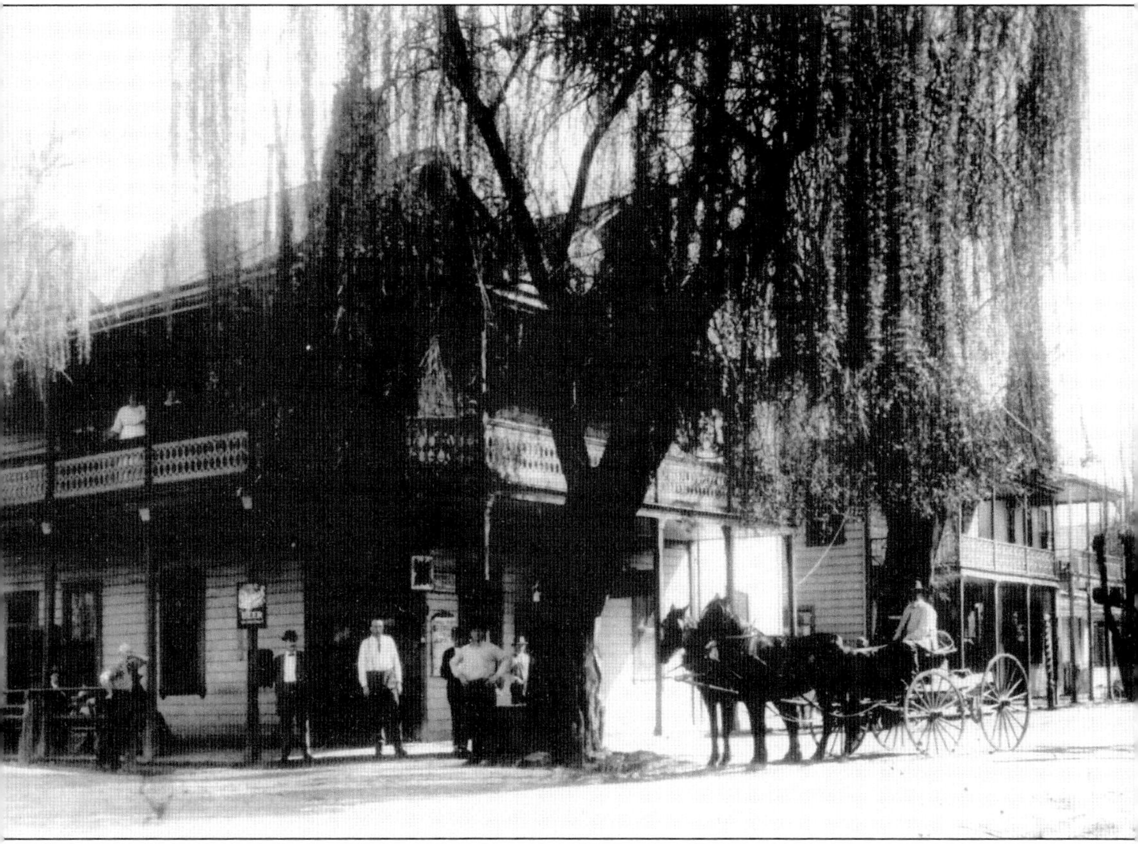

The Hotel Willow, named for the giant willow trees which graced its corner for many years, was the premier hostelry in Jamestown from its beginnings in 1896 to recent years. Constructed by John Pereira to take advantage of the new influx of travelers he anticipated as a result of the railroad's arrival, it replaced his earlier hotel on the site, which burned in 1863. The business was immediately leased to C. C. Stone. By the end of 1897, Frank and Pauline Mayer, natives of Germany, had acquired the business, purchasing the building for $4,000 in 1899. In this view, about 1900, a driver awaits his fare while employees pose outside the front entry. Their daughter, Amelia, continued to maintain the family interest with various managers until her death in 1933. (Courtesy Gary Wilson.)

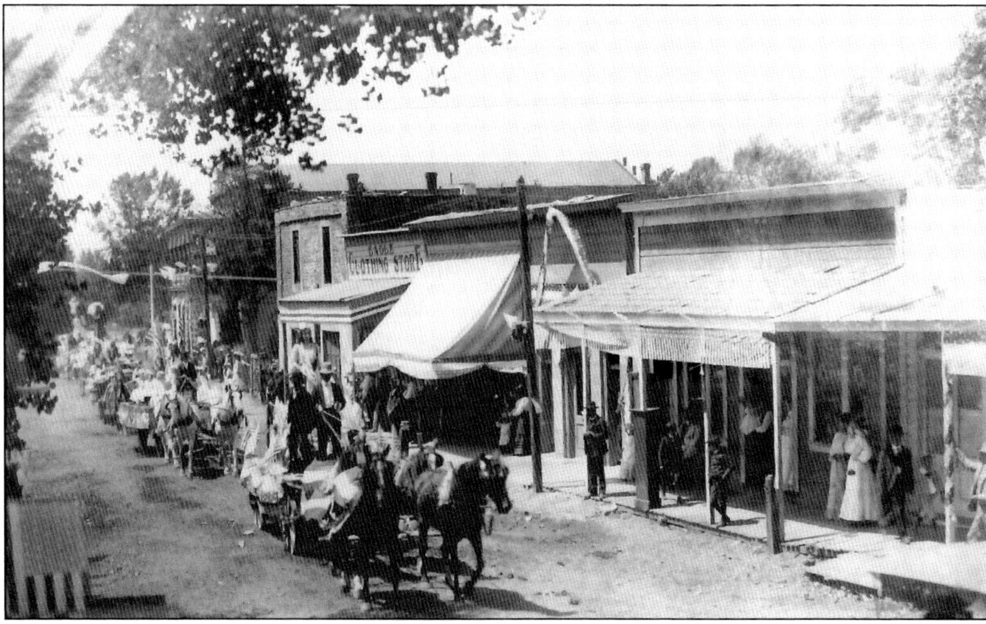

On July 4, 1897, the people of Jamestown celebrated with a parade, bunting, American flags, Chinese lanterns, and horse-drawn floats. The Ramirez Building is on the left, behind the float. To the north was the Oleander brothers' Eagle Clothing Store, whose business started in 1901 in the 1870s building; Flanders' Drug Store, still a one-story stone building; and two frame, false-fronted stores, which are no longer in existence. (Courtesy Gary Wilson.)

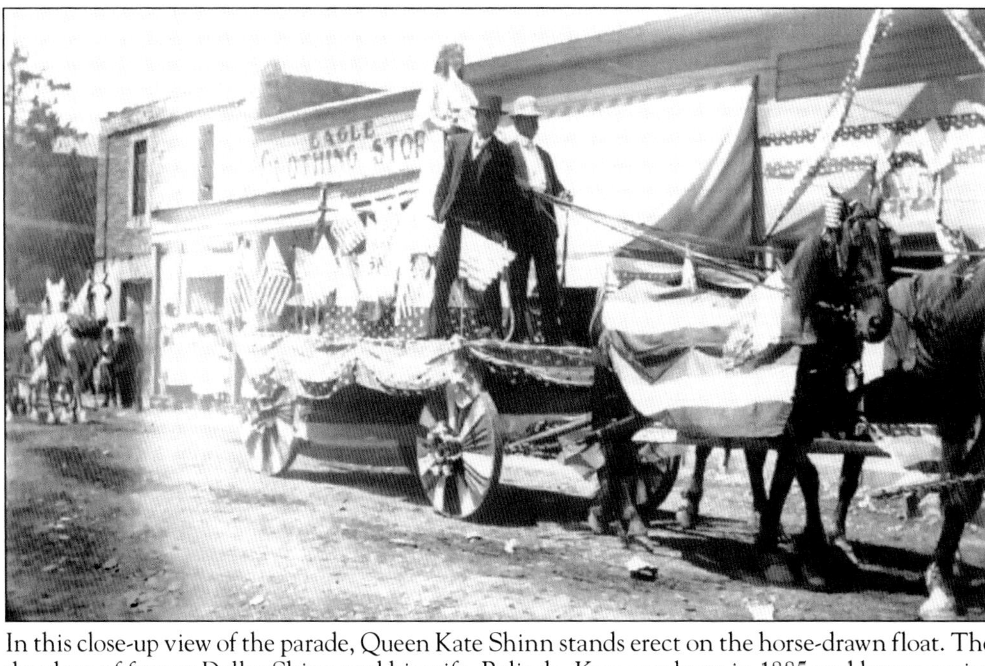

In this close-up view of the parade, Queen Kate Shinn stands erect on the horse-drawn float. The daughter of farmer Dallas Shinn and his wife, Belinda, Kate was born in 1885 and later married Joseph Marchaud. The Ramirez Building, then owned by A. B. Preston, the last Master Mason of the lodge that once occupied the building, and later by postmaster Howard Preston, is visible to the left. (Courtesy Gary Wilson.)

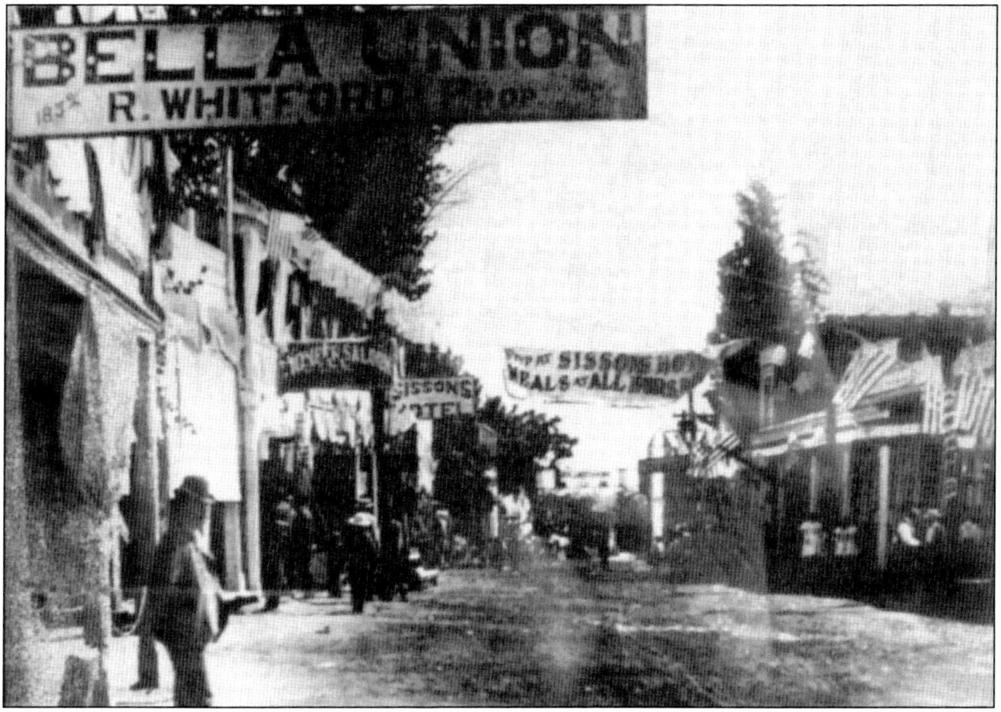

This view south on Main Street was taken from Seco Street at street level about 1898. The dapper gentleman in the bowler hat stands in front of the Bella Union Saloon, and Sissons Hotel's banner advertises "meals at all hours." The Independent Order of Odd Fellows (IOOF) building would not be built for another two years. (Courtesy Stephen Willey.)

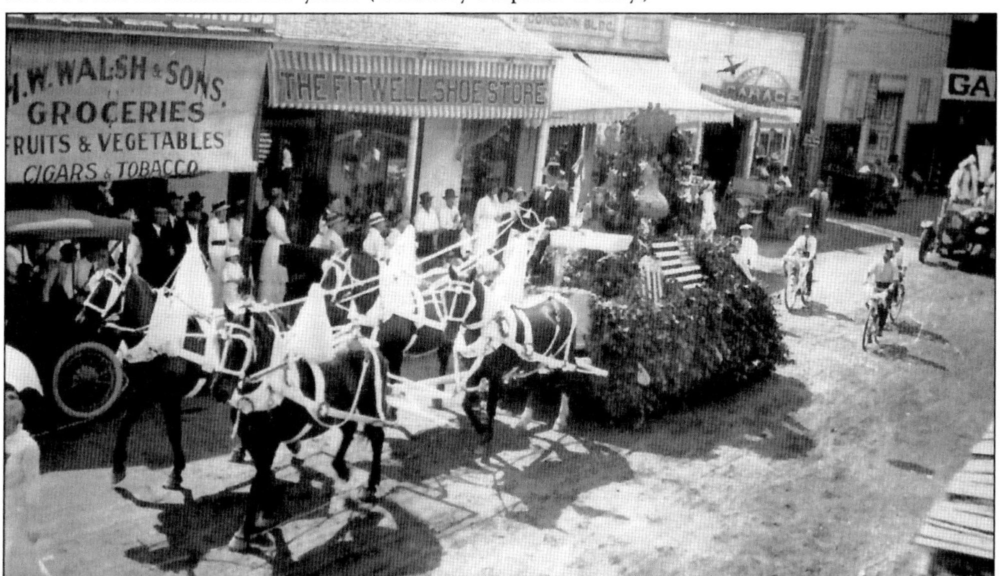

Jamestown loved its parades, and this one in the 1910s featured not only a horse-drawn float, but the automobile that would soon take its place, as well as boys on bicycles. The Walsh and Sons Grocery, Fit Well Shoe Store, and two garages signaled the modern era. (Courtesy Tuolumne County Museum.)

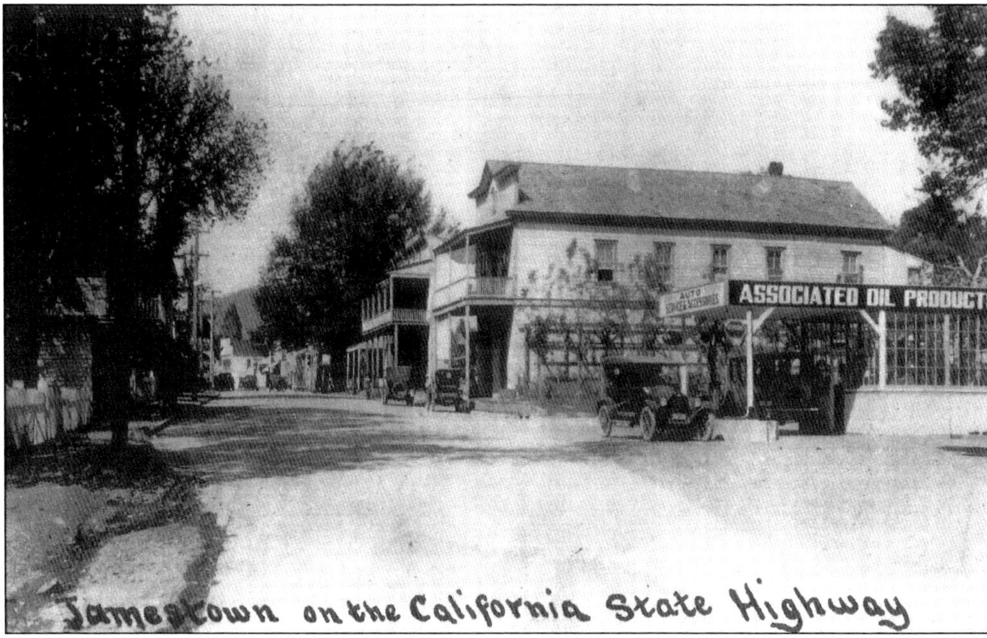

This photograph from around 1925 looks north on Main Street, old Highway 108/49. Today Donovan Street intersects on the immediate right where the Associated Gasoline was located. The large building on the right was built by Col. William Donovan in 1854, but by the 1890s, it was operated as the Marengo Hotel until the upper story burned in a fire in 1937. (Courtesy Stephen Willey.)

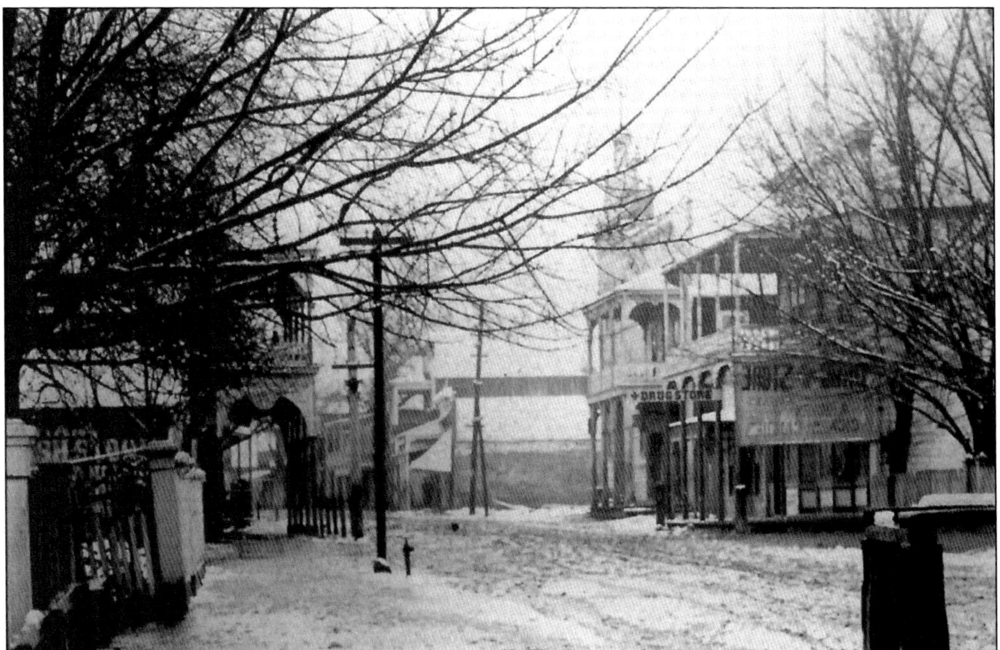

Slightly farther up Main Street, the Durgan Building and the National Hotel were photographed on a rare snowy day in Jamestown. (Courtesy Tuolumne County Museum.)

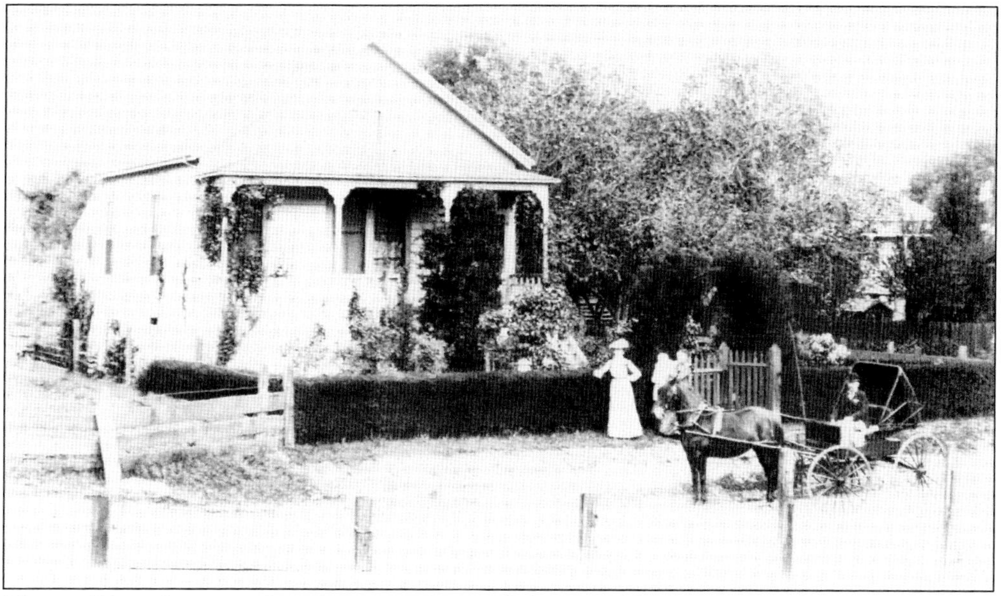

This well-kept home and garden, complete with boxwood hedge, foundation shrubbery, and vernacular Greek Revival architecture, was one of the lovely homes that graced upper Main Street in the early 1900s. At this time, Jamestown, with its business buildings, residences, hotels, schools, churches, and a newspaper, was described in *Tuolumne County, California* (issued by the *Union Democrat* newspaper in 1909) as "a fine little mining town of about 1000 inhabitants." (Courtesy Gary Wilson.)

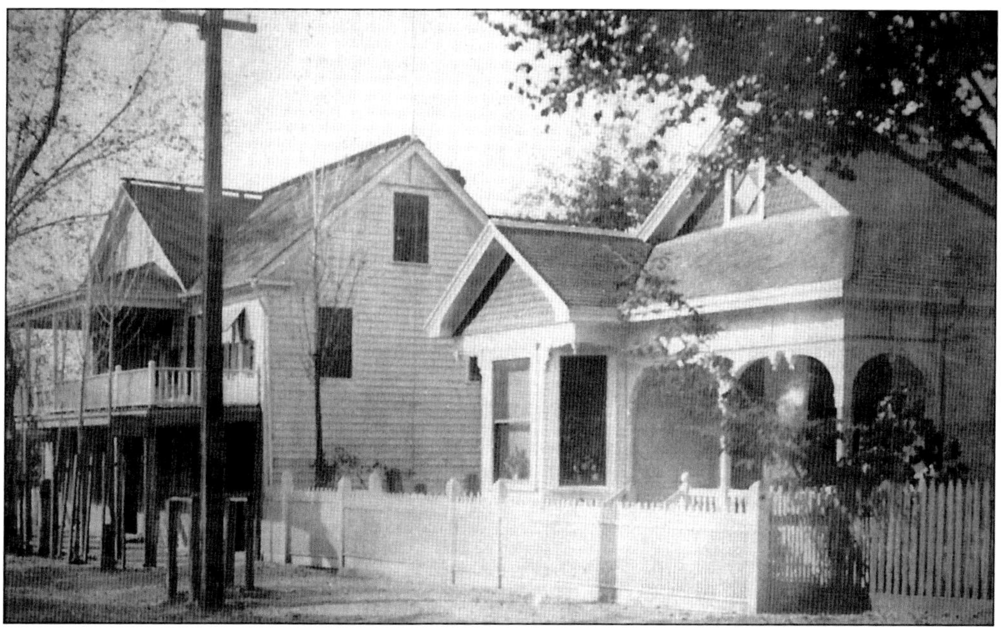

Many of the nicer homes built in the 1890s and early 1900s hard rock mining era in Jamestown were designed in the Queen Anne architectural style, with their asymmetrical facades, patterned shingles, bay windows, and gingerbread elements. The Butterfield house, built for Melvina "Minnie" Butterfield next to her family's Butterfield Store on the south end of town, was completed in 1906. (Courtesy Tuolumne County Museum.)

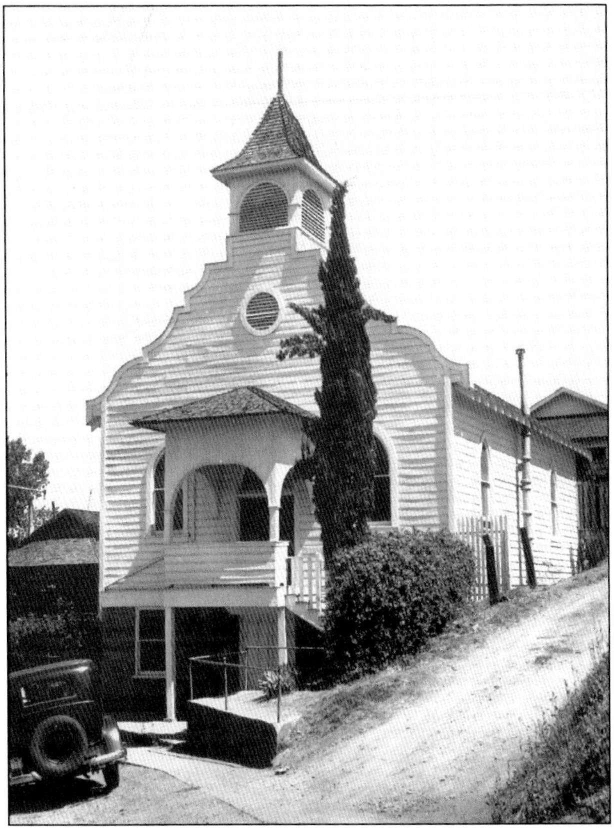

One of the oldest churches in California, the Methodist Episcopal Church was erected in the Greek Revival style in the 1850s. In 1916, what had been a pathway alongside the church was widened to a driveway, and the building was completely reconstructed to face the road in the Mission Revival style (then sweeping California), with a "witch's cap" affixed to the bell tower. (Courtesy Stephen Willey.)

The Jamestown Grammar School, a Greek Revival building erected in 1862, had two front doors: one for boys and one for girls. Located on the knoll above the old Stockton Road on the O'Donnell property, it served the Jamestown pupils until 1929, when it burned. The school was replaced at its current location on Fifth Street by a brick building the following year. (Courtesy Stephen Willey and Tuolumne County Museum.)

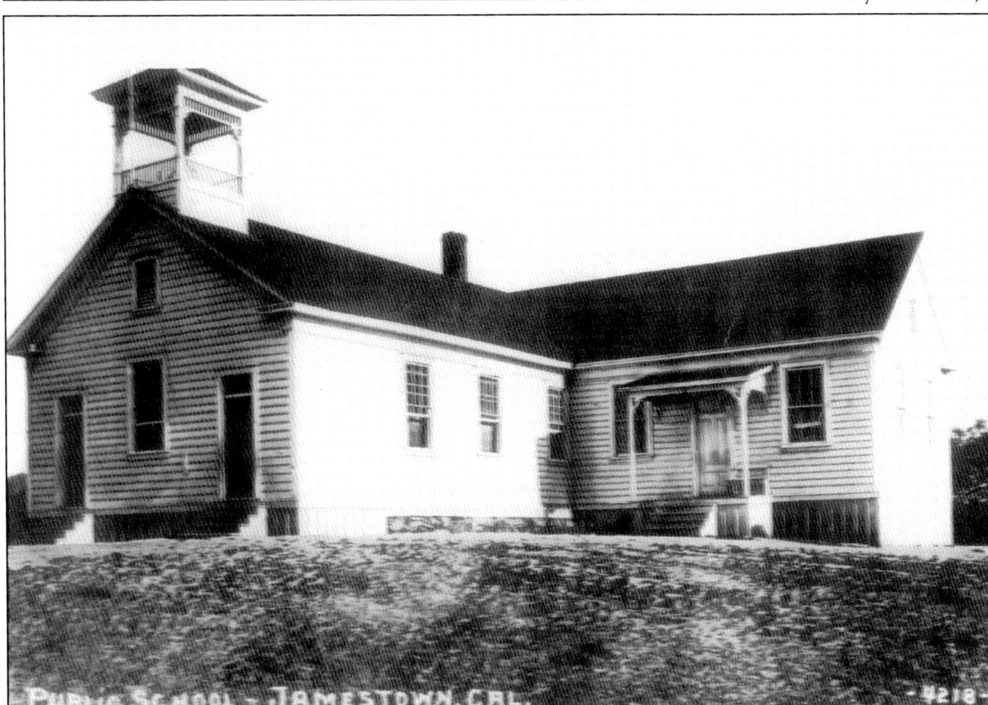

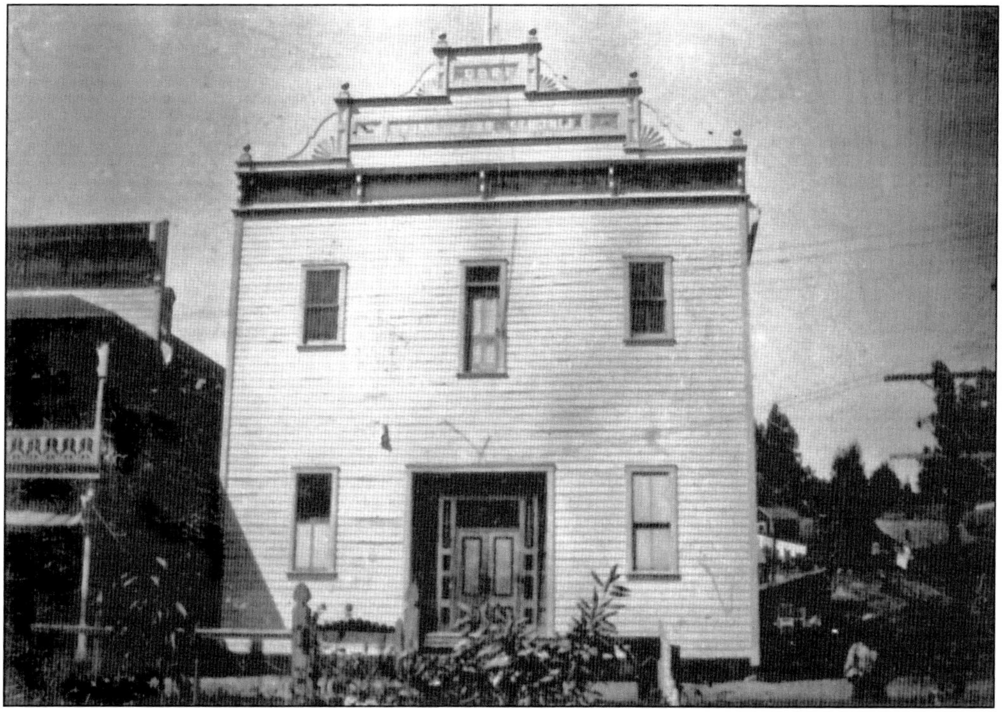

Fraternal lodges were important organizations in the mining camps of the West and provided a brotherhood of like souls with whom to associate when men were far from home and family. The Independent Order of Odd Fellows (IOOF) and the Free Masons were the two most prevalent in the Mother Lode. This undated view was printed in reverse; the National Hotel should be to the right. (Courtesy Tuolumne County Museum.)

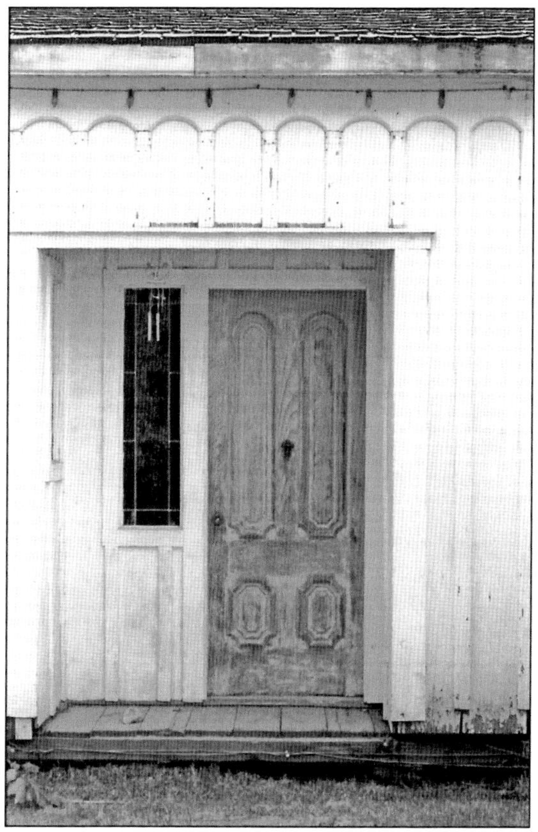

The facade of the Dr. M. T. Dodge home, probably built in 1854 by Edwin Rogers, features beveled and scalloped board-and-batten siding and was reputedly shipped around the Horn and assembled on site, as were many other homes in the gold country. This was later the home of liveryman Joseph Daigle and then the Whyte family, whose descendants reside there today. (Courtesy Scott Weber.)

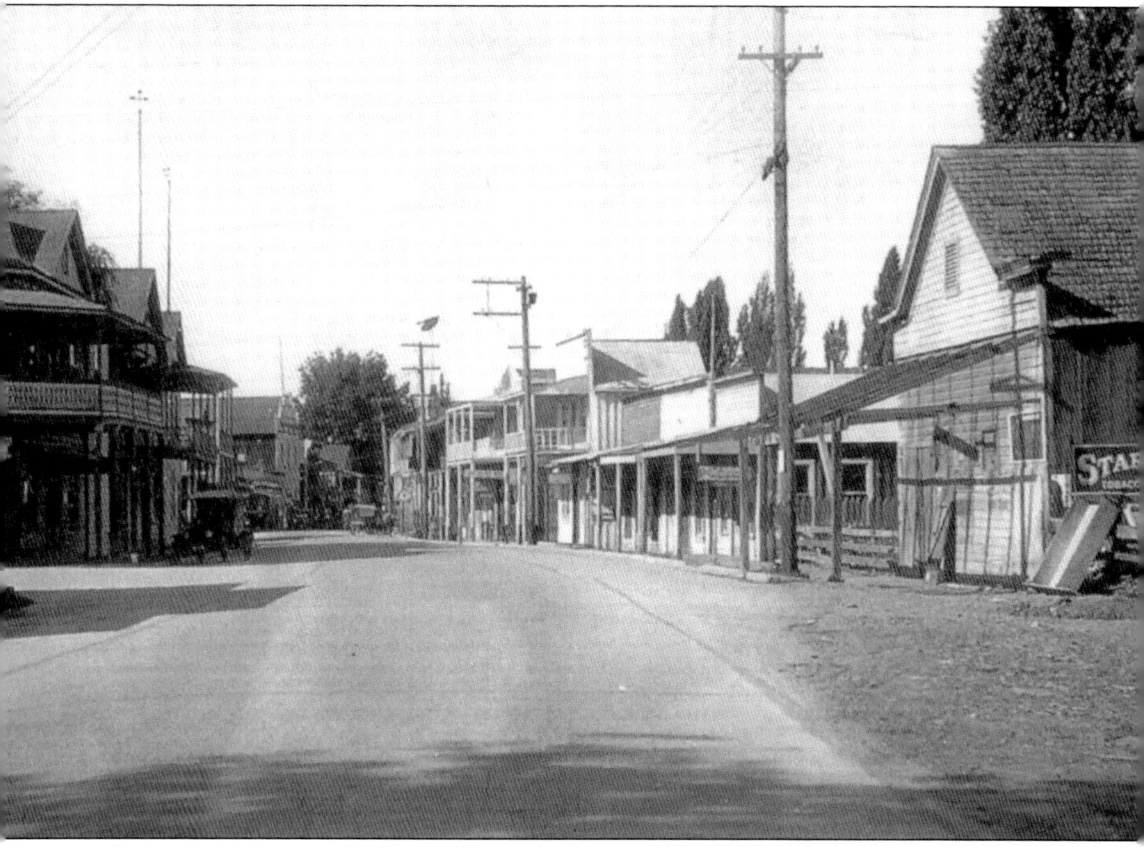

In this 1923 photograph of Main Street, the Hotel Willow, with its second-story balcony, is seen on the left. Next to it is a two-story hotel, and the Odd Fellows Hall is farther down the street beside the National Hotel. On the west (right) side of the street, proceeding south, were the Pioneer Livery Stable; three small false-fronted buildings housing a saloon, harness shop, and cobbler; a two-story building with a restaurant and lodgings; and the Marliani Building, with its peaked false front. (Courtesy Bancroft Library.)

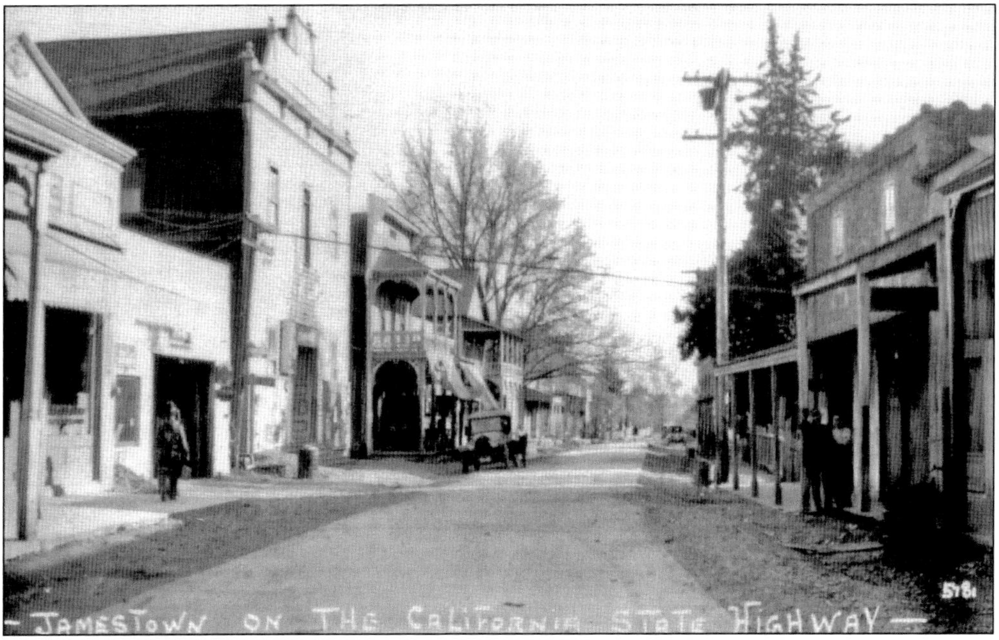

In about 1925, the Congdon Building is partly visible to the left, followed by Roy Rushing's garage, the Odd Fellows Hall, the National Hotel and Restaurant, the Durgan Building, and the Jamestown Hotel down the street. The Ramirez/Preston Building is seen to the right in the photograph. (Courtesy Stephen Willey.)

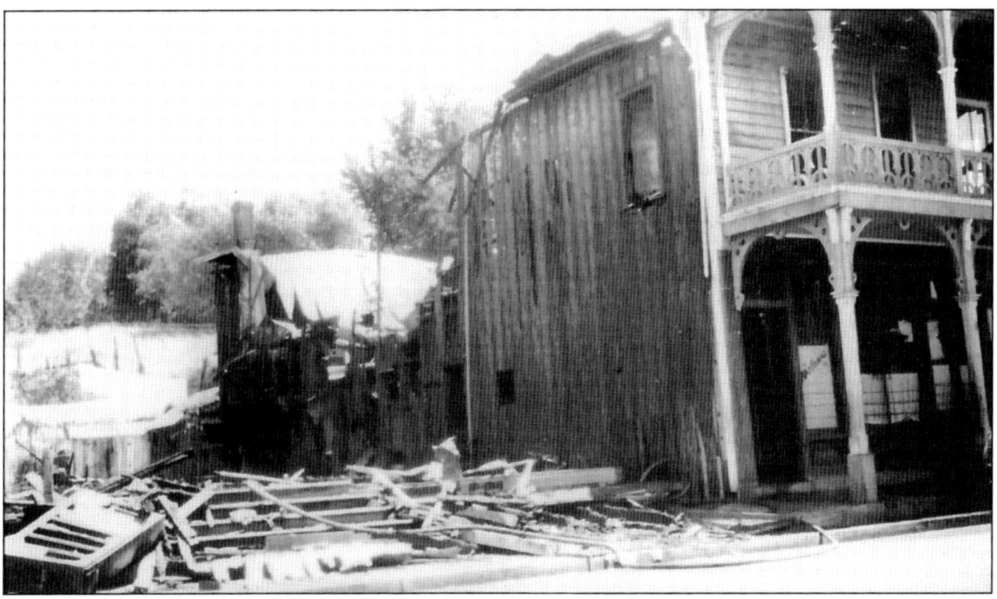

The Odd Fellows Hall and the National Hotel were photographed in 1927, just after they had been consumed by fire. The Odd Fellows rebuilt their lodge hall in concrete, which in subsequent years served as the Kerr Hatchery, managed by the Sayer family. The National Hotel was also rebuilt in fireproof concrete the following year. (Courtesy Tuolumne County Museum.)

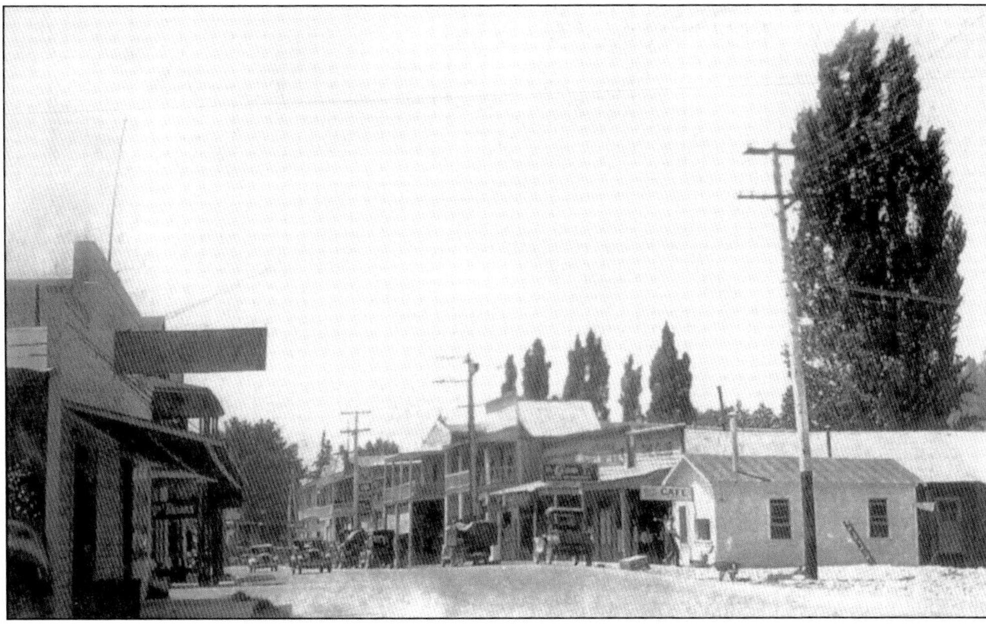

By the time this 1928 image of the west side of Main Street was taken, the Little White Café had replaced the Pioneer Livery, and down the street were The Club, the New York Café, the Tuolumne Inn, the Marliani Building, and The Pioneer (now Community Hall). A bakery is seen to the left, and several emporiums are advertising soft drinks, a paean to Prohibition. (Courtesy Bancroft Library.)

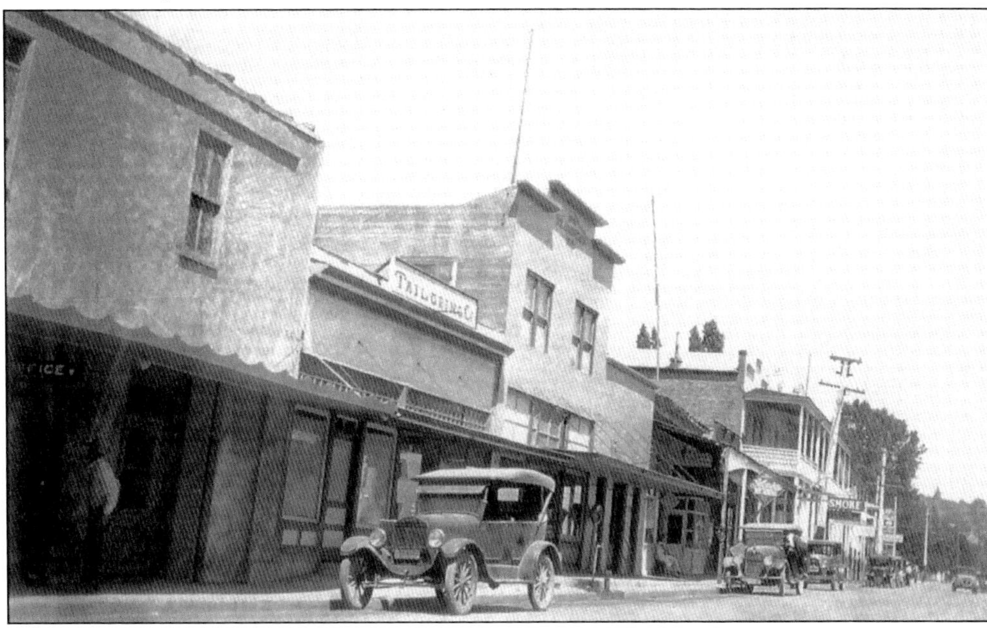

The view from the opposite end of Main Street, when it had been built up with several two-story concrete buildings, is depicted in this 1928 photograph taken from the south by Jesse Brown Cook. The Ramirez/Preston Building is seen to the left, along with the Eagle Mercantile, the Flanders Building with its new second story, Flanders Office Building, and several buildings that were later consumed in the 1966 fire. (Courtesy Bancroft Library.)

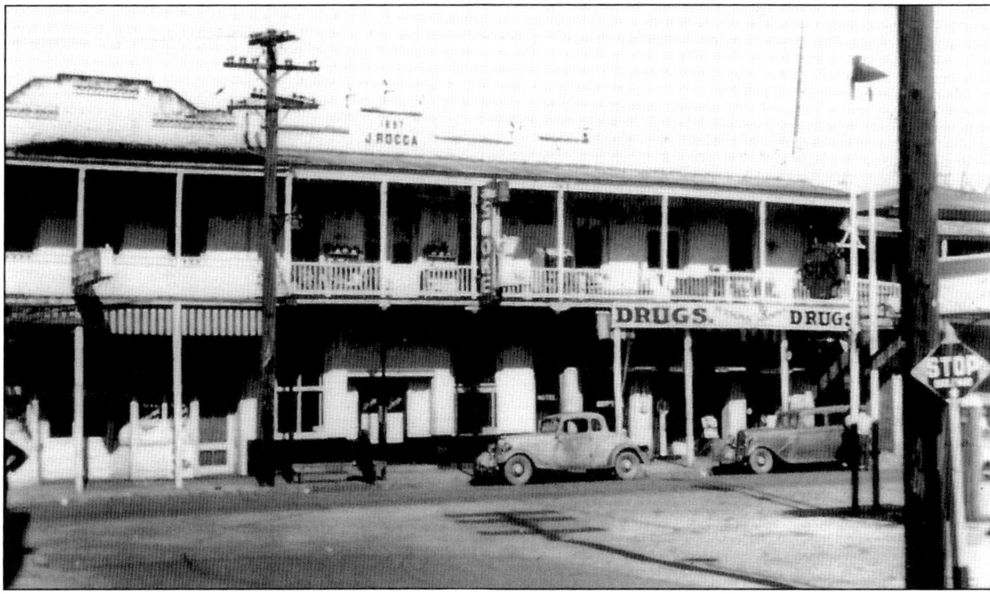

Anchoring the west side of the north end of Main Street, the J. Rocca Building was a long, rectangular two-story building with overhanging porches. Capped with a Mission-style pediment, it was home to numerous businesses over the ensuing years following its construction in the late 1890s. The Jamestown Drug Store occupied the north end of the building for many years, while The Smoke, the most famous of the town's restaurants and saloons in those years, occupied the center. The Gold Nugget Saloon occupied the southern corner during the 1950s and early 1960s, before the building burned in 1966. The site is now occupied by Rocca Park. The adjacent concrete building, which survived the fire and was home to a later incarnation of The Smoke, belonged to Hap and Edna Collard and is visible to the right. It was the home of Dodsworth's Hardware and then Baker's Candy Kitchen, a favorite of the local children, which was operated for over 30 years. (Courtesy Tuolumne County Museum.)

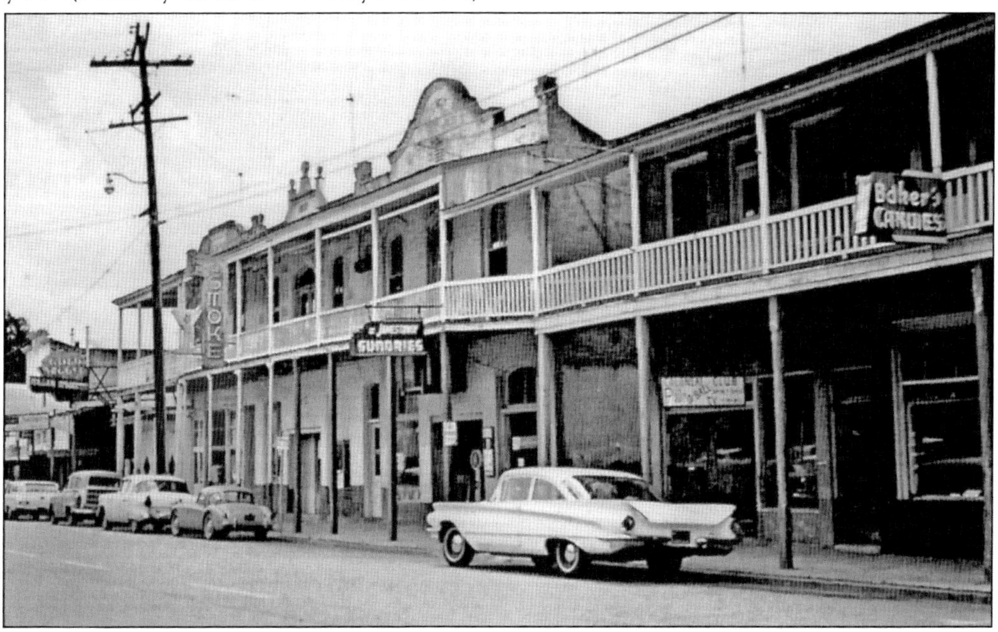

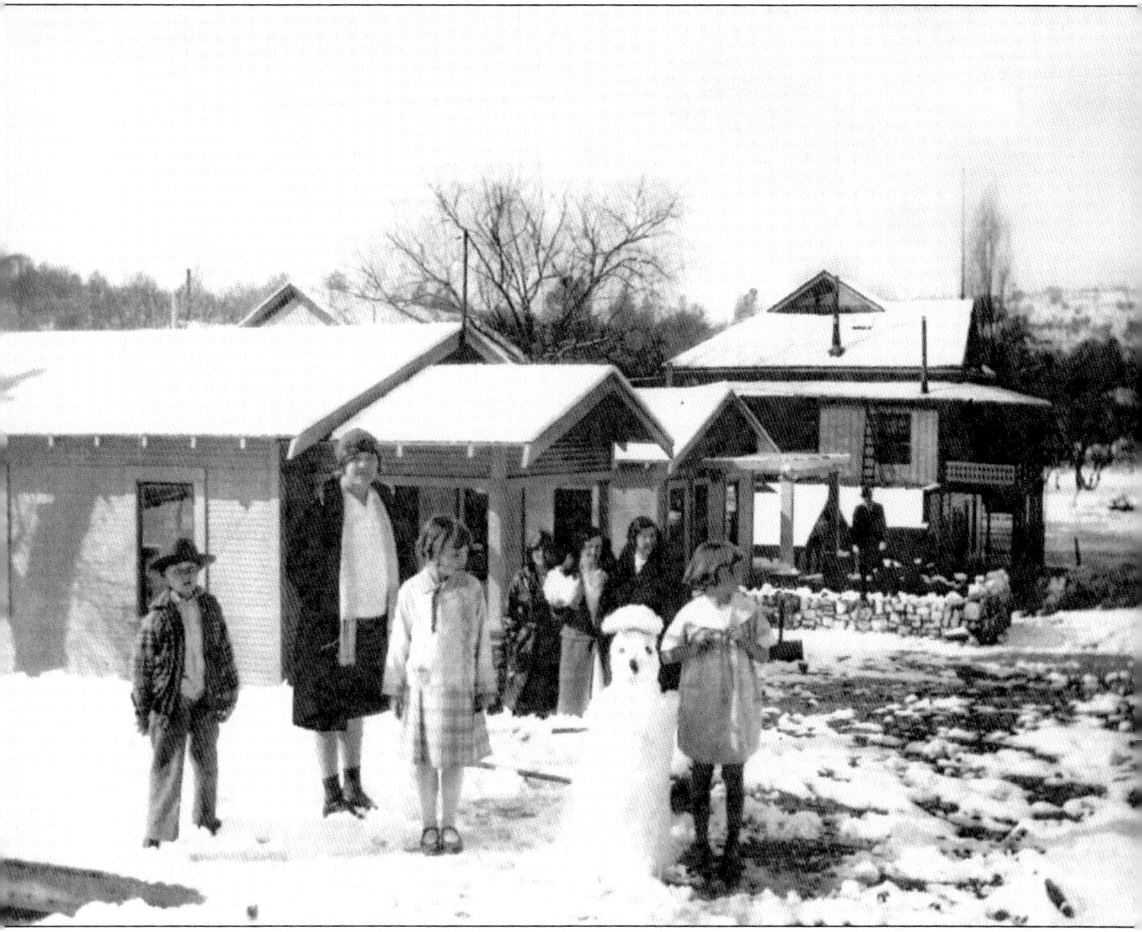

In 1927, Amelia Mayer, who had inherited the Hotel Willow from her parents, was married to Andy Froelich, who brought his four daughters and one son to the union. On an unusual snowy day in 1929, the family built a snowman in front of the Froelich Cottages behind the hotel. (Courtesy Gary Wilson.)

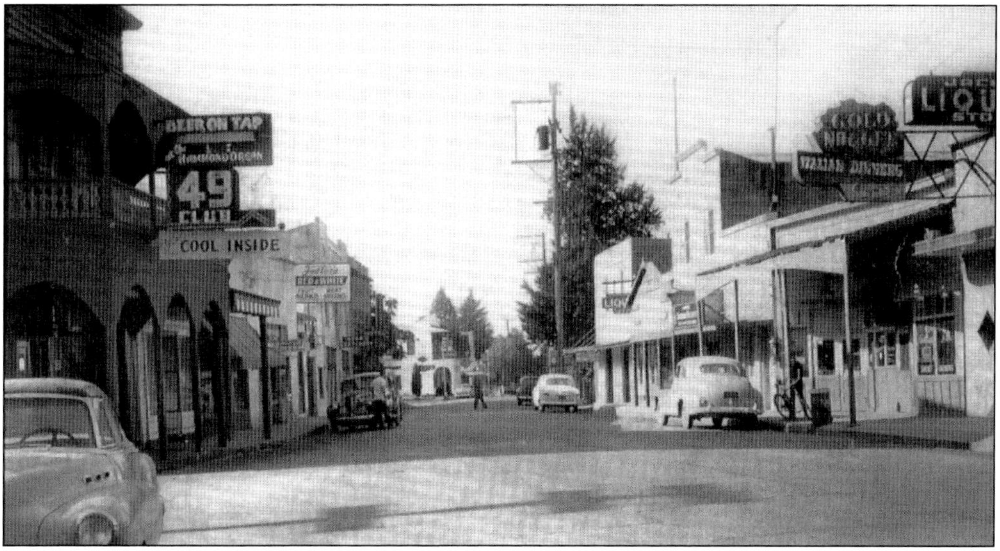

One of Jamestown's most famous watering holes, the Commercial Saloon owned by Johnnie Gandolfo, is seen on the left. It became the 49er Club when Arthur Pardina took it over and was eventually razed in 1966. Farther south down the street were the Kerr Turkey Hatchery (formerly the 1928 Odd Fellows Hall), the National Hotel, and the Jamestown Hotel, visible to the rear. (Courtesy Jim Yeisley.)

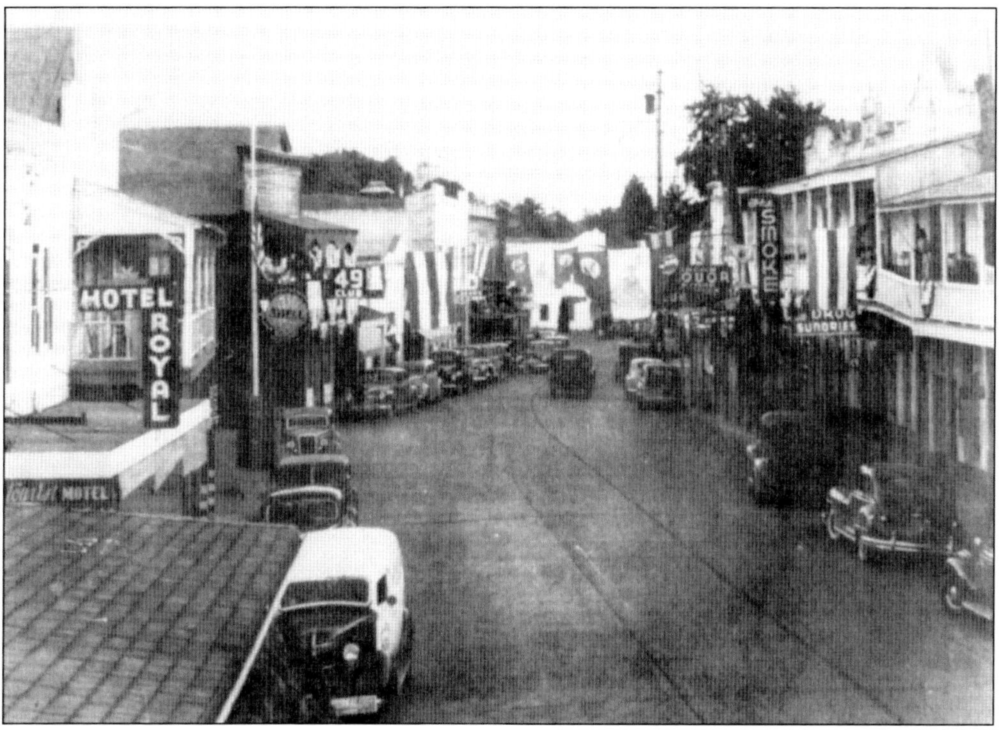

By the late 1940s, Jamestown's Main Street was once again populated with bars and saloons, advertised with the neon signs of the times. The Rocca Building is seen on the right; the former Schiffman's Men's Clothing Store, at this time home to the public library and another saloon, is on the left. (Courtesy Gary Wilson.)

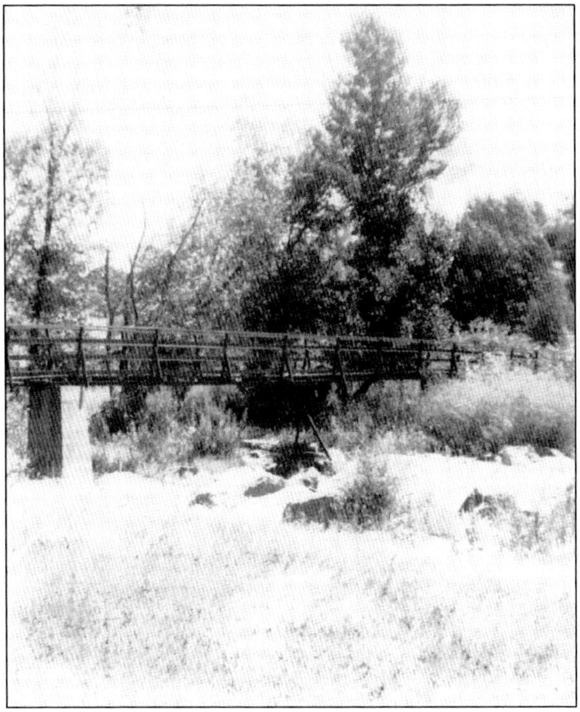

The footbridge to Butterfield Flat, located west across Wood's Creek, provided access to residences there. So called because it was the site of B. F. Butterfield's 1849 store before it burned, prompting his move across the creek, the flat was also the location of the 1849 Bellingham Store (page 111). This 1957 photograph was taken by Jim Yeisley, a Bellingham descendant. The concrete supports of the structure remain today. (Courtesy Gary Wilson.)

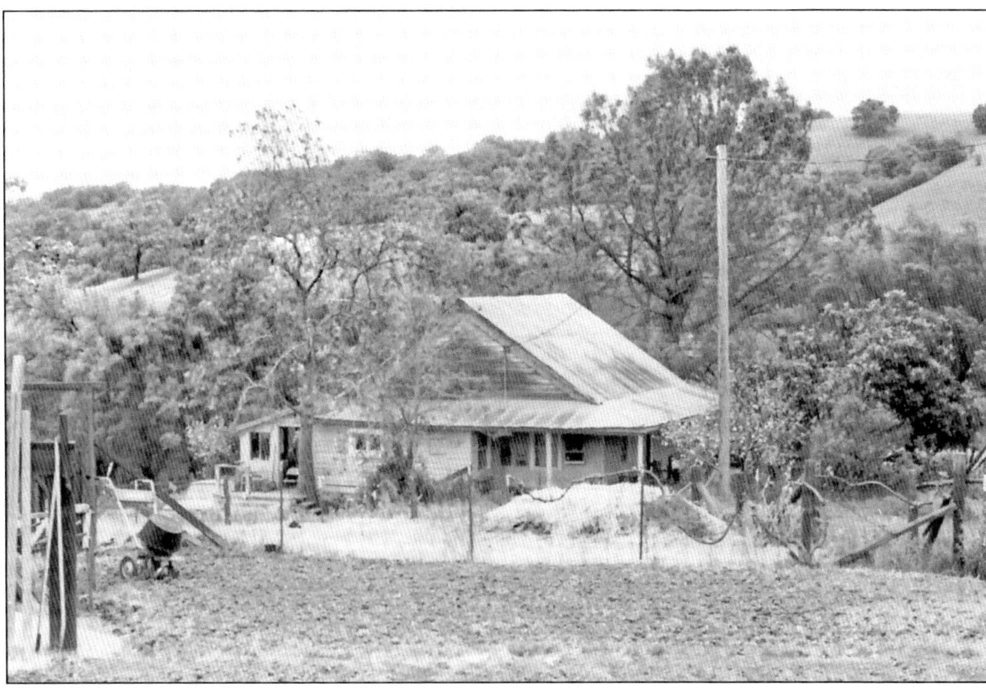

The home of John App was located south of Jamestown and near his famous App Mine (App-Heslep) on Quartz Mountain, which produced over $6 million in gold. His wife, Leanna Donner App, was famous for surviving the cold winter of 1847 at Donner Lake during the ill-fated attempt to cross the Sierra in winter. She died in Jamestown in 1929 at the age of 95. (Courtesy Scott Weber.)

Four

THE SECOND GOLD RUSH

Lode mining began in the early 1860s along the Mother Lode vein, but little appreciable gold was produced for another two decades. This was to change with the advent of the hard rock mining boom of the late 1880s, which continued until most of the mines were shut down for World War I. This boom was occasioned by the improvements in mining and milling technology (such as air drills, explosives, pumps, and the introduction of electric power), enabling many more lode deposits to be profitably worked, especially large, but low-grade accumulations. The introduction of rock crushers, an increase in size of stamp mills, and new concentrating devices such as vanners lowered milling costs, while cyanidation was introduced in 1896, soon replacing the chlorination process.

The second gold rush occurred around Jamestown from about 1893 to 1906, with around 300 stamps dropping those years. Among the most productive lode mines in the Jamestown District were the App-Heslep, Dutch Sweeney, Harvard, Jumper, Rawhide, Santa Ysabel, and Eagle-Shawmut, with total production estimated at $30 million by 1975.

Most of these mines were to close during World War I, some never to reopen and others to be consolidated into the Harvard Mine on Whiskey Hill. There was some activity during the 1920s, and more during the 1930s. Jamestown, along with the rest of the gold regions in California, experienced sporadic mining activity until 1942, when nearly all gold mines in the area were shut down by the U.S. government as nonessential, war-related industries. Prospecting and development began again after the war, but Jamestown mines remained stalled for many years.

High gold prices in the late 1970s renewed interest in the Mother Lode, with geologists conducting exploratory drilling in the old Jamestown district. Results were promising, and in 1983, a group of Canadian geophysicists incorporated Sonora Mining Corporation with the sole purpose of purchasing and developing the Jamestown (Harvard) Mine. During 1986, a 7,000-ton-per-day gold processing facility was erected adjacent to the Harvard pit, where the first ore was processed in February 1987. The mine shut down in the 1990s, and the land is being reclaimed.

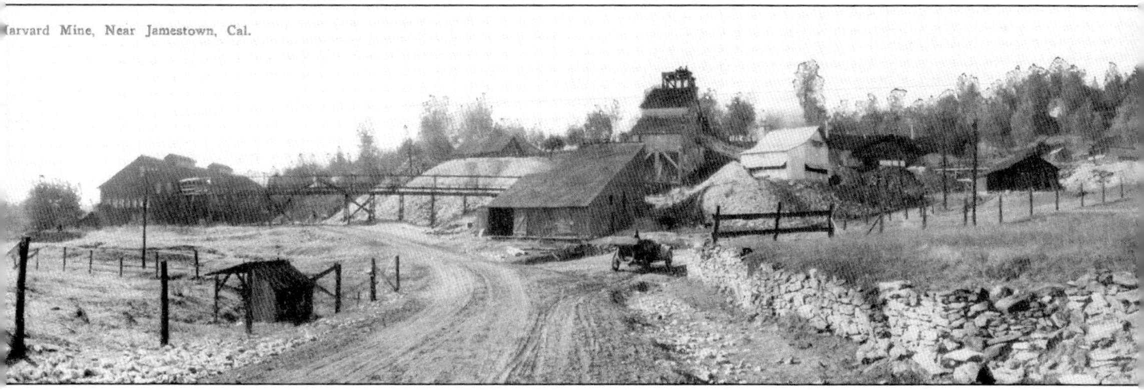

After the Harvard Gold Mining Company paid $350,000 in 1902 for the Erin Go Braugh and Cloudman Mines on Whiskey Hill, the mill was enlarged to treat the combined ores. The mine eventually comprised several other claims including the Trio, Crystalline, Sobrante, McCann, Mooney, and others. The lode was very prominent, with massive quartz outcroppings of 100 to 300 feet wide, with veins 10 feet wide. This photograph was taken in 1914 when the mine had a 300-horsepower double-drum electric hoist, Rix compressors, and an auxiliary steam plant; the ore was hoisted in 2-ton skips and crushed by two Blake crushers. Equipment in the mill consisted of 60 stamps, weighing 1,200 pounds apiece, dropping 100 times per minute. (Courtesy Sharon Marovich.)

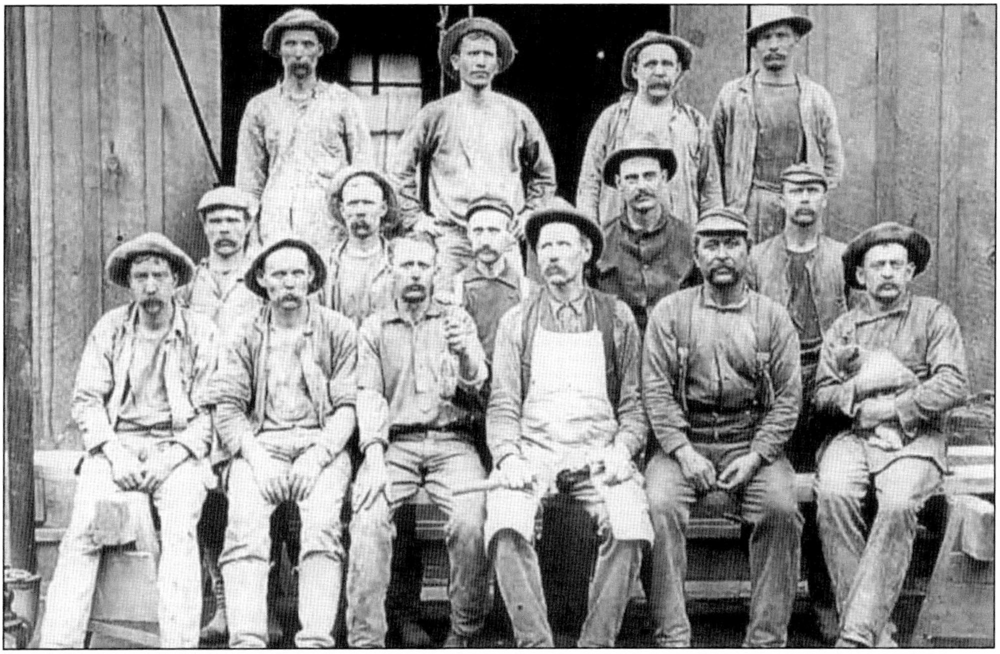

The mining crew posed for photographer A. H. Gilfillan at the Harvard Mine in 1928. They wore no hard hats or steel-toed boots and worked underground 8–12 hours a day, six days a week, for an average wage of $3.64 a day, with bosses making about $1 more. The blacksmith, who sharpened the drills on a regular basis, is depicted in the center of the front row, wearing his leather apron. (Courtesy Bancroft Library.)

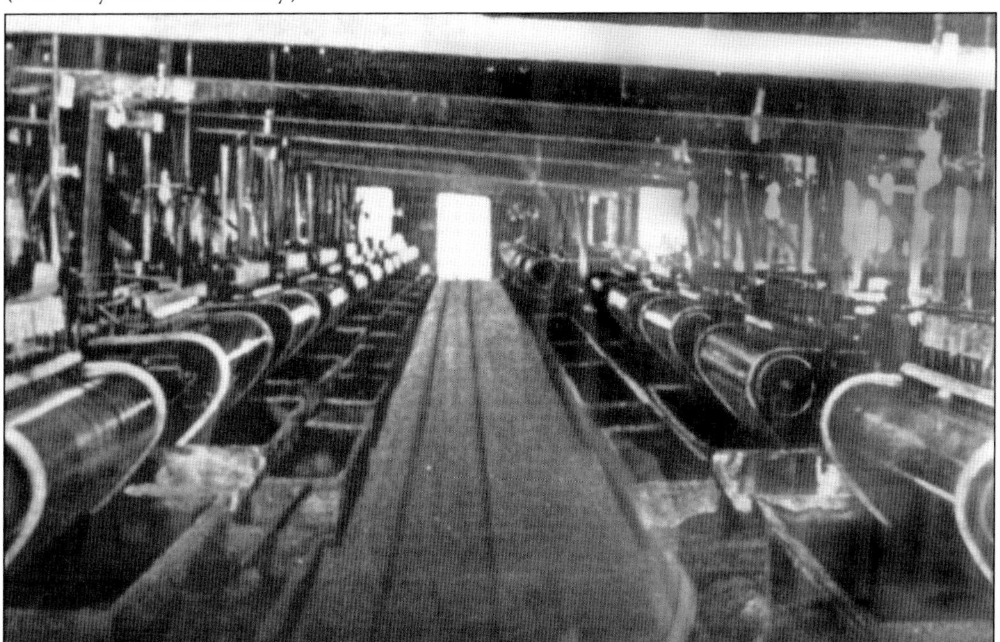

After passing through the stamps, the pulp from the batteries was concentrated by twenty-four 6-foot Johnston vanners, which extracted 86 percent of the ore, assaying at $30 per ton. At this time, a force of 116 men were employed by Harvard Mine, Inc. (Courtesy Stephen Willey.)

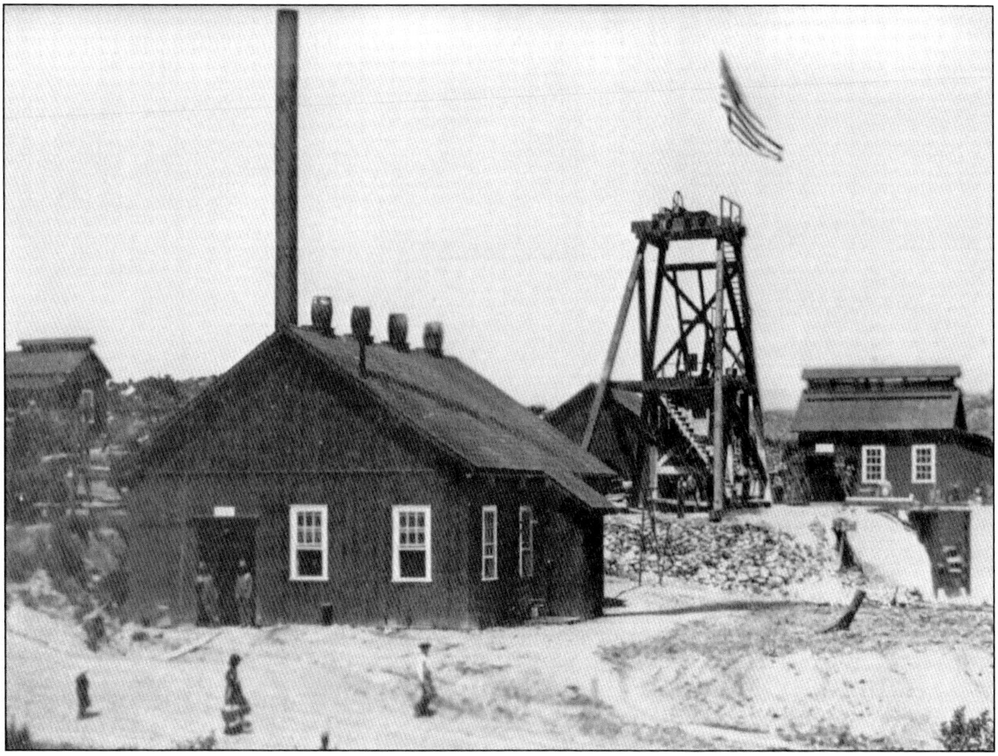

The photographer caught this image of the Alameda Mine at Quartz on the Fourth of July in 1890. The head frame, flying the American flag, is in the center of the photograph, with the engine room in the foreground. By 1914, the mine was idle and the workings caved. (Courtesy Tuolumne County Museum.)

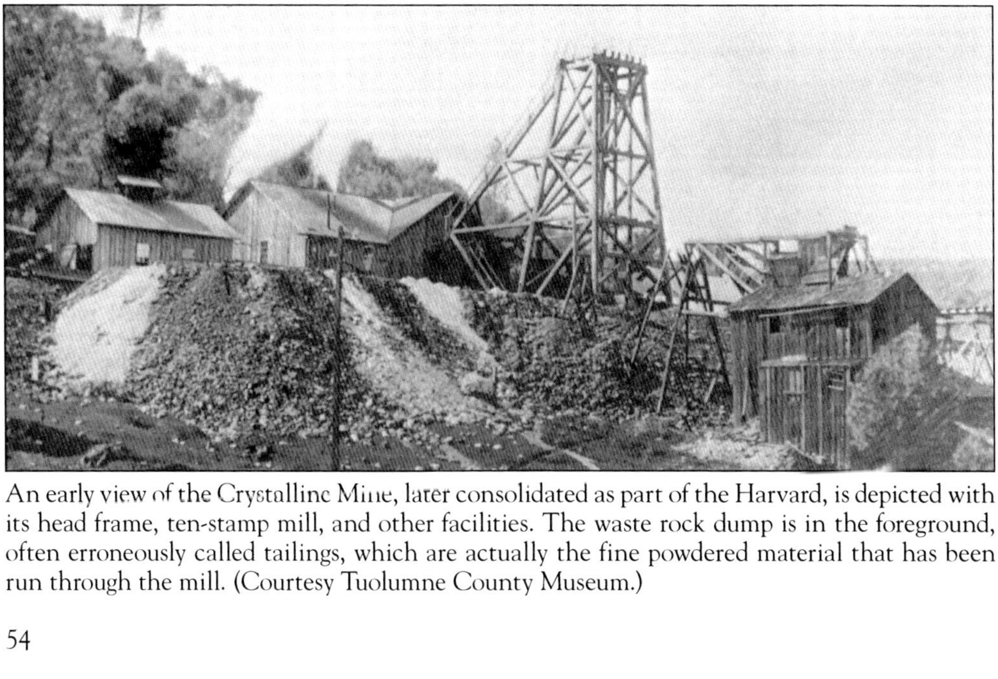

An early view of the Crystalline Mine, later consolidated as part of the Harvard, is depicted with its head frame, ten-stamp mill, and other facilities. The waste rock dump is in the foreground, often erroneously called tailings, which are actually the fine powdered material that has been run through the mill. (Courtesy Tuolumne County Museum.)

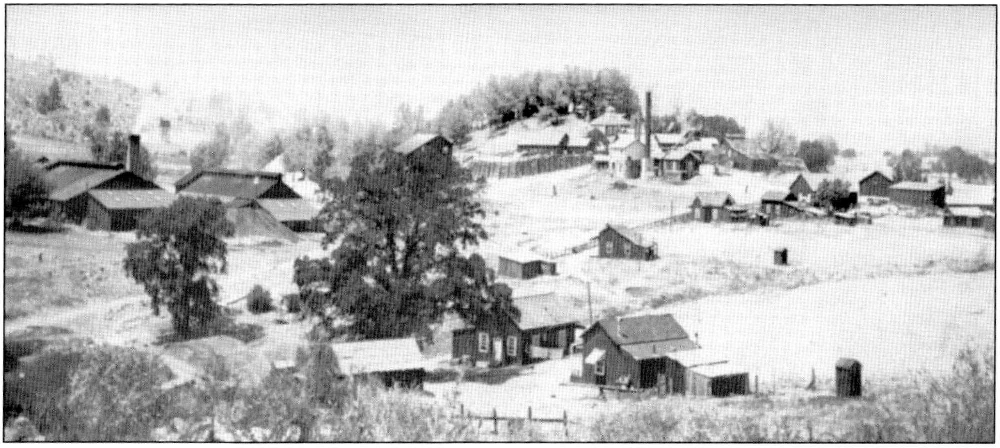

Situated about 2 miles northwest of Jamestown and north of Table Mountain, this view of the Rawhide Mine was probably taken in the 1890s. Led by William Nevills, who also constructed the Hotel Nevills at the Sierra Railway depot, the mill was operating with 30 stamps and a chlorination works. In this northward view, the head frame and hoisting works are in the right center, surrounded by the homes of the miners. At this time, the south, or working, shaft was sunk on vein to a depth of 2,000 feet, with levels driven north and south on the vein every 100 feet, comprising many miles of drifts. (Courtesy Tuolumne County Museum.)

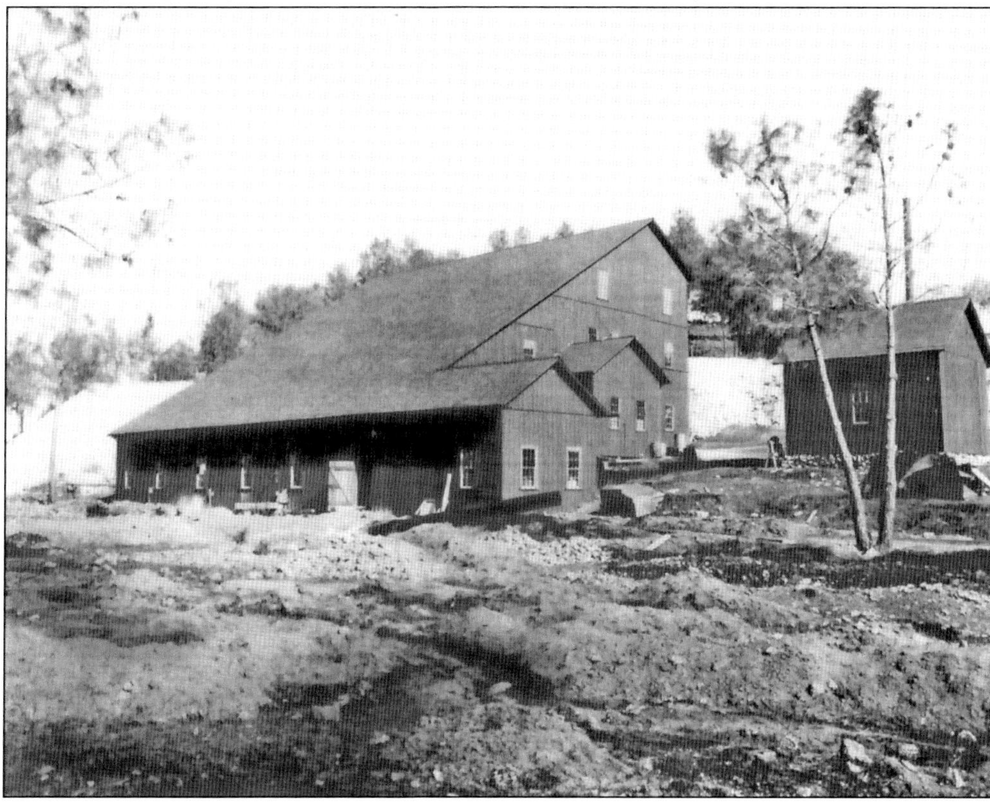

The modern mill building of the Rawhide Mine was photographed in the early 1900s. The mill operated with 40 stamps, with gold production reported to have been $6 million. (Courtesy California State Library.)

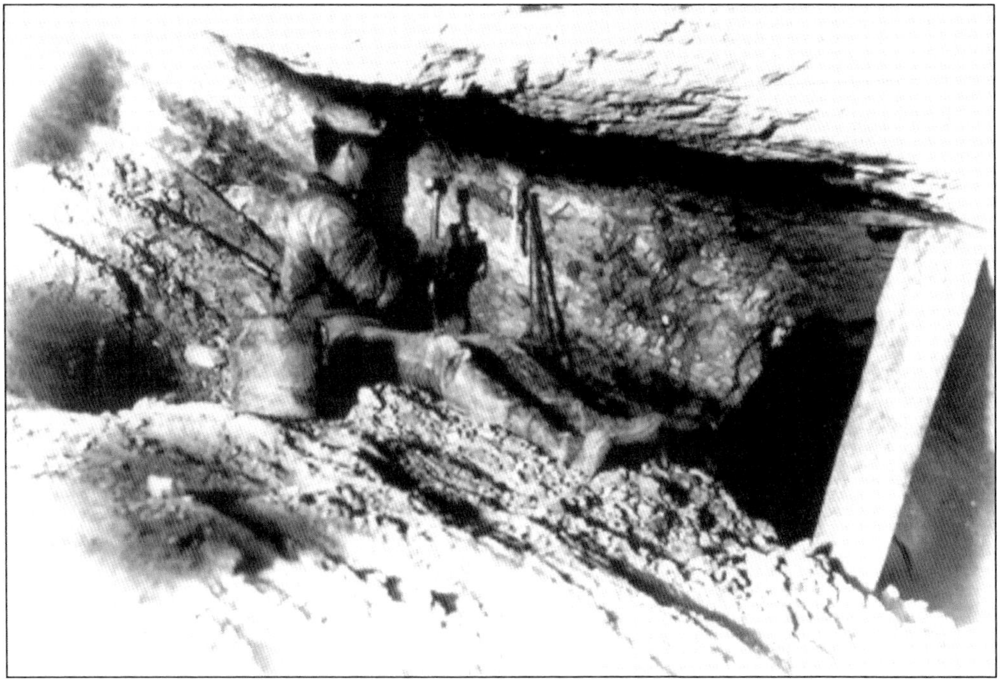

Working deep underground, this miner is single-jacking a hole for the dynamite before blasting. In an inclined vein, between the head wall and the footwall, most of the vein has been mined out, and a piece of timber is in place to keep the head wall from collapsing. (Courtesy California Department of Conservation.)

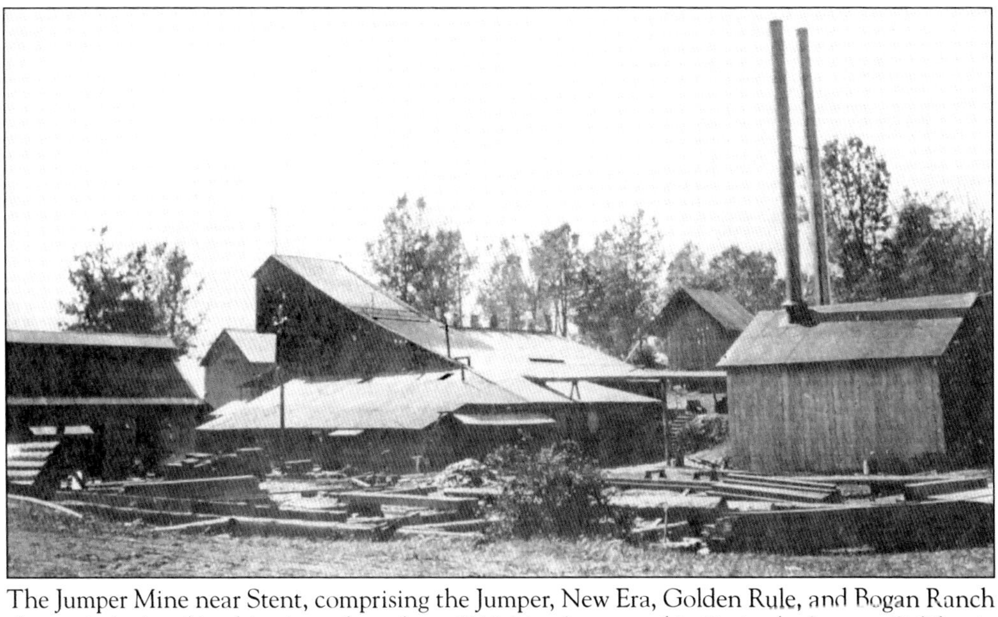

The Jumper Mine near Stent, comprising the Jumper, New Era, Golden Rule, and Bogan Ranch claims, is depicted in this view taken about 1910. Headquartered in Paris, the Jumper California Gold Mines Company employed 28 men at this time. Noted for its rich pockets of gold, often chiseled off shafts in sheets and piled "waist high to a man," the mine produced over $5 million during its heyday. (Courtesy California State Library.)

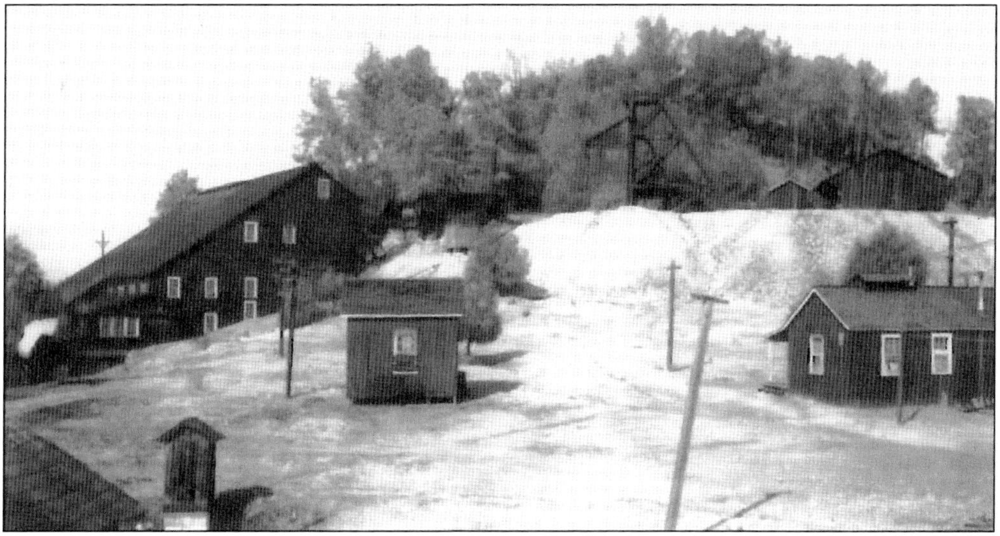

The Santa Ysabel was one of the several productive mines at Quartz Mountain, which had a population of over 800 during the boom years. On the Mother Lode vein, it controlled the Knox and Boyle, Gray Eagle, Miller and Holmes, and Nyman claims, comprising 100 acres. The mine, with an average vein width of about 6 feet, was developed by three incline shafts. (Courtesy Charla Francis.)

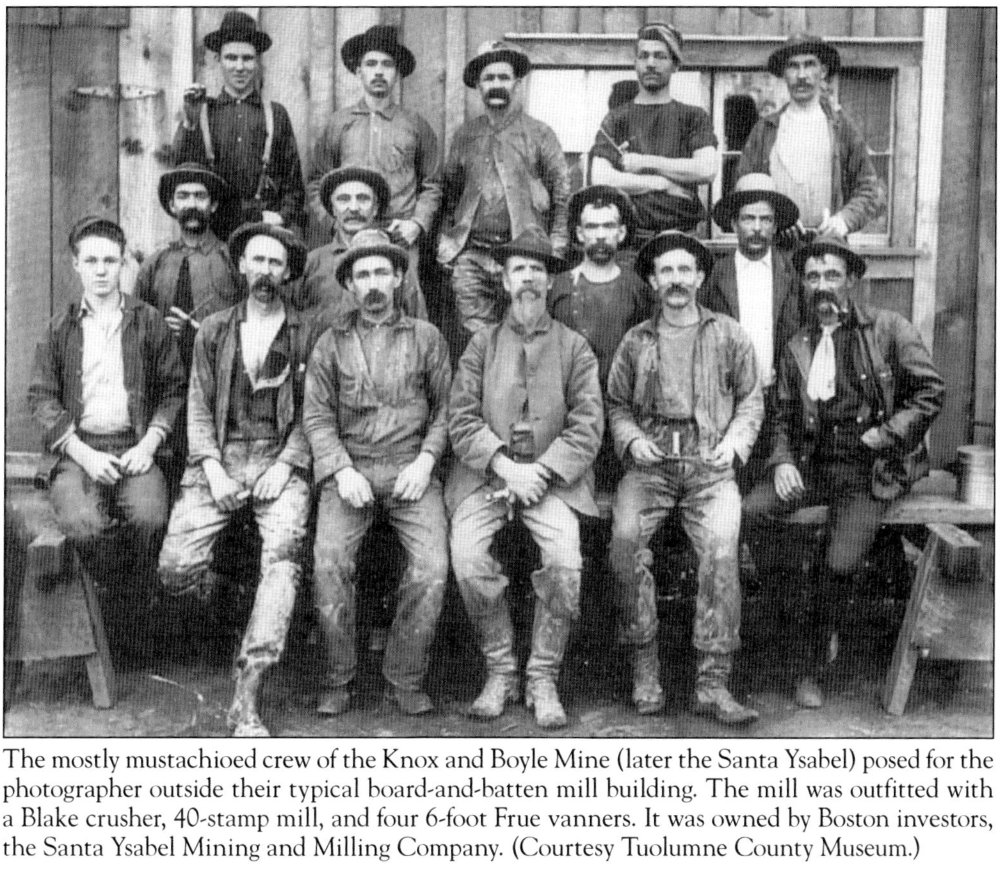

The mostly mustachioed crew of the Knox and Boyle Mine (later the Santa Ysabel) posed for the photographer outside their typical board-and-batten mill building. The mill was outfitted with a Blake crusher, 40-stamp mill, and four 6-foot Frue vanners. It was owned by Boston investors, the Santa Ysabel Mining and Milling Company. (Courtesy Tuolumne County Museum.)

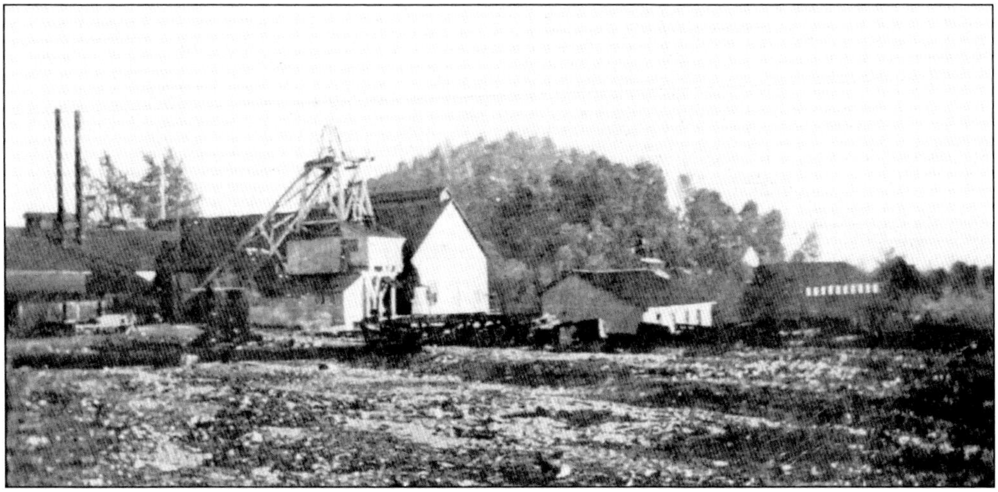

The Dutch Mine, also at Quartz Mountain, was one of the big producers during the 1890s, comprised of the Dutch and Sweeney claims and later combined with the 60-stamp App Mine as the Dutch-App. Concentrates assayed at $36 per ton, with total operating costs of $2.50 per ton. C. H. Segerstrom of Sonora was the manager of the 64 men employed, who produced a total output of $3 million. (Courtesy Gary Wilson.)

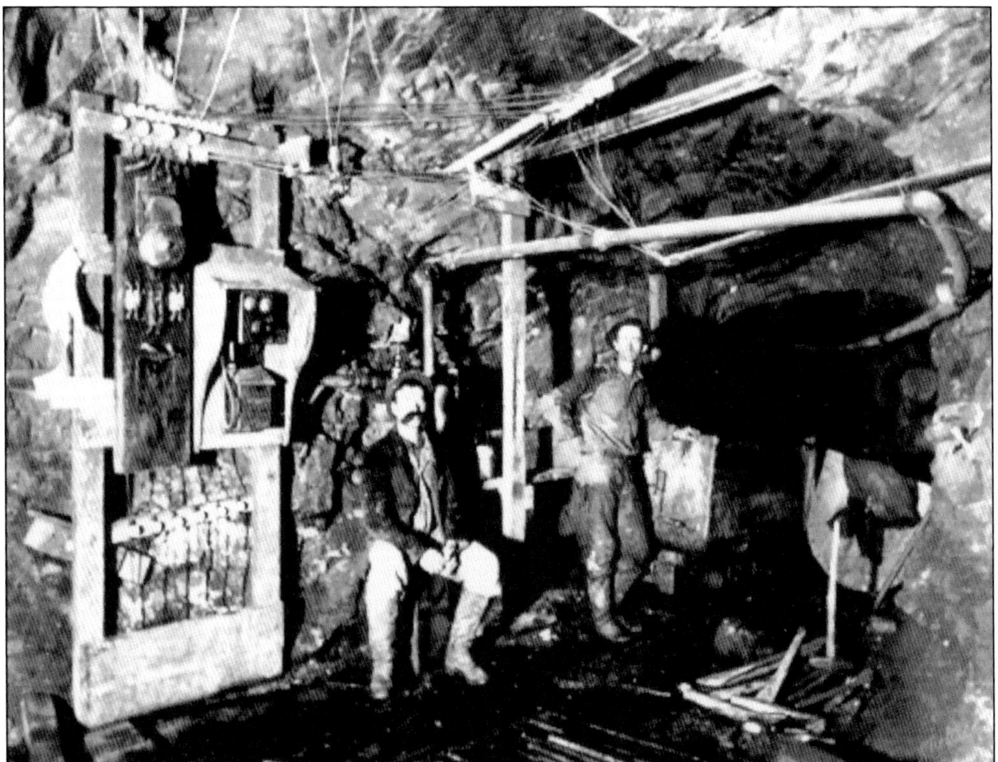

In this up-to-date 1890s underground mine, the telephone and the electrical transformer, which operated the lights, are depicted at left. While the shift boss sits, the miner poses by his ore car. A pile of drill steel and tools are in the right foreground. (Courtesy California Department of Conservation.)

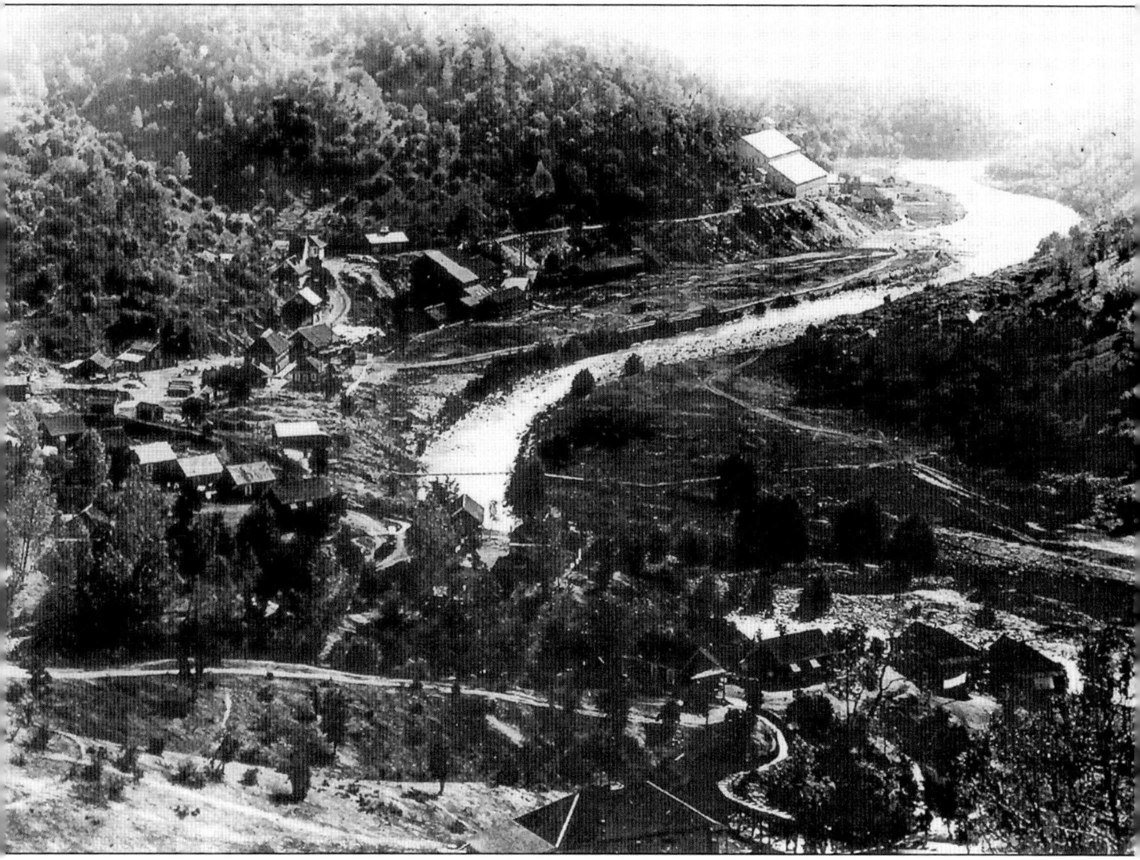

The Eagle-Shawmut Mine, located in the Jacksonville Mining District on the Tuolumne River southeast of Jamestown, was formed from the consolidation of two claims worked as early as the 1860s and combined about 1895. The Eagle-Shawmut was the largest, if not the richest, gold mine operating in Tuolumne County in the late 1890s, eventually producing over $8 million in gold. In 1900, the plant was described by the *Mining and Scientific Press* on January 27, 1900, as "extensive and excellent and housed in ample buildings." The following year, with a seemingly unending body of ore, the company expanded its mill to 100 stamps, with an incline tramway built to take ore from the No. 2 shafts at the top of the hill to the mill. By the following year, 260 men were employed at the new mill, which was crushing five tons per stamp per day. A chlorination plant was built on the west bank of Wood's Creek directly across from the mill, connected by an aerial tramway. Workers' cottages, boardinghouses, and the community of Jacksonville are seen in the foreground. (Courtesy Jim Yeisley.)

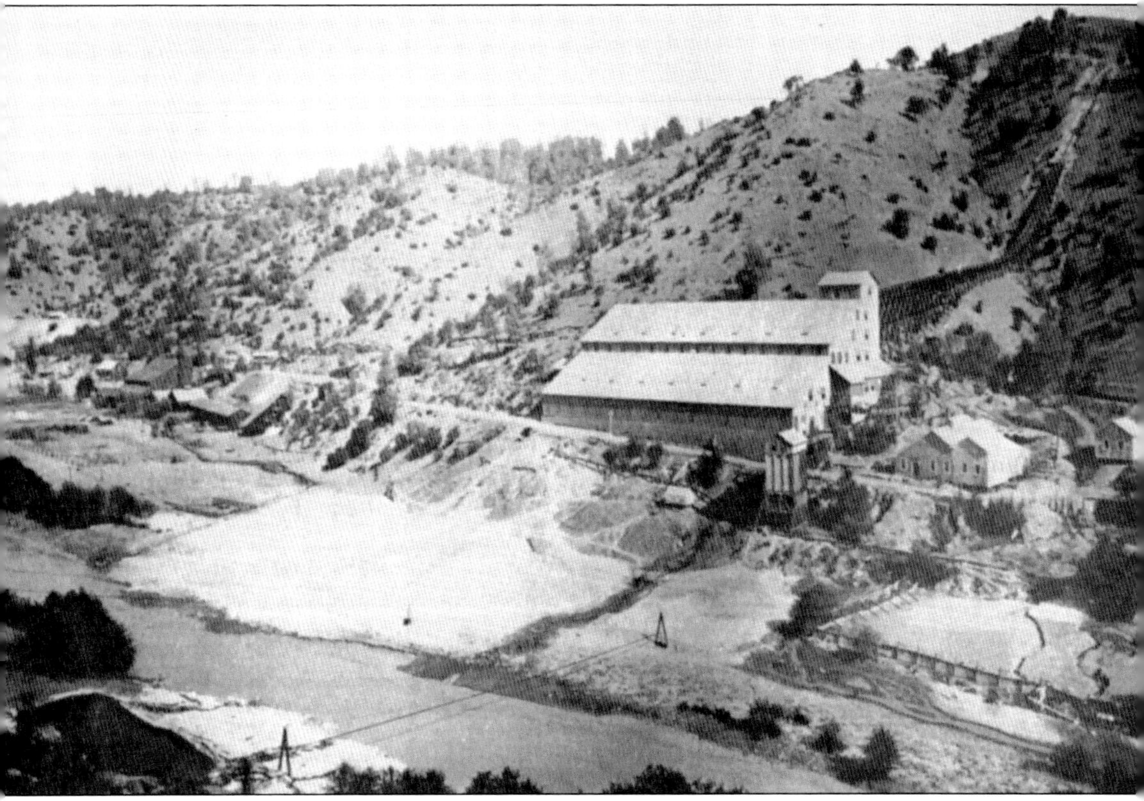

A water-powered plant at the mine, driven by a Pelton wheel, generated electricity for the tram, hoists, crushing machinery, and lights; 2 miles of 10-inch pipeline from the Sierra and San Francisco Power Company brought water to the mine. Rich strikes were made in the 1910s, but increased costs after World War I caused the mine to go idle in 1926. It was reopened in 1938 and operated until 1947, with the largest year of production in 1942. The concentrates, which carried 2 to 3 ounces of gold per ton, were hauled by truck to the Selby smelter near Vallejo, and, because this type was needed, the Eagle-Shawmut was one of the few gold mines allowed to operate during the war. Increased costs after the war made it unprofitable to continue, so all work was stopped November 1, 1947. This northeast view, taken in 1914, depicts the tramway, 100-stamp mill, and the tailings pond on the Tuolumne River. The Tarantula Mine, which produced $100,000, is seen at left, and the community of Jacksonville farther left. (Courtesy Tuolumne County Museum.)

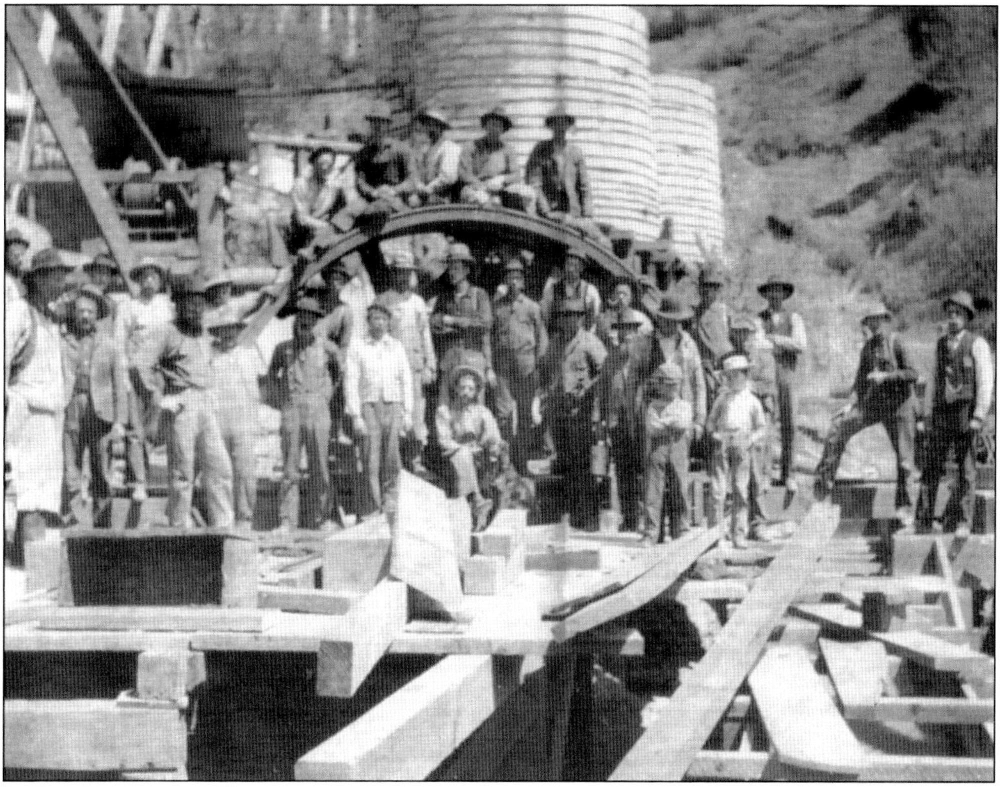

In this view, men and boys are standing in front of the water tanks, evidently about 1901, when the new mill was under construction. The 40-stamp mill was increased to 100 stamps, and the large frame tramway was erected. New workers' homes were also built, and a large tonnage of equipment was installed. The mill, and Jacksonville, disappeared under the waters of New Don Pedro Reservoir in the early 1970s. (Courtesy Jim Yeisley.)

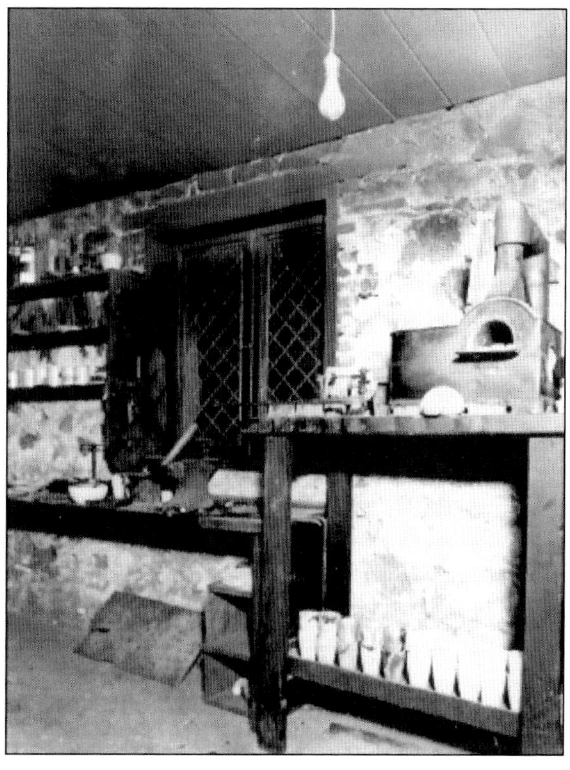

If the gold was not visible to the naked eye, an assay was required to determine if precious metals were present in a rock. The rock was first pulverized, then poured into fire clay crucibles, placed in a muffle furnace, formed into slag, placed into cupels with bone ash, formed into a bead, and finally, fired. The tiny prill that remained was the *doré*—gold and silver. (Courtesy California Department of Conservation.)

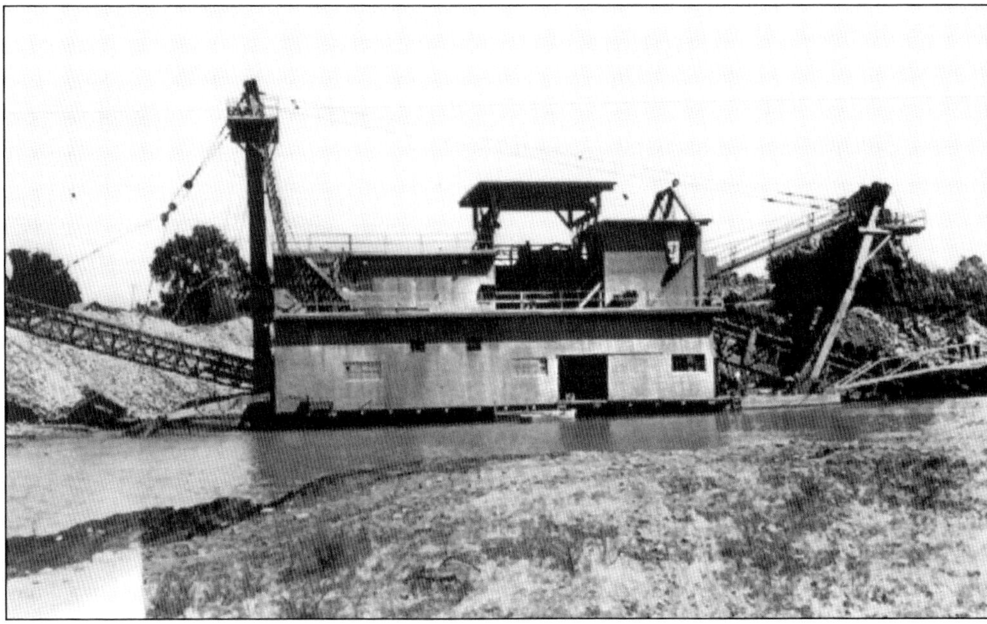

A combination of sand dredge and gold-saving equipment, a marriage of a boat and sluice, gold dredges operated throughout the Mother Lode beginning in the early 1900s and continuing through the Depression. Buckets scooped gravel in front of the dredge, then processed in a manner similar to sluicing to recover the gold, with the rocks and boulders discharged aft. (Courtesy California Department of Conservation.)

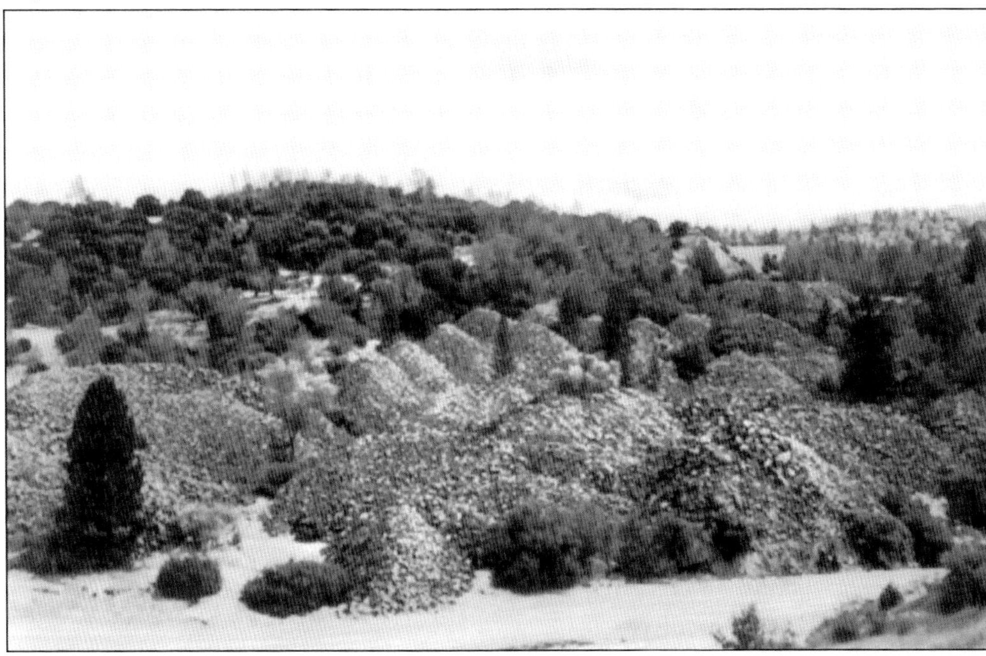

Dredging was well-suited for placer gravels that were relatively flat and not very deep, with dredges crisscrossing shallow-gradient river valleys and wider parks, operating easily with very little water. Dredging left behind continuous piles of waste rock, most readily seen on the Tuolumne River banks near the county's southwestern boundary. (Courtesy California Department of Conservation.)

Five

Routes to the Mines

Most of the major highways and corridors in California followed the routes of Native American trails, based largely on resource location. In Tuolumne County, these routes were generally followed by the early explorers and cartographers and included State Route 49 and probably portions of State Route 108, later used by the miners and prospectors on their way to the mines. Present Route 49 was designated as such in 1934 and extends 295 miles from Oakhurst on the south to Vinton in the north, passing through the most important mining communities of 1849.

The majority of the travelers to Jamestown and Sonora traveled by rail or steamer to Stockton, then over the Stockton to Sonora Road or the Stockton to Angels Camp Road. From there, they took the ferry roads to Knights Ferry, O'Byrnes Ferry, and Central Ferry to the mines in Tuolumne. The Stockton Road connected the mines and communities in Tuolumne County with the port city of Stockton, where passengers, freight, foodstuffs, and all manner of materials were transshipped from San Francisco and the world. Stagecoaches departed Stockton daily for the Southern Mines; after the advent of the railroad to Oakdale, travelers continued eastward by coach and horses. From the north, another stage service ran from the Southern Pacific terminus at Milton to Copperopolis and crossed the Stanislaus River at O'Byrnes Ferry by toll bridge to join the Sonora Road and proceed eastward.

Among the early local roads, which may have followed early Native American trails, was the Mule Trail, established by 1850, leading from Green Springs to Montezuma Junction near Mountain Pass. The road to Chinese Camp is also one of the earliest roads, with a stage running daily from Sonora to Stockton via Montezuma, Chinese Camp, and Knights Ferry beginning in September 1850. Its junction with the Stockton Road is now known as Yosemite Junction, reflecting the importance of Yosemite National Park to the tourist industry. In the early 1870s, the Nevada Stage Company established the Yosemite Run from Milton through Copperopolis, O'Byrne's Ferry, and Chinese Camp.

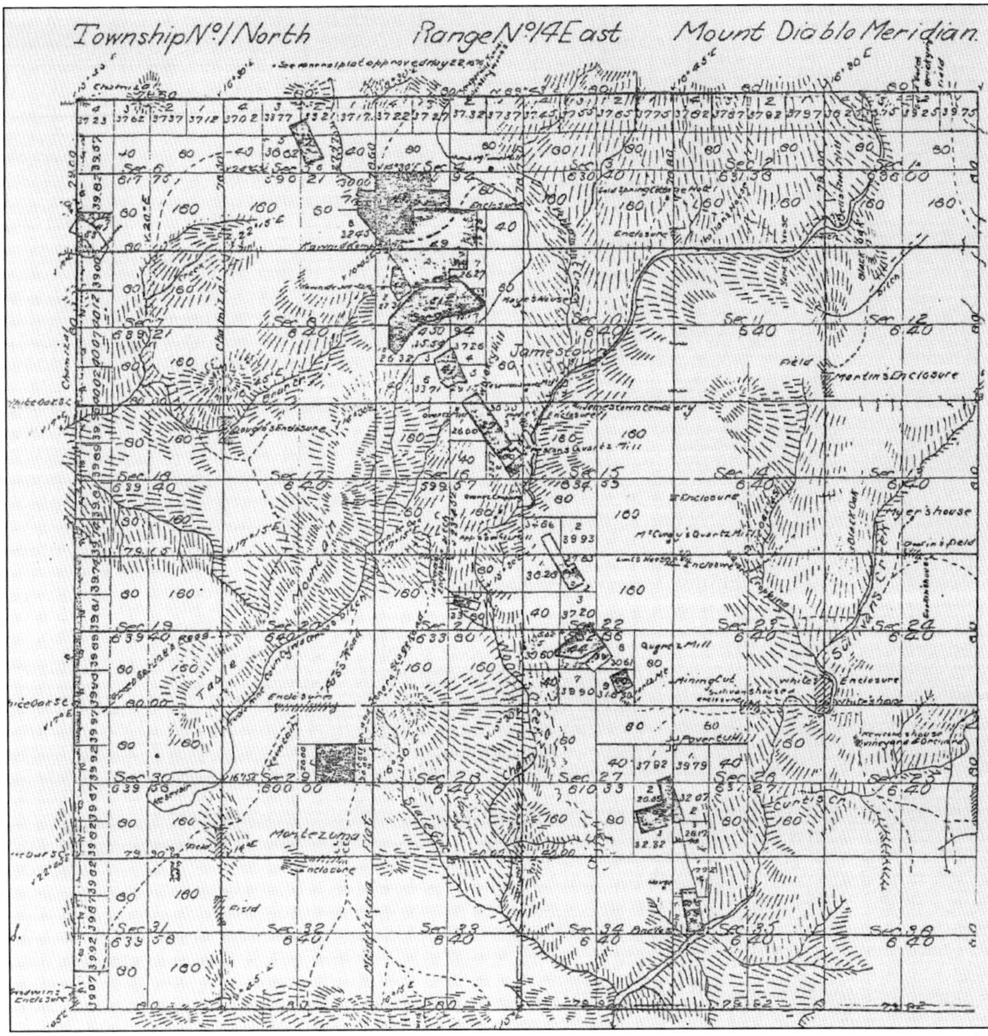

In this 1876 General Land Office plat, all roads lead to Jamestown and Sonora. Depicted are the Stage Road from La Grange, the Pass Road (State Route 108), Green Springs Road, Rawhide Road, Coulterville Road (State Route 49), Sonora Road, and other more localized routes. (Courtesy Tuolumne County Surveyor's Office.)

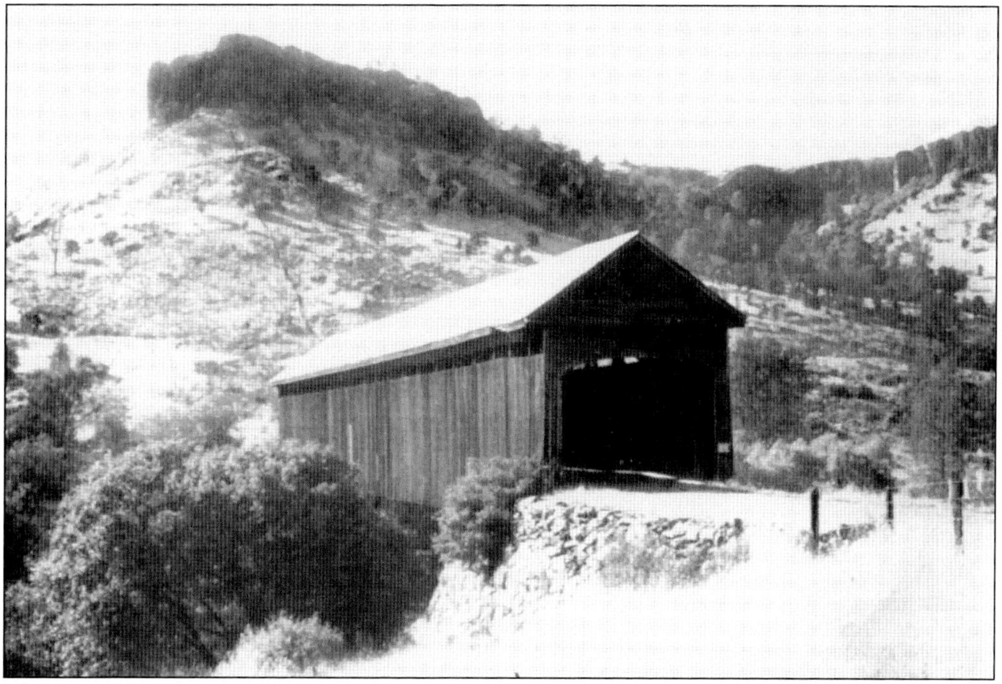

The covered bridge at O'Byrnes Ferry was one of the important early crossings of the Stanislaus River on the road to the mines in Jamestown and Tuolumne. Built in 1863 by the Union Bridge Company, it was a toll bridge until purchased by the counties of Calaveras and Tuolumne in 1902 and was demolished in 1959, when Tulloch Reservoir was raised. (Courtesy Gary Wilson.)

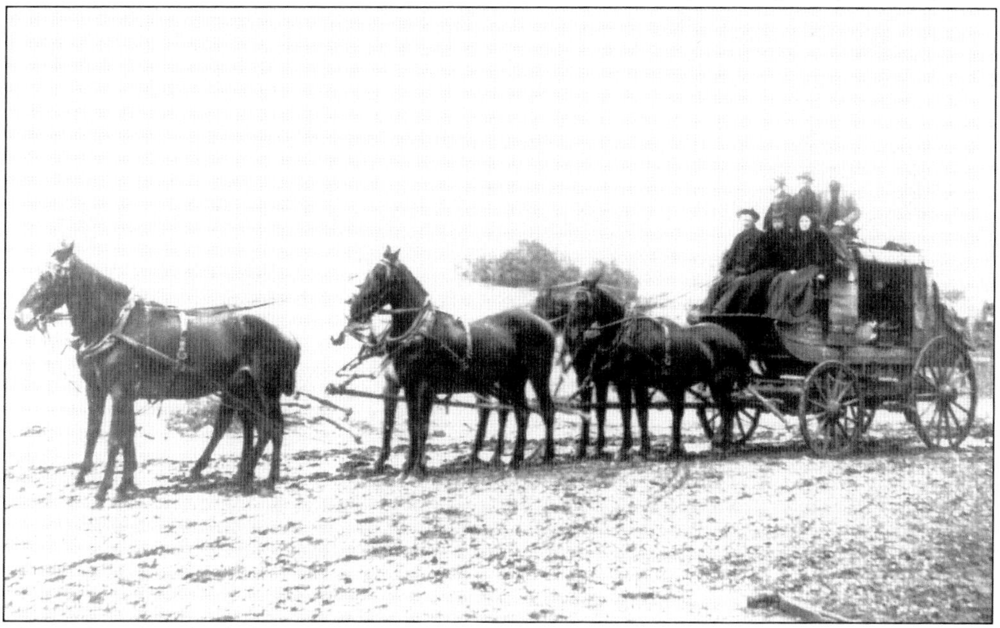

The preferred method of transportation from Stockton, this stagecoach was photographed on its way to Jamestown with a full load of passengers, including two ladies riding shotgun. At this point in time, they had probably taken a river steamer to Stockton, transferred to one of the railroads, and were on their way from the station to their destination. (Courtesy Gary Wilson.)

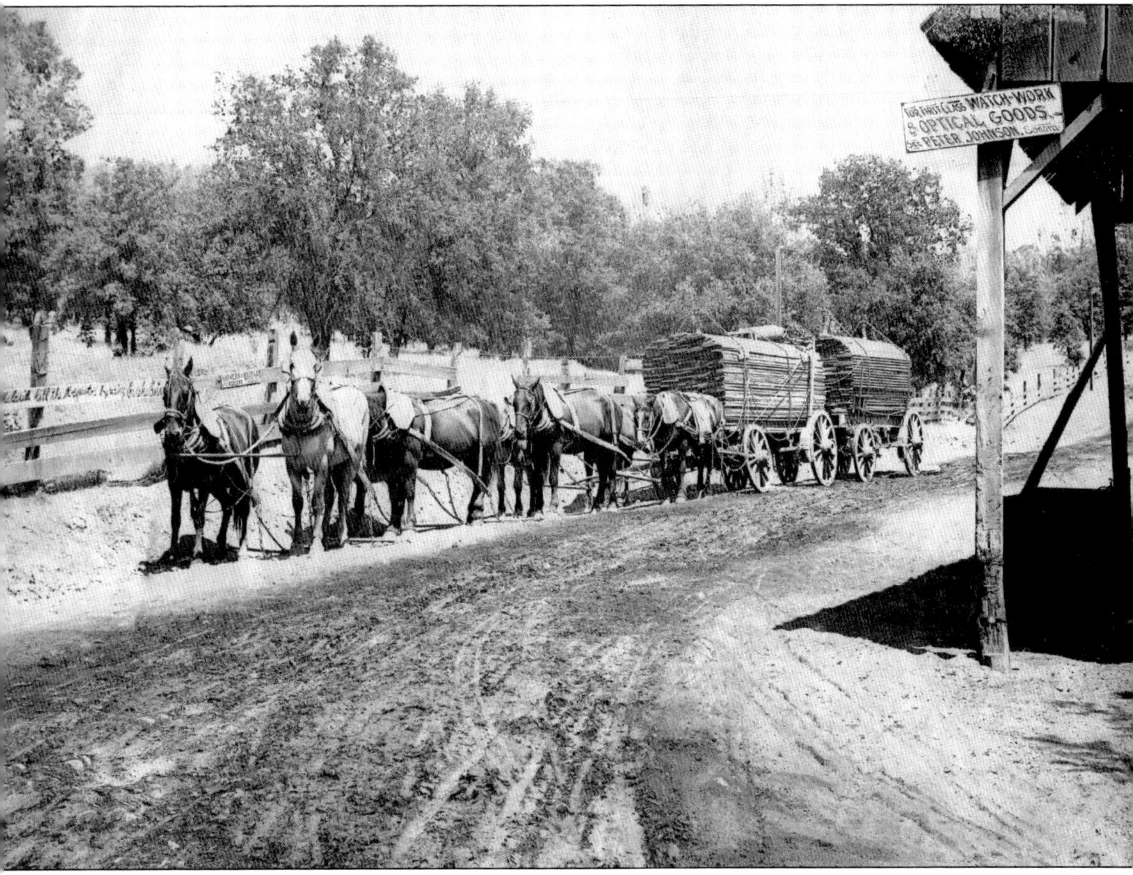

The early roads were dry and dusty in the summertime and muddy and rutted in the winter months. With teams of horses hauling freight and stages over the roads, they often became impassable or, at the least, very difficult. In this view of a freight wagon hauling lumber, the road appears to be in fairly good condition. The team was parked by the side of the Jacksonville Road at Quartz; the driver no doubt partaking of refreshments at Dan Mann's Saloon across the road. The Jacksonville Road connected the communities of Sonora and Jamestown with the mines and settlements on the Tuolumne River. (Courtesy Tuolumne County Museum.)

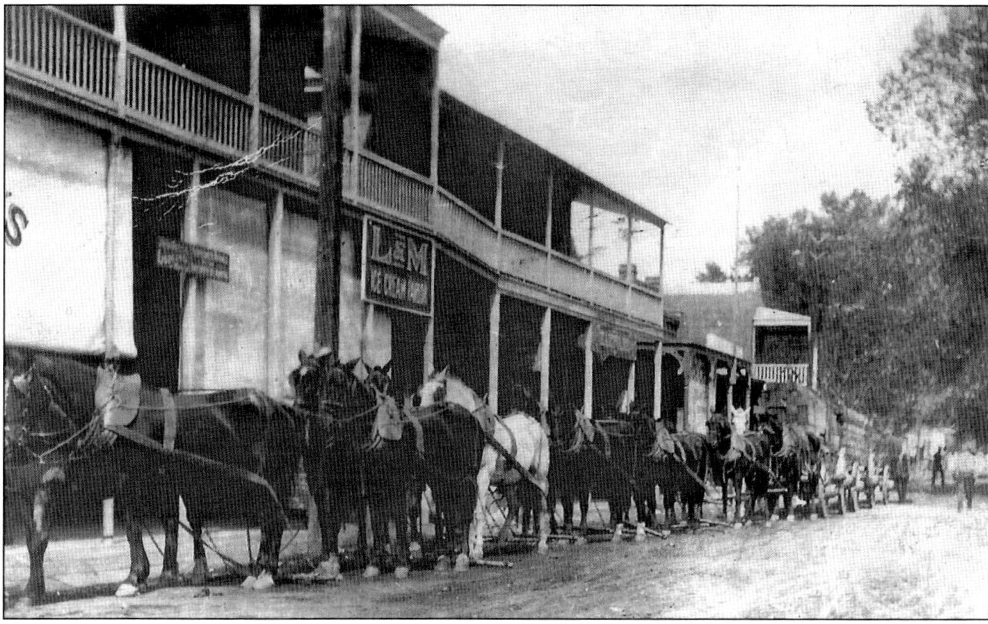

This team of 12 horses and one lead horse has just pulled into Jamestown, hauling a load of logs and lumber. Probably a warm day, this driver was evidently treating himself to some ice cream from the L&M Ice Cream Parlor. (Courtesy Jim Yeisley.)

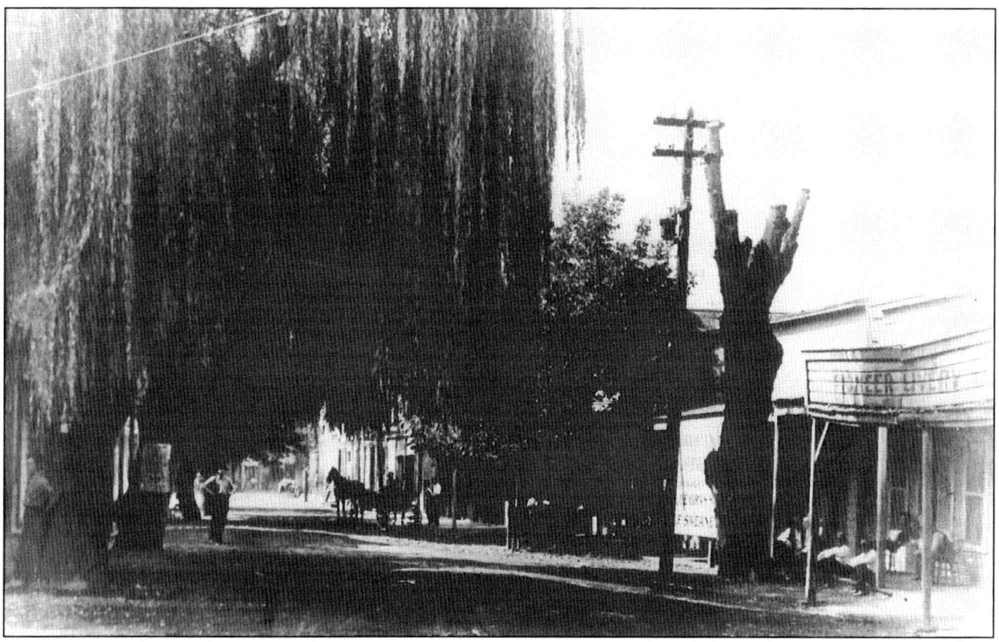

Livery stables, where horses were fed, watered, and changed, were important enterprises in every town from the 1850s through the 1910s. In this photograph taken about 1910, the Pioneer Livery Stable is located across from the Hotel Willow and undoubtedly served its patrons as well as others. (Courtesy Stephen Willey.)

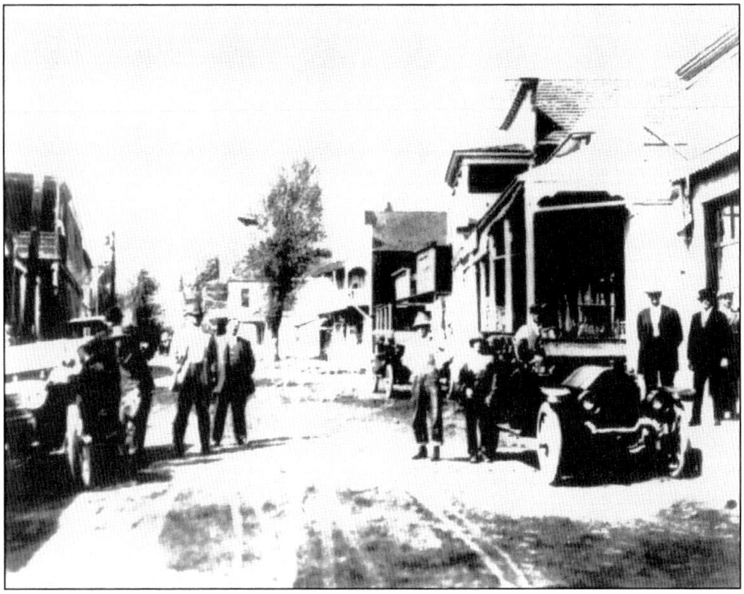

By the time of this 1910s photograph, the automobile had replaced the horse as the preferred means of transportation. The roads, however, were still earthen and rutted. In this view looking north on Main Street, the Congdon Building is prominent on the right. (Courtesy Tuolumne County Museum.)

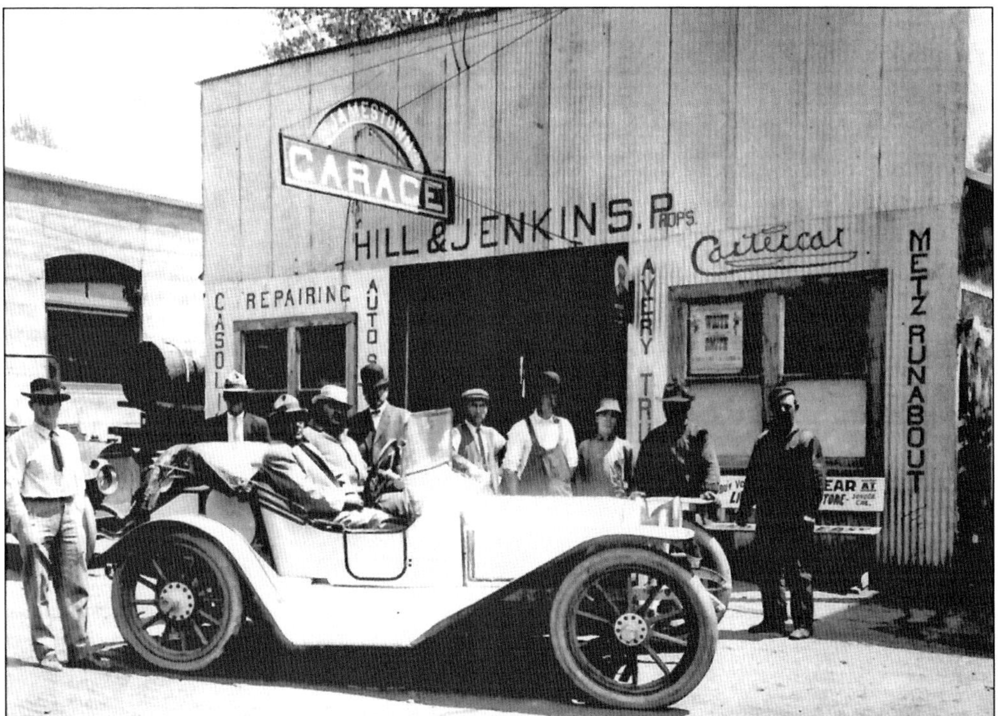

Automobiles often broke down in those early years, necessitating repair shops and garages, such as the Hill and Jenkins Jamestown Garage depicted here in the 1910s, to keep them operating. The frame building was replaced by E. Booker's concrete garage in 1922. (Courtesy Tuolumne County Museum.)

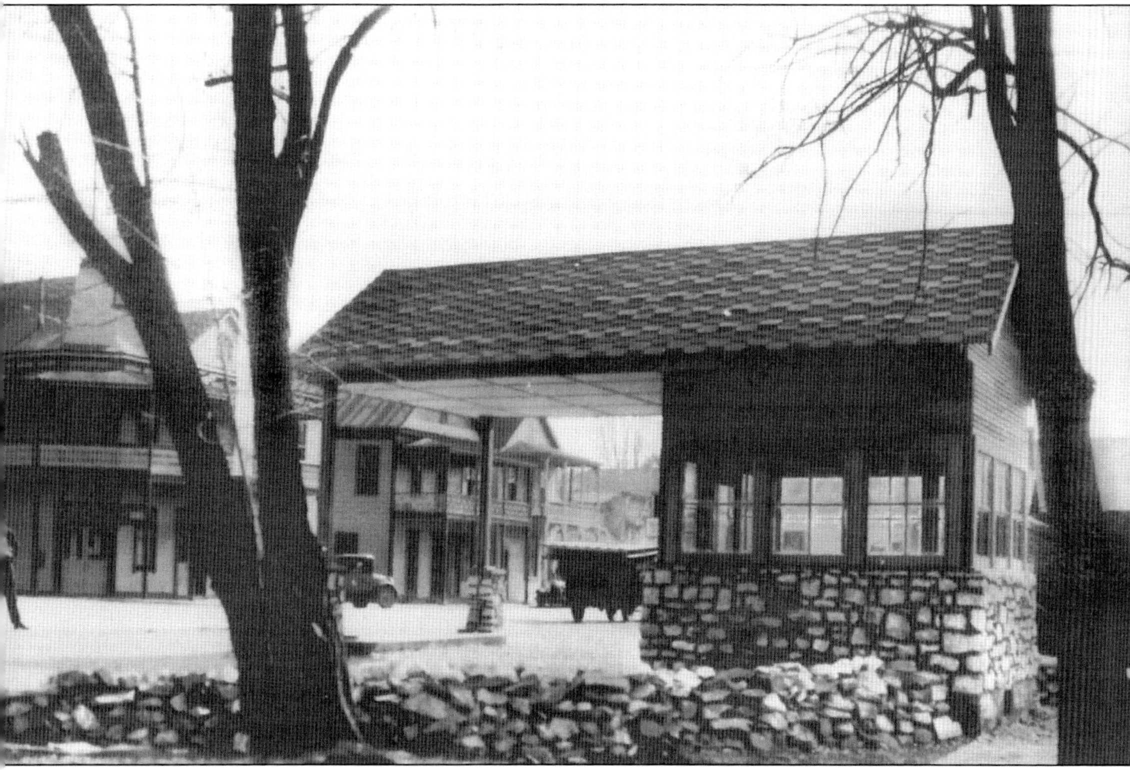

With the advent of the automobile, the need for regular gasoline stations became imperative, and they were erected in each community and way station. Lovelace's gasoline station, photographed in the 1920s, was located on the west side of Main Street, opposite the Hotel Willow (left). Although much altered, it is still extant. (Courtesy Donn Blount.)

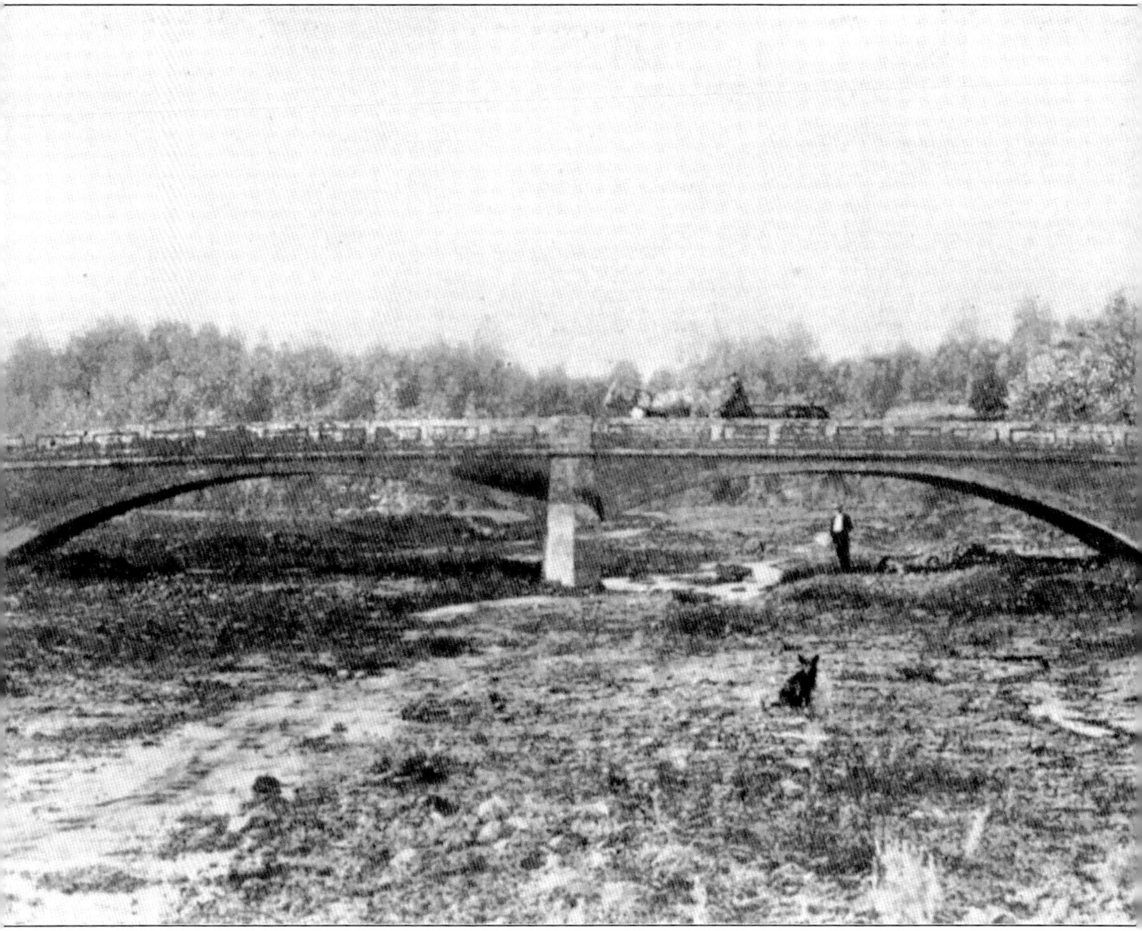

The Rawhide Road Bridge over Wood's Creek, which replaced an earlier span, was designed by Tuolumne County engineer N. J. Pickle in 1908. It is the oldest multiple-span, reinforced-concrete, spandrel arch bridge in the southern Mother Lode area of California and was evaluated as eligible for listing on the National Register of Historic Places by Caltrans in 1986. (Courtesy Tuolumne County Museum.)

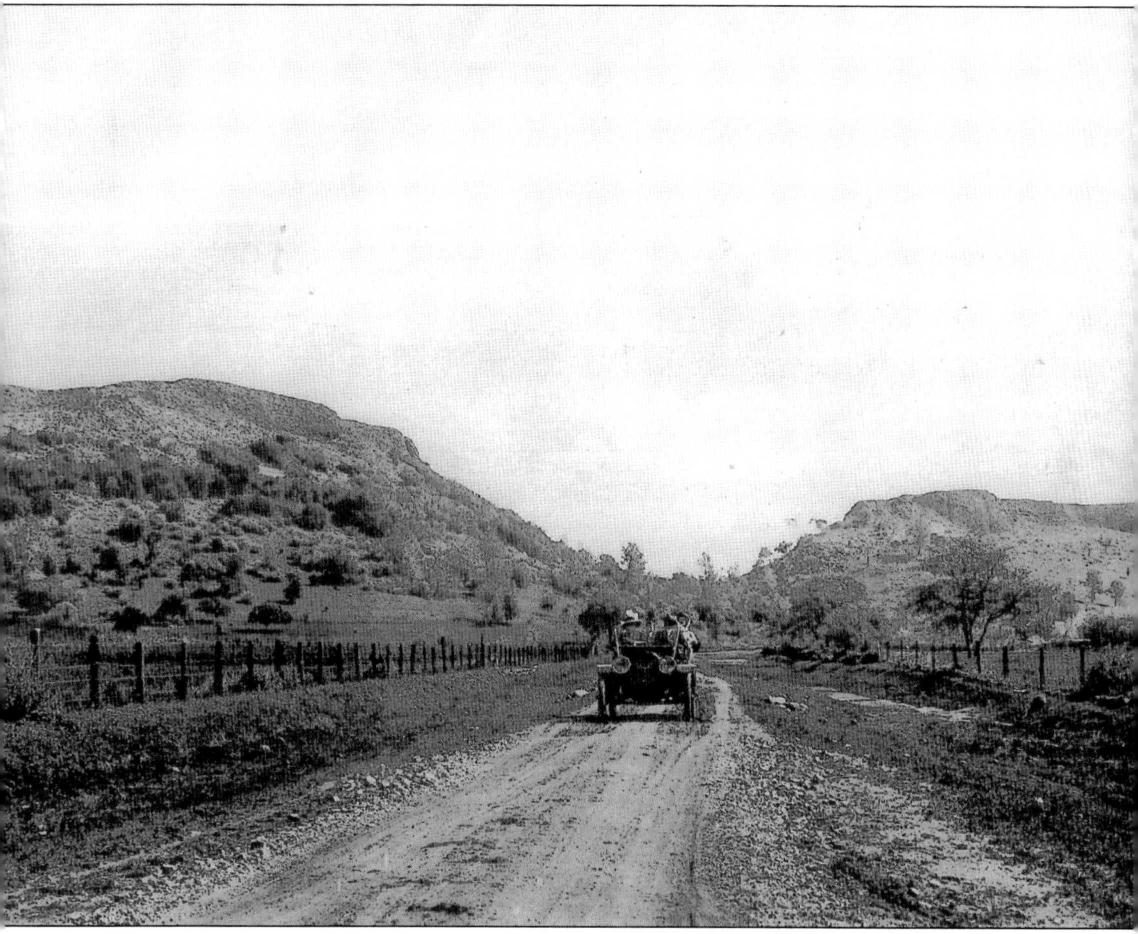

Some folk in a 1910s automobile take a spin down the Stockton Road near Yosemite Junction at Mountain Pass. The ancestral Wood's Creek bisected Table Mountain at this point as it headed south toward the Tuolumne River. (Courtesy Donn Blount.)

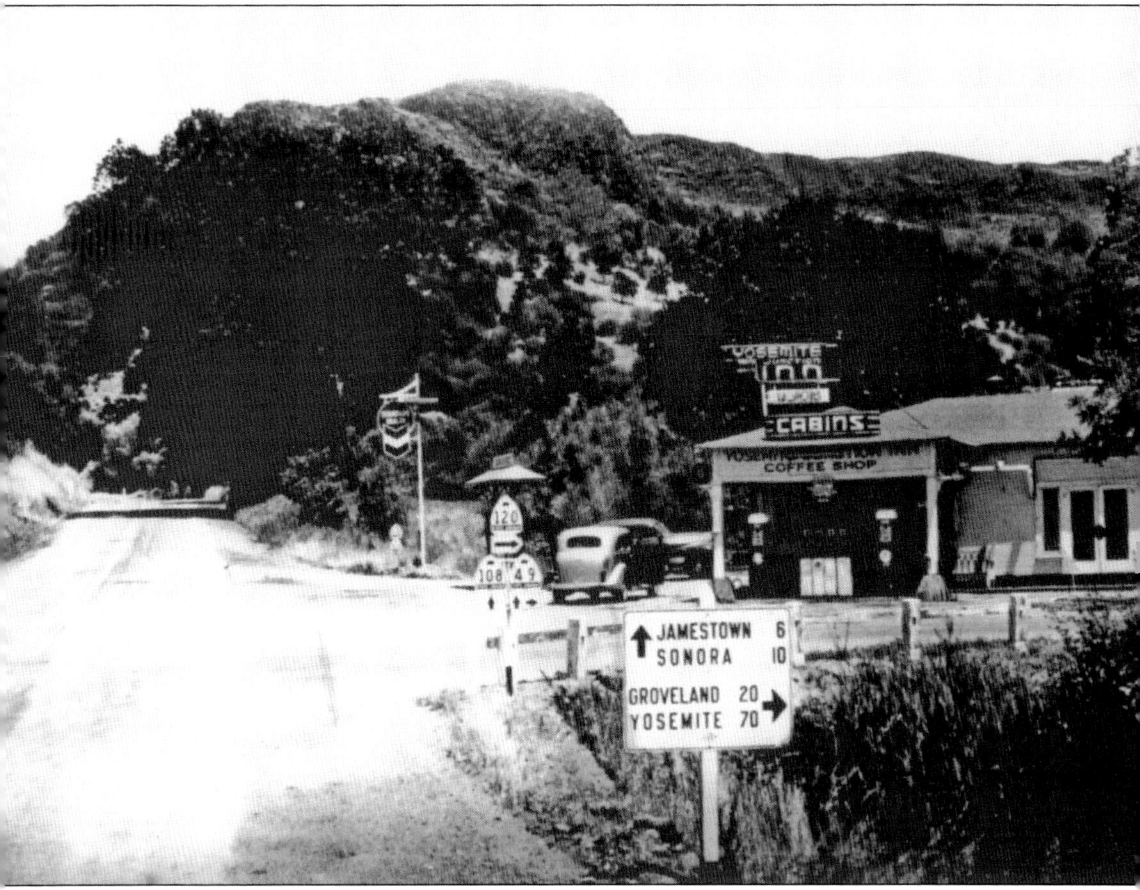

Located at the former junction of State Routes 49, 108, and 120, Yosemite Junction was a busy stopping place in the 1930s. Claude Weaver operated the restaurant in the 1940s, advertising "special chicken and steak dinners." Owned by Rubye and Dave Bonavia since 1952, the inn burned in 1956, but was rebuilt in 1966. The Bonavias retired in 1989. (Courtesy Stephen Willey.)

Six

The Iron Horse Comes to Town

In the 1890s, with many mines in production and lumbering underway, a group of wealthy investors incorporated the Sierra Railway Company on February 1, 1897. Principals were Thomas S. Bullock, a New York capitalist; William Crocker, a San Francisco banker; and Prince André Poniatowski, a delegate for a group of wealthy French industrialists. The company intended to construct and operate a railroad to carry passengers and freight from the Southern Pacific Company's line at Oakdale in Stanislaus County northwest approximately 65 miles to a point in Angels Camp in Calaveras County.

Selected as the site for the roundhouse, freight buildings, and railroad shops, Jamestown was the pivot point of encircling quartz mines. Soon Bullock announced plans to build three extensions from Jamestown: to Sonora, Jacksonville, and Angels Camp. The line reached Jamestown in November 1897, Sonora in February 1899, and Summersville (Tuolumne) in 1900, with that depot located only a few hundred yards from the West Side Flume and Lumber Company's mill, operated by the same three men. In the early decades of the 20th century, shipping wood products from the West Side mill and the mountain mills of the Standard Lumber Company, as well as the Sugar Pine Railroad, provided the largest source of revenue for the railroad.

The company reached its peak just before World War I, when as many as 10 trains a day ran over the line. By the end of the war, only one train a day was operating; the burning of Hotel Nevills in 1915, competition from trucks and automobiles, the Great Depression, high interest payments, and other factors combined to force the company into receivership in 1932.

Passenger service was abandoned in 1939, along with the Angels Branch, and during the coming decades, operations were concentrated on serving the lumber industry. The last steam engine arrived in Jamestown in 1952, long having been replaced by diesel locomotives. The Jamestown facilities were sold to the California Department of Parks and Recreation in 1982. It is now known as Railtown 1897 State Historic Park, with authentic roundhouse and repair shops, offering scheduled steam engine rides from April through October.

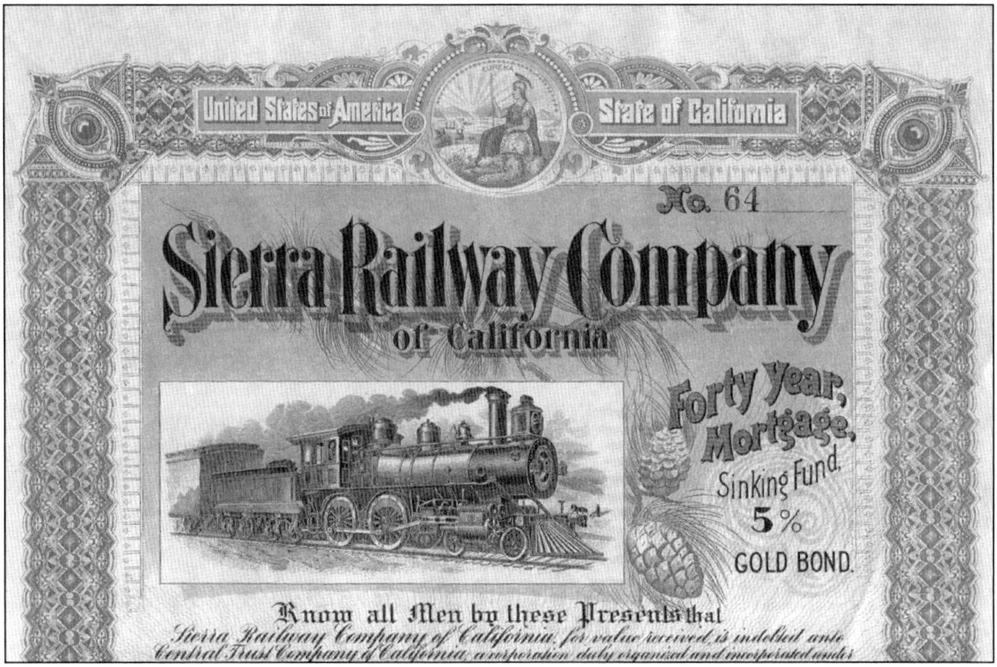

The Sierra Railway Company sold gold bonds, with a 40-year mortgage, to finance construction of the line. Capital stock was $5 million, of which Sidney Freshman had subscribed $50,000, and $18,500 each by the other four directors. Backed by Crocker interests, Thomas S. Bullock had recently promoted the West Side Flume and Lumber Company, while William A. Nevills, owner of the rich Rawhide Mine, financed the hotel. (Courtesy Wally Motloch.)

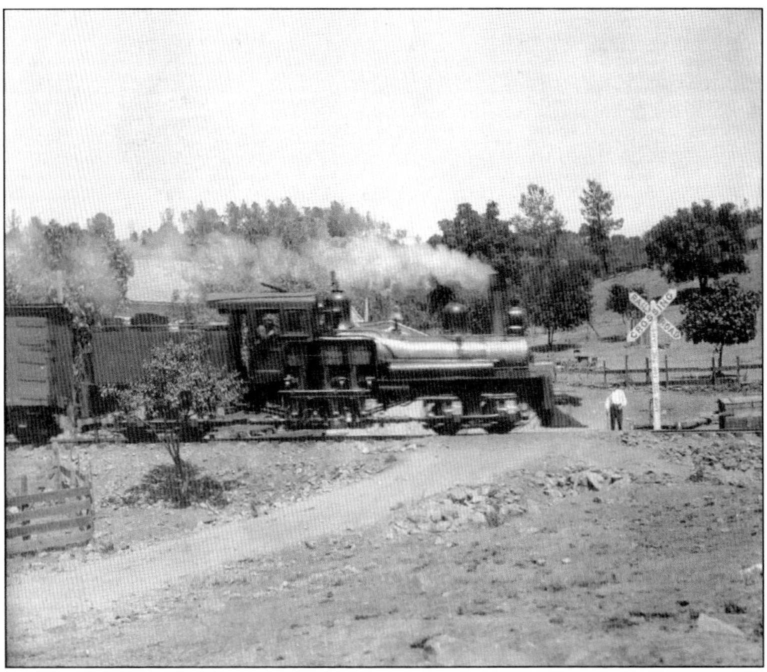

In this vintage photograph, a man waits for the train to cross before wending on his way. Construction of the line began in Oakdale on March 24, 1897, with 400 men and 300 horses and mules working from dawn to dusk, seven days a week. (Courtesy Wally Motloch.)

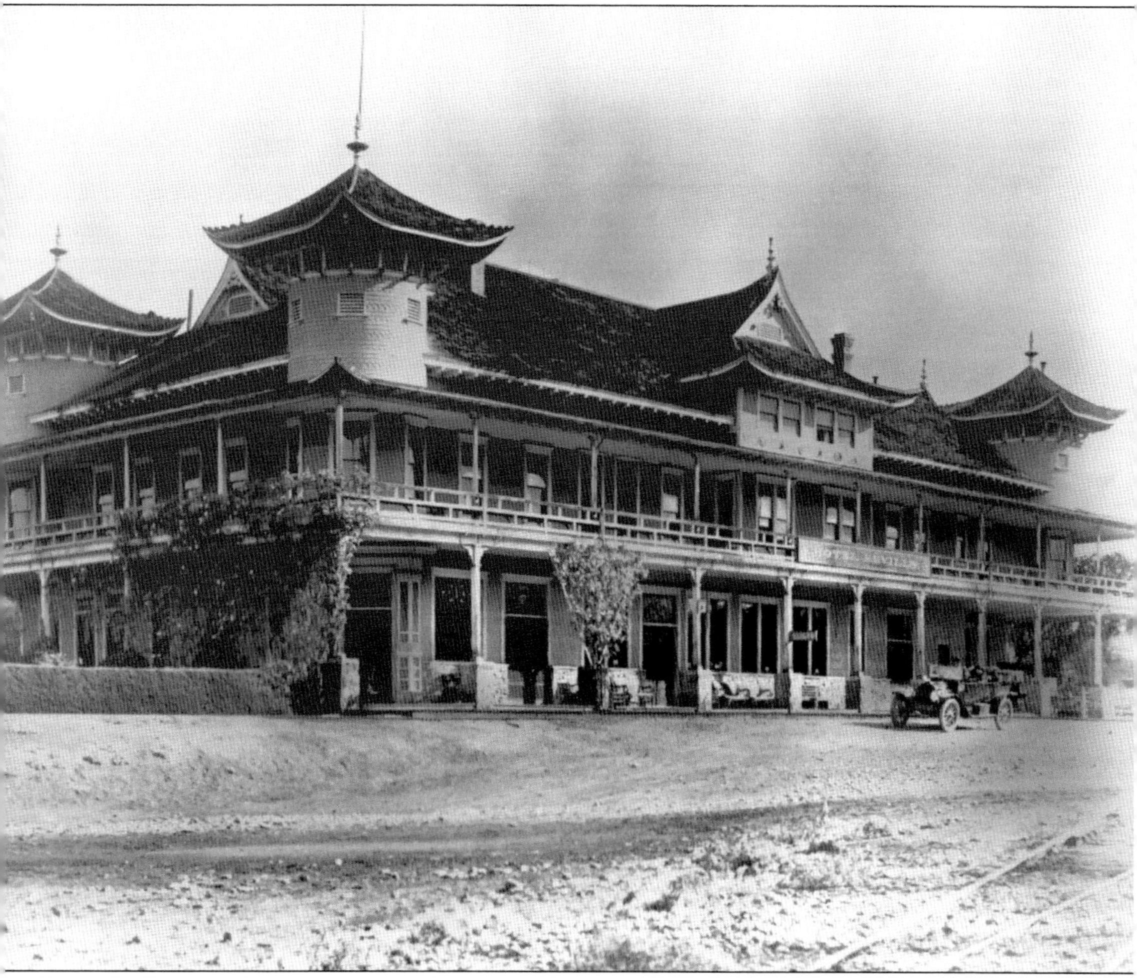

General offices of the company were located in Jamestown and housed in the railway's large depot, situated next to Hotel Nevills, which, with its country club atmosphere, served as the base for tourists wishing to take trips to the Yosemite Valley or other nearby attractions. Hotel Nevills, a large three-story Japanese-style building, was erected in 1898 of local products, including marble, quartz, and Ponderosa pine from quarries and forests belonging to the railroad barons. The 60-room hotel, the largest ever constructed in Tuolumne County, burned in 1915 and was never rebuilt. (Courtesy Stephen Willey.)

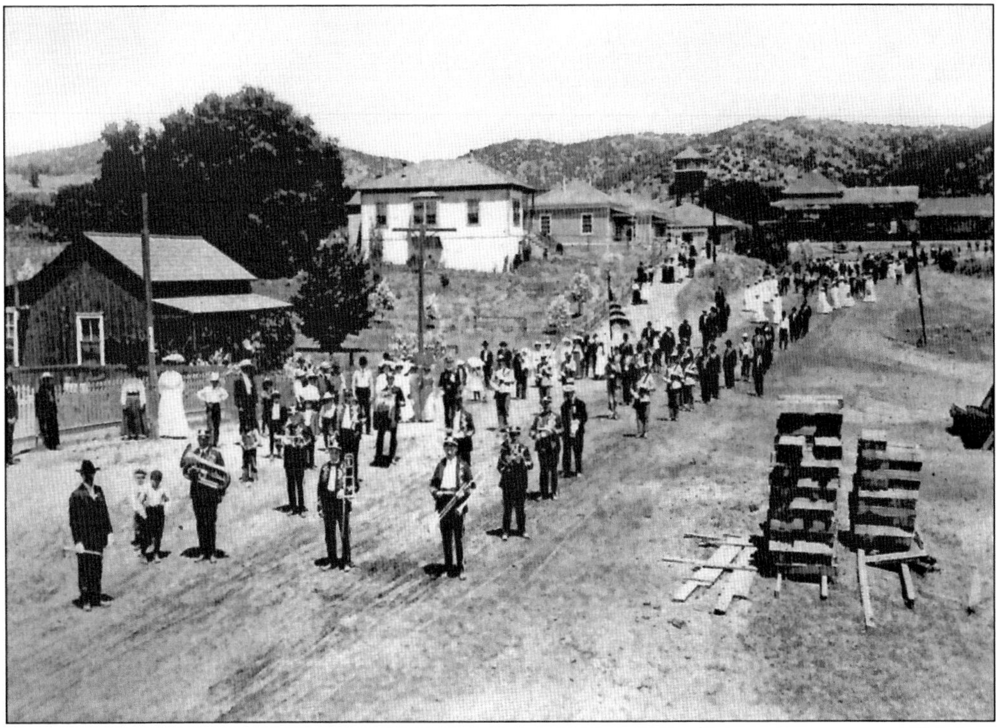

It was a big day for Jamestown when the iron horse came to town. The community turned out to celebrate its arrival on November 10, 1897, with a full band and parade from the station, down Ninth Street, to town. Some 4,500 people came to witness the arrival of the first train over the new line. (Courtesy Tuolumne County Museum.)

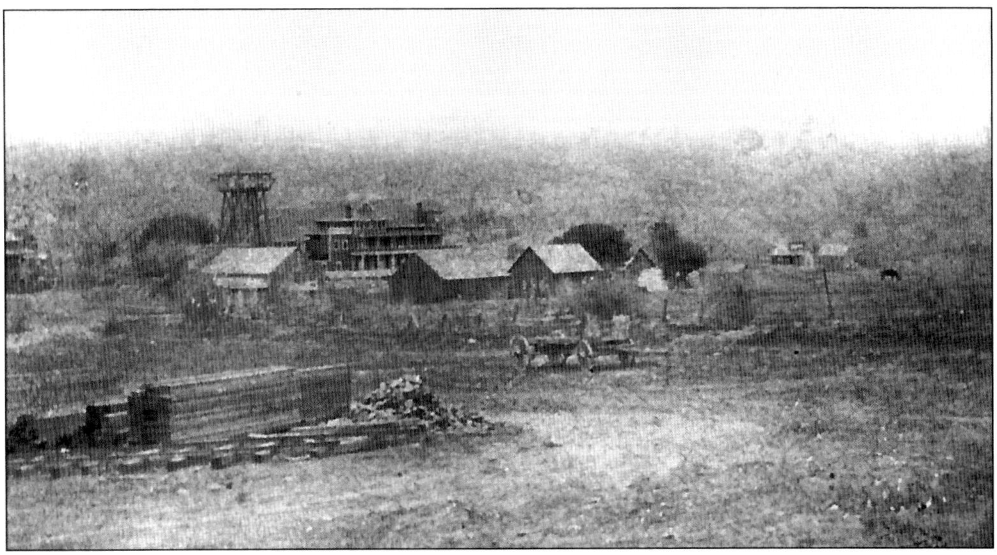

In this early photograph, Hotel Nevills is seen in the background while construction of the line to Tuolumne continues in the foreground, with rails and timber awaiting installation. During this period, the Southern Mother Lode and East Belt Mines provided a major source of revenue. Sulphurets from mines without chlorination or cyanided plants were hauled to reduction works nearby or to the Selby works near San Francisco. (Courtesy Tuolumne County Museum.)

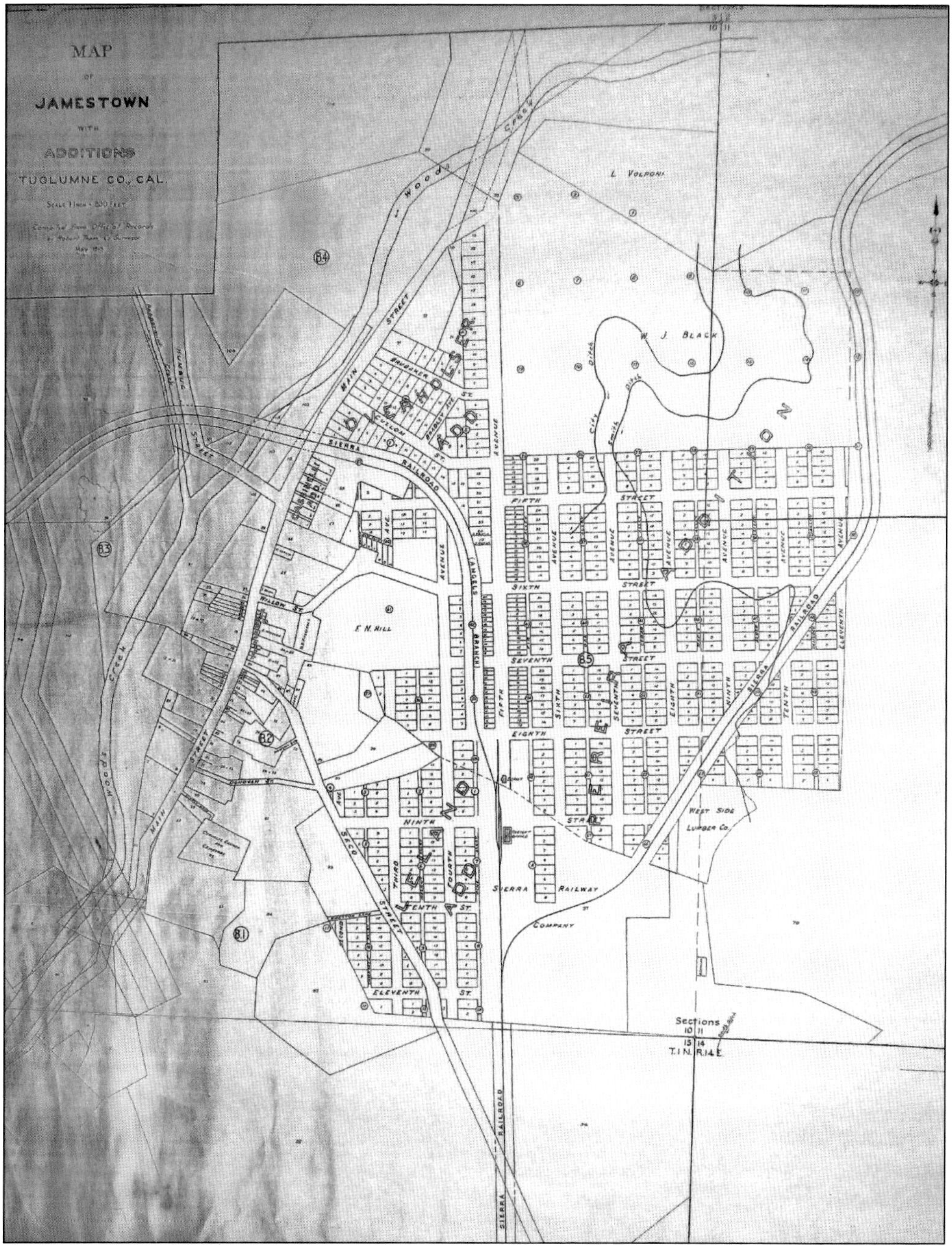

Anticipating the town's growth, Bullock, Crocker, and Poniatowski, with local partners, formed the Jamestown Improvement Company to develop 120 hillside acres as a residential area near the depot. Known as the Pereira Addition, it was named for pioneer John Pereira who originally owned the land. The Leland and Overholser Additions were platted at about the same time period, all intended to house railroad workers and their families. Jamestown was to be converted to a modern town with avenues and streets properly laid out and water, electric, and sewer systems. With streets numbered north and south and avenues numbered east and west, the additions were quickly built out with craftsman bungalows surrounding the station. (Courtesy Lori East.)

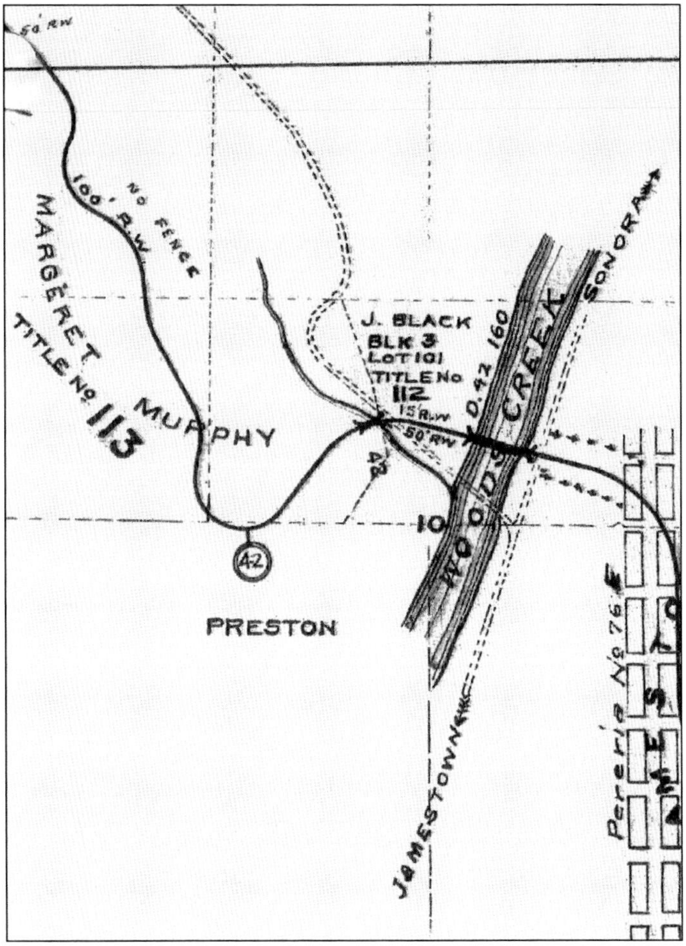

Branching west from the Jamestown depot, the tracks crossed Wood's Creek at the north end of town before climbing Table Mountain at its lowest point. Curving northward to the Tuttletown station and continuing past the station at Omega, the railroad crossed the 700-foot Stanislaus River chasm to Melones, Carson Hill, and Angels Camp, the 18th station of the Sierra Railway. The trip employed five switchbacks, grades up to 4.15 percent, and 27- to 28-degree curves. (Courtesy California State Railroad Museum.)

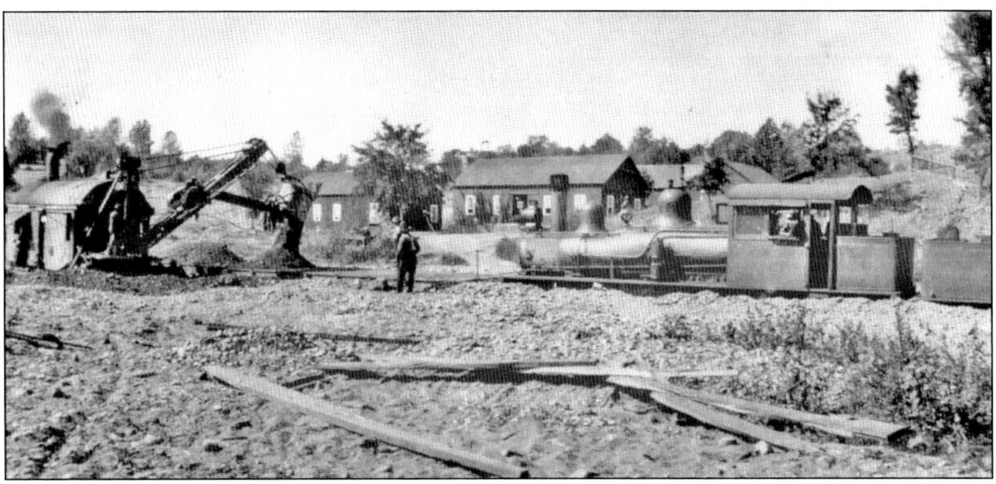

A steam shovel works on the railway line west of Jamestown. This line reached Angels Camp on September 10, 1902, with over 3,000 people coming to see the first train. Only five minutes late, No. 10 roared into the depot with two coaches loaded with railroad "brass" and guests. (Courtesy California State Railroad Museum.)

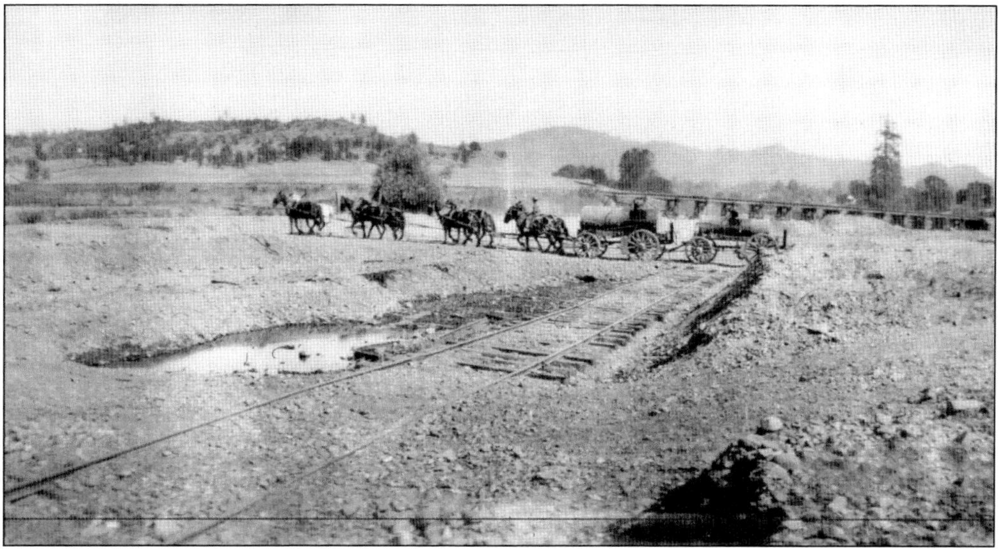

The Wood's Creek bridge of the Angels Camp branch of the Sierra Railway is depicted in the background of this photograph, with two water-tank cars pulled by a team of horses in the foreground. Note the extensive gravel beds, remnants of the early placer mining days, along the creek. The daily operation continued until the last train service was discontinued in March 1939. (Courtesy California State Railroad Museum.)

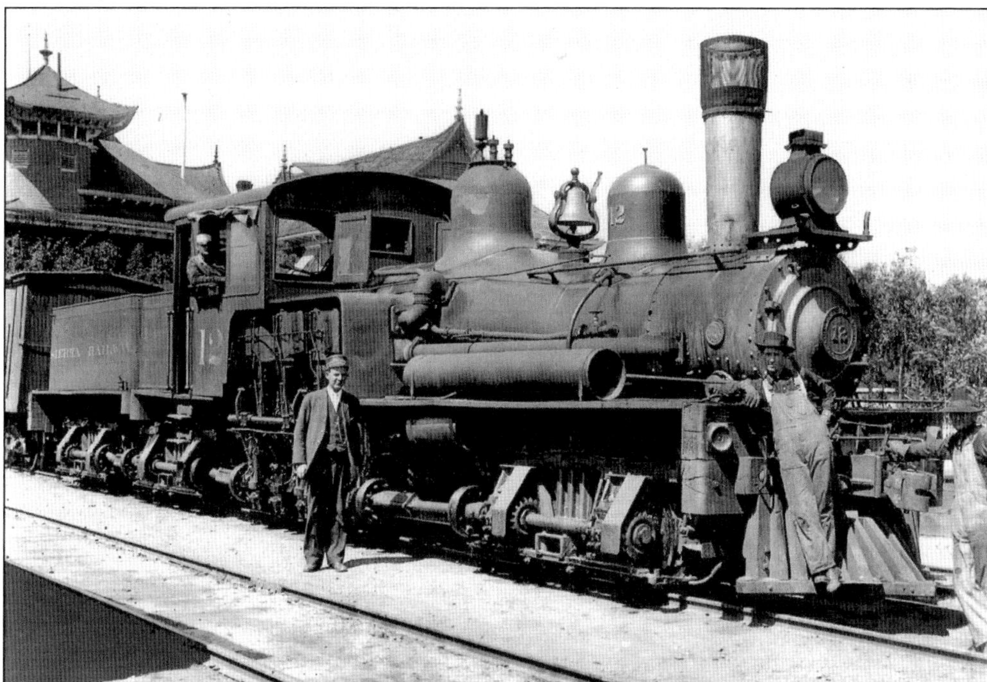

Sometime before 1915, H. F. Clouette and Joe Moir pose for the photographer with engine No. 12, a Lima Shay built in 1903, in front of Hotel Nevills in Jamestown. Several pieces of vintage rolling stock, including locomotives, coaches, passenger cars, a caboose, boxcars, and numerous other cars, are still found at Railtown 1897 State Historic Park, and steam engines ply the rails for tourists. (Courtesy California State Railroad Museum.)

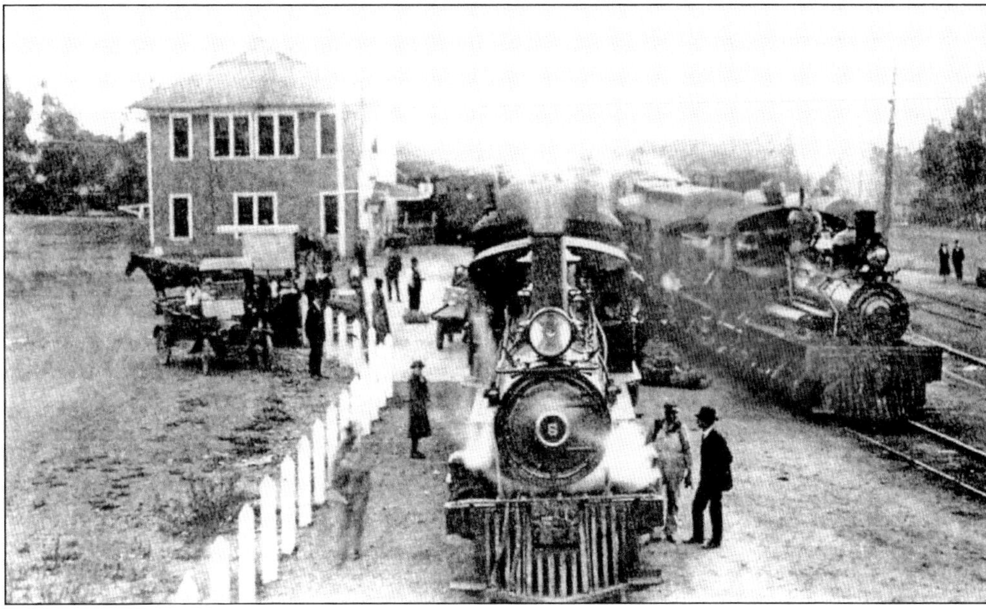

In 1910, the old roundhouse burned, and a new one with eight electrified stalls was constructed. All locomotive repairs were performed in the roundhouse, with car repairs completed in the nearby car shops; other facilities included a turntable, machine shops, and sheds. In this image, the rebuilt Jamestown depot and Sierra Railway trains arrive about 1916, after the destruction of Hotel Nevills by fire. The Oakdale train is arriving on the left, while the train to Angels Camp waits to the right. The second Jamestown depot, a utilitarian structure that replaced the original soon after it burned in 1913, was reduced to ashes on November 23, 1978, in an arson fire and was not rebuilt. (Above, courtesy Guy L. Dunscomb, from the Al Moreno Collection; below, courtesy Gary Wilson.)

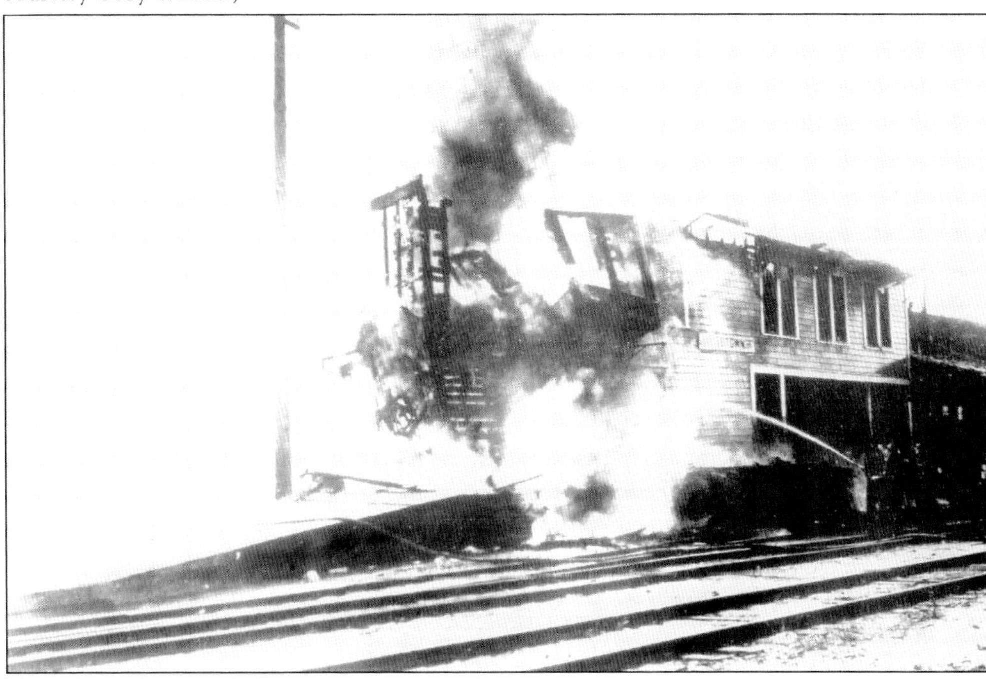

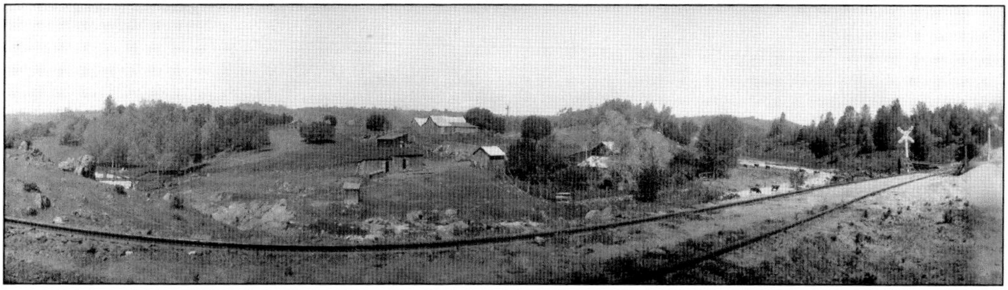

Seen through a wide-angle lens, the Sierra Railway line traverses the foreground, with Wood's Creek in the middle and the Mooney property at Wood's Crossing in the background. The crossing of present Bell Mooney Road is denoted by the crossing sign to the right. (Courtesy California State Library.)

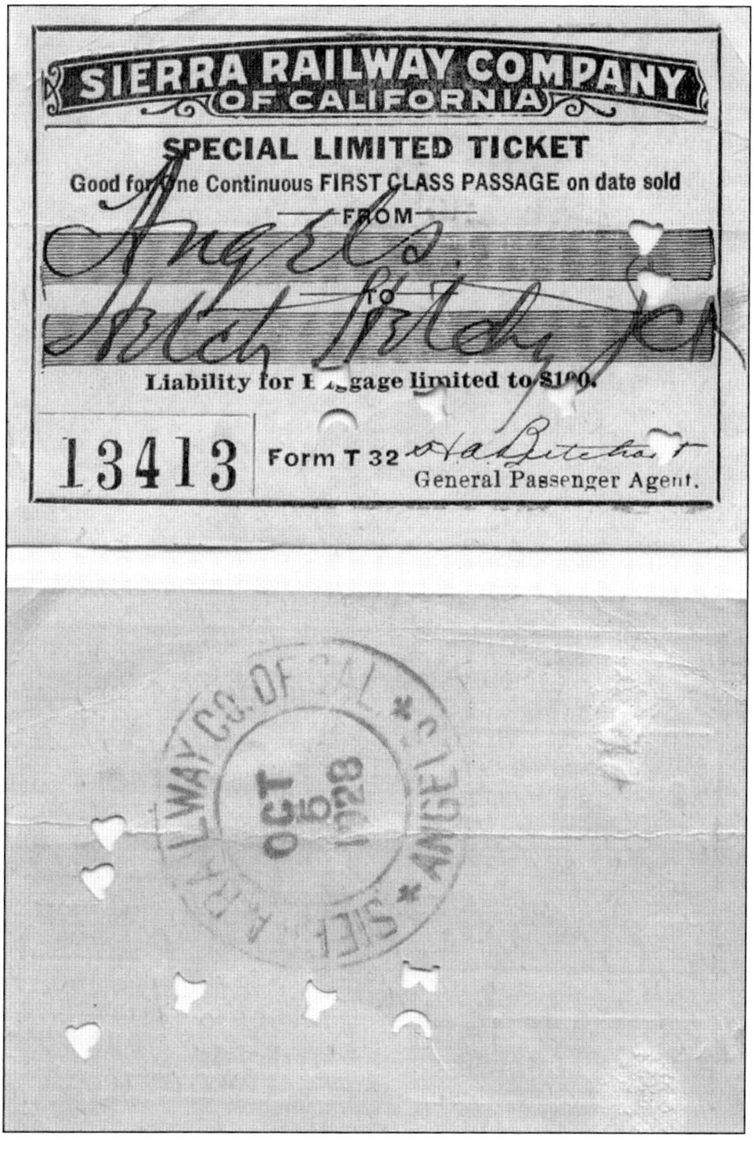

In 1928, this first-class ticket was purchased to Hetch Hetchy Junction. The Hetch Hetchy Railroad was completed in 1917 to the Hetch Hetchy Valley in Yosemite National Park, where a dam was built to provide water to San Francisco. During the 1930s, when the dam was raised to store more water, the railroad operated as a division of the Sierra Railway, which reached its record length of 140 miles of track. (Courtesy Wally Motloch.)

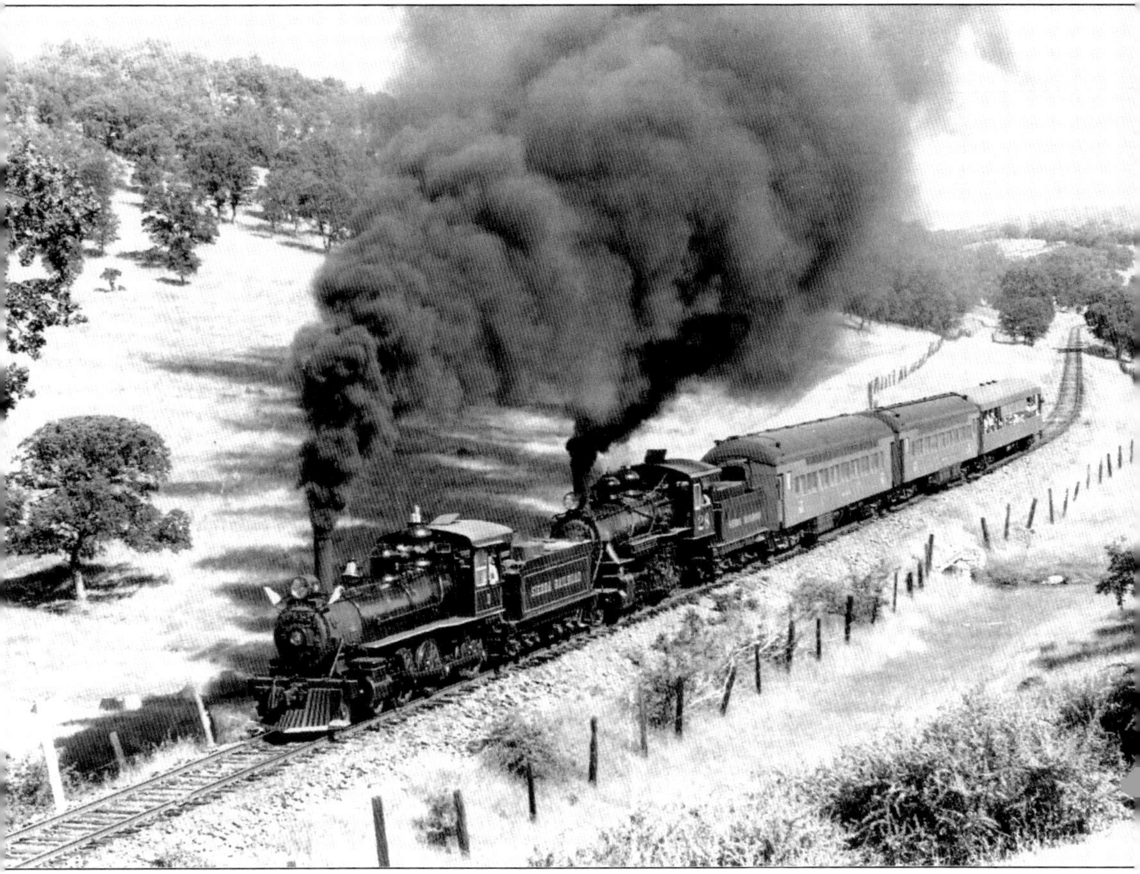

In this 1950s image, "Movie Star" Engine No. 3 makes its way toward Jamestown through the ranch lands near Keystone. A "Farewell to Steam" celebration was held in Jamestown on April 17, 1955, with 600 passengers arriving from the San Francisco Bay Area on a 13-car steam excursion train, sponsored by the Pacific Coast Chapter of the Railroad and Locomotive Historical Society. This photograph was taken during the heyday of the line as a location for over 200 films, including *The Virginian*, *Rage at Dawn*, *Duel in the Sun*, *High Noon*, and *Unforgiven*, as well as the television shows *Death Valley Days*, *Petticoat Junction*, and *Little House on the Prairie*. The Rogers No. 3 locomotive was built in 1891 and continues to operate for service and film and television work. (Courtesy Gary Wilson.)

Seven

Hostelries, Emporiums, and Ranches

The majority of the commercial and industrial development in Jamestown was directly related to the mining and railroading industries, with hotels, boardinghouses, and the ubiquitous saloons representing the preponderance of the business enterprises from the beginning, catering to locals and visitors alike.

The town was first occupied/populated by miners and travelers, then in the 1890s by those who traveled on or worked for the railroad and in the hard rock mines, and finally, by tourists to Yosemite and those attracted by the nostalgia for the Gold Rush during its centennial.

Commercially, most of the establishments in Jamestown were either general merchandise stores, providing virtually all the needs for a miner and his family, or specialty shops, such as gunsmiths, jewelers, cigar stores, butcher shops, hardware, and so on. Many of the other businesses were related to transportation: livery stables, blacksmiths, or harness and saddle makers. Tailors, barbers, milliners, dressmakers, and launderers provided for the personal needs of many, while doctors and dentists cared for the ills of the body.

Shortly after the discovery of gold, agriculturalists from the eastern states and foreign countries were drawn to the area to provide the fresh fruits, vegetables, and meats to feed the hungry hoards of miners. Many farms were also started by miners who stayed behind, producing everything needed to feed their families on lands that were free for the taking simply by filing agricultural land claims or homesteads. A few cooperative Italian gardens and prominent orchards and vineyards were located in the area, with small acreages and truck gardens producing fruits and vegetables for the local market, while extensive livestock ranches were located farther afield.

Always critical as a supporting service and industry, and at times the most important source of income, ranches were established in the early years, when animals provided much of the labor, and massive production of hay and grasses was necessary to feed the cattle, oxen, and horses that drew the wagons and stagecoaches to the mines. Wheat, barley, and oats, which could be grown without water or much attention, were produced, while grasslands were used for the grazing of cattle, sheep, and goats.

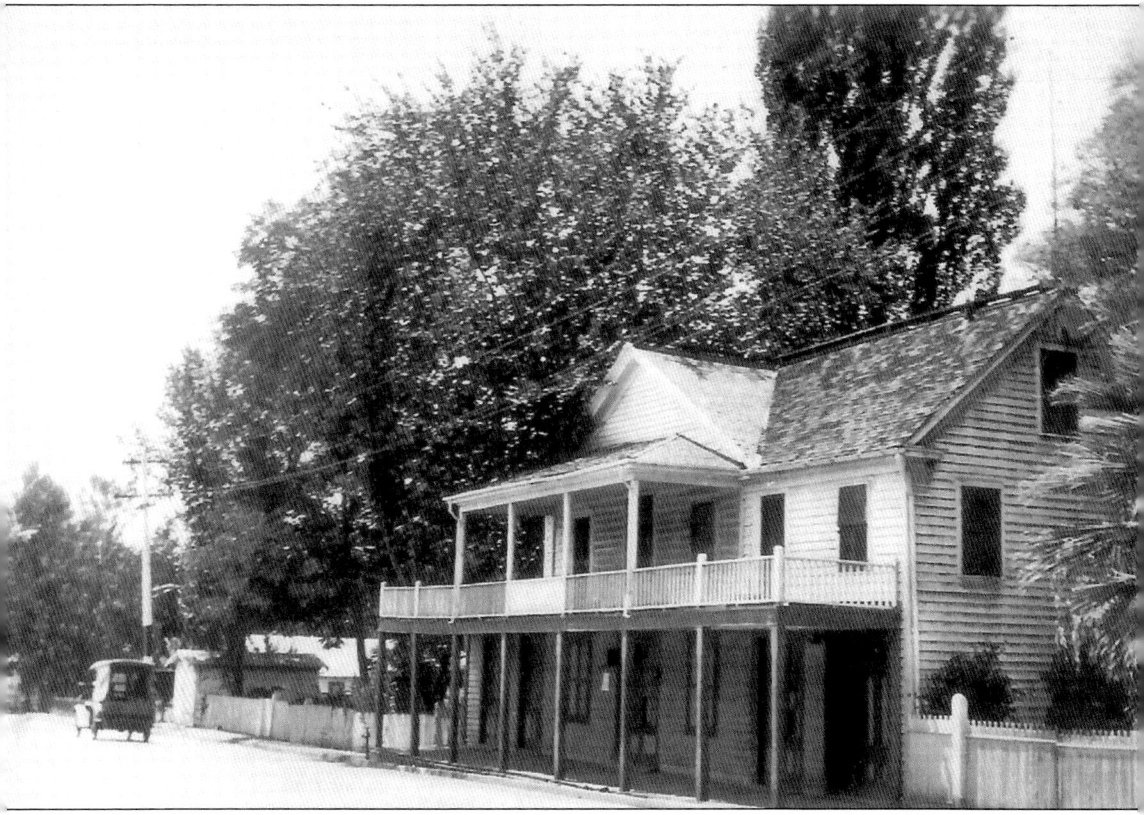

One of the first and longest-lasting establishments in Jamestown was that of B. F. Butterfield, who opened the Butterfield Mercantile Company store on Butterfield Flat, west of Wood's Creek, in March 1849. There he erected a building made of logs and canvas, installed a stock of goods, and began business. When that building burned, he moved across the creek and constructed this building of Virginia pine, brought around the Horn in the 1850s, where Butterfield advertised, "Honest goods at honest prices." The family resided on the upper floor, and the children continued to operate the business after the death of their parents. In 1909, it was noted that the store had never closed its doors, being the oldest in the county. At that time the store was a large frame building, carrying an immense stock of general merchandise, including dry goods, clothing, groceries, hardware, mine supplies, and other necessities. The store closed in 1919, was taken over by the Mines Supply Company in 1939, and closed again in the 1990s. (Courtesy Bancroft Library.)

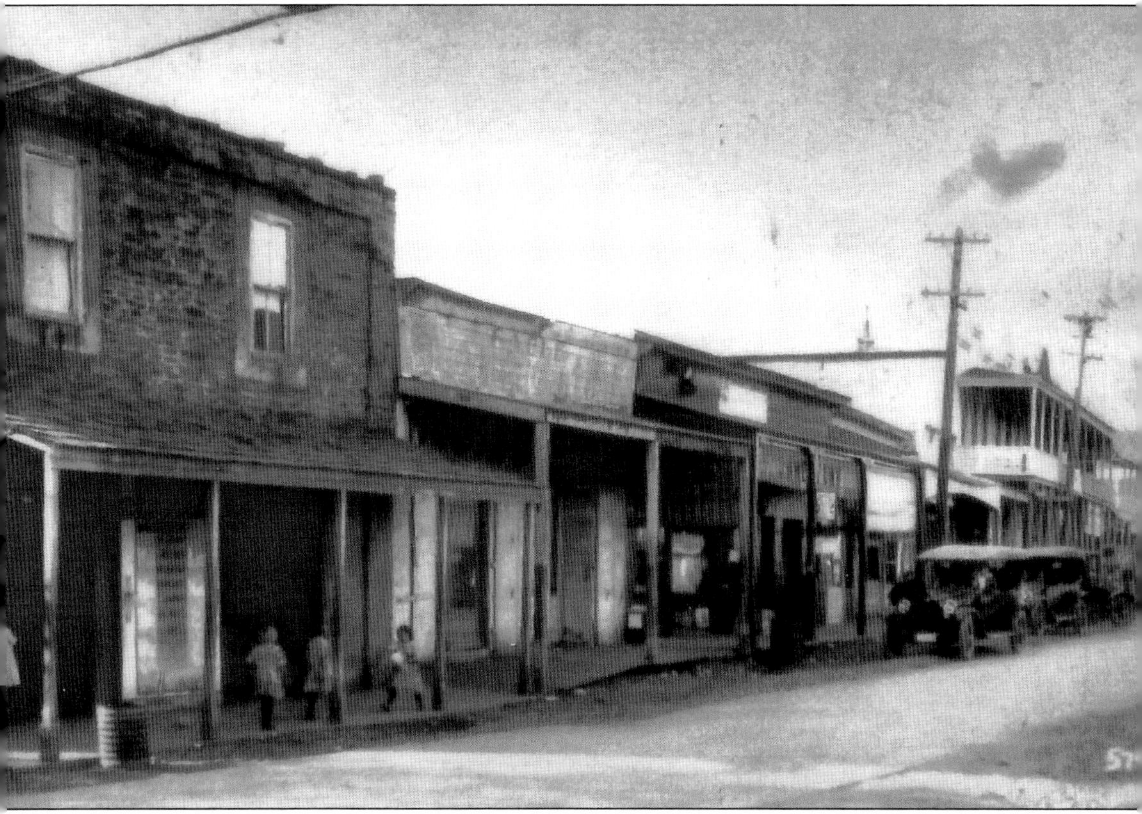

What may be the oldest–remaining stone building in Jamestown is depicted here in the 1910s, when it served as the post office. The building was erected for Doña Ignacia Ramirez in the 1850s; Ramirez was one of several Mexican women in Tuolumne County who operated their own establishments, owned mines, and were successful businesswomen. In the 1860s, the building was leased to the short-lived St. James Masonic Lodge No. 54, which held its own in the early 1860s, but was down to 26 members by the end of the Civil War. Membership fluctuated in the late 1860s, but was down to seven Master Masons by 1875, when it shut down forever. In this view, the Ramirez Building, the 1870s Raspi Store, 1880s one-story Gonzales and Carlon's Store, and other buildings that are no longer extant progress north up the west side of Main Street. (Courtesy Donn Blount.)

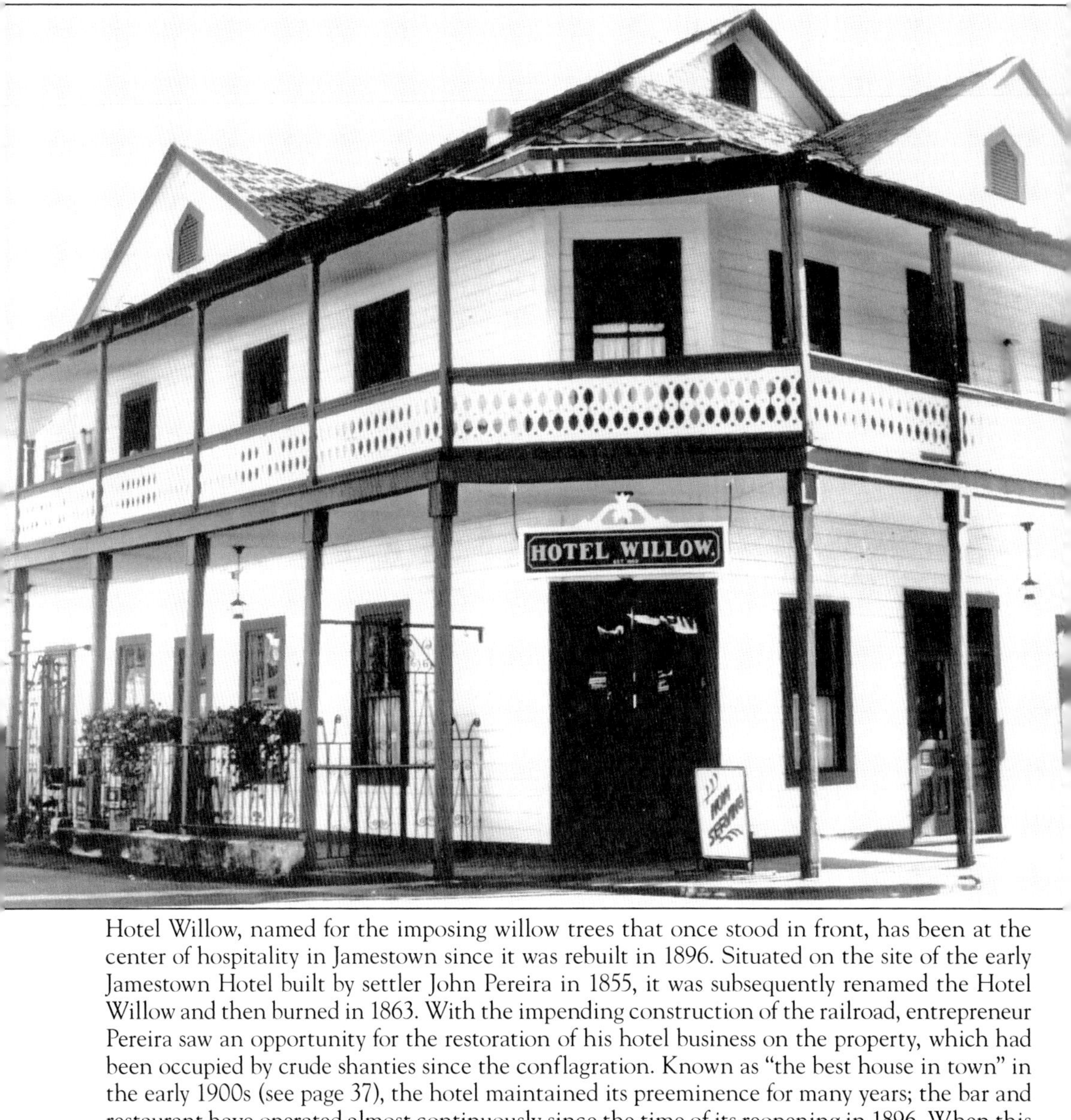

Hotel Willow, named for the imposing willow trees that once stood in front, has been at the center of hospitality in Jamestown since it was rebuilt in 1896. Situated on the site of the early Jamestown Hotel built by settler John Pereira in 1855, it was subsequently renamed the Hotel Willow and then burned in 1863. With the impending construction of the railroad, entrepreneur Pereira saw an opportunity for the restoration of his hotel business on the property, which had been occupied by crude shanties since the conflagration. Known as "the best house in town" in the early 1900s (see page 37), the hotel maintained its preeminence for many years; the bar and restaurant have operated almost continuously since the time of its reopening in 1896. When this photograph of Hotel Willow was taken in 1974, the building was quite spiffed up and prosperous looking. The second story was consumed in a 1978 fire, but the lower floor retains many of its original architectural elements. (Courtesy Gary Wilson.)

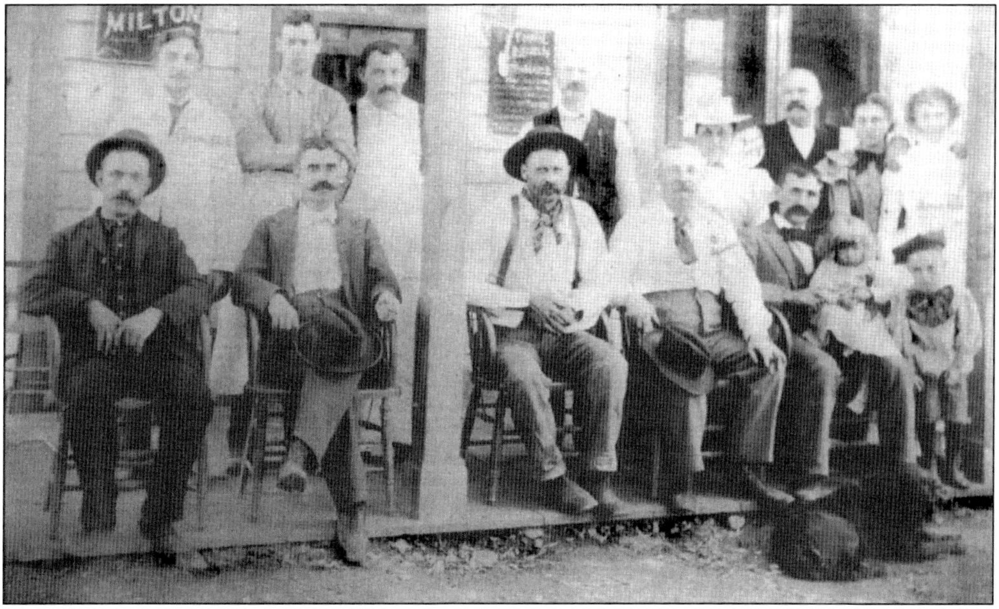

Employees and townsfolk, with the obligatory dog, pose on the front porch of Hotel Willow sometime after 1897. Posted in the background is an advertisement for the Sonora and Milton Stage, where people could pick up the stage to travel northeast to Sonora or northwest to Milton, via Copperopolis. (Courtesy Gary Wilson.)

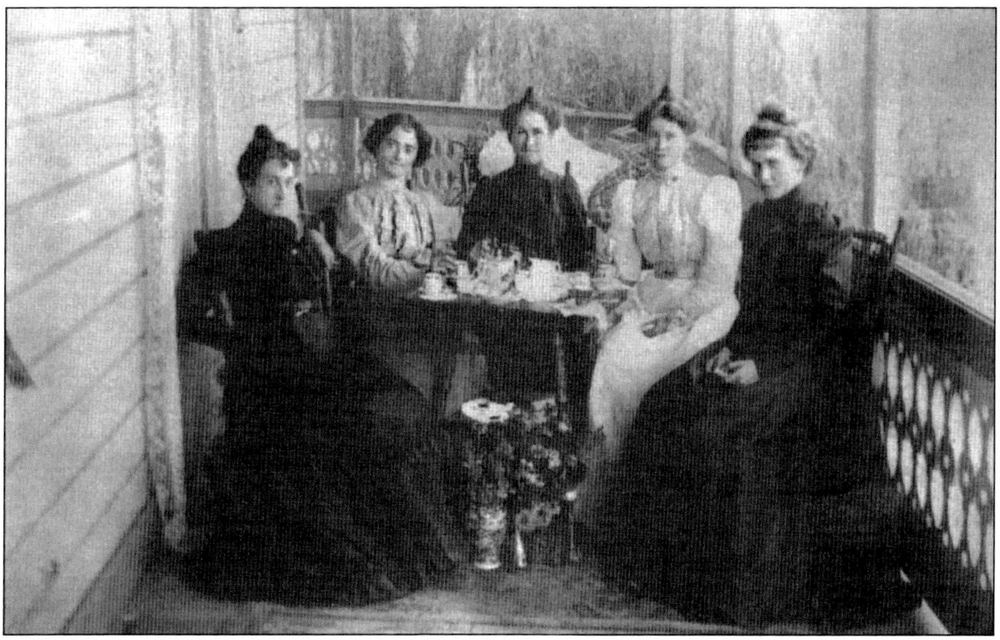

Dressed in their finery, members of the Mayer family (Hotel Willow proprietors in the early 1900s) and friends take a respite from work to have tea on the balcony. The women evidently preferred to be seated on the pleasant upper balcony, in contrast to the men who inhabited the lower story near the saloon. (Courtesy Gary Wilson.)

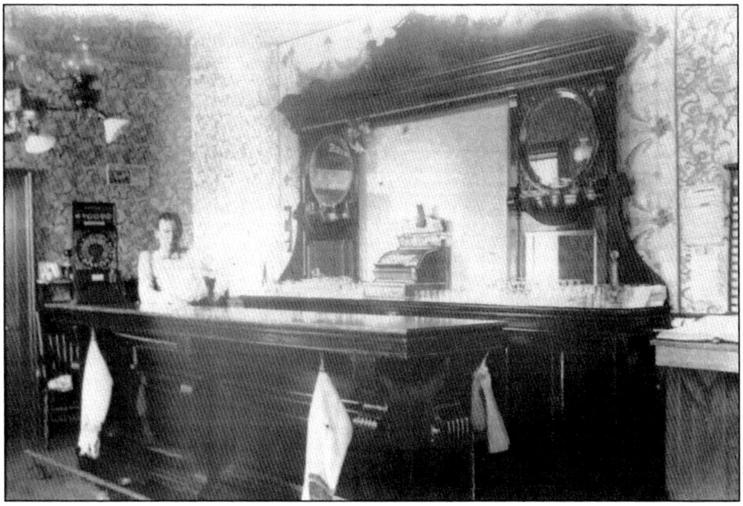

In these two early views of the Hotel Willow saloon, improvements to the bar correlate with the increase in business and change of operators. The early bar was much shorter than the latter, with a simpler mirrored back bar, gas and electric lighting, floral wallpaper, and towels for the patrons. (Courtesy Gary Wilson.)

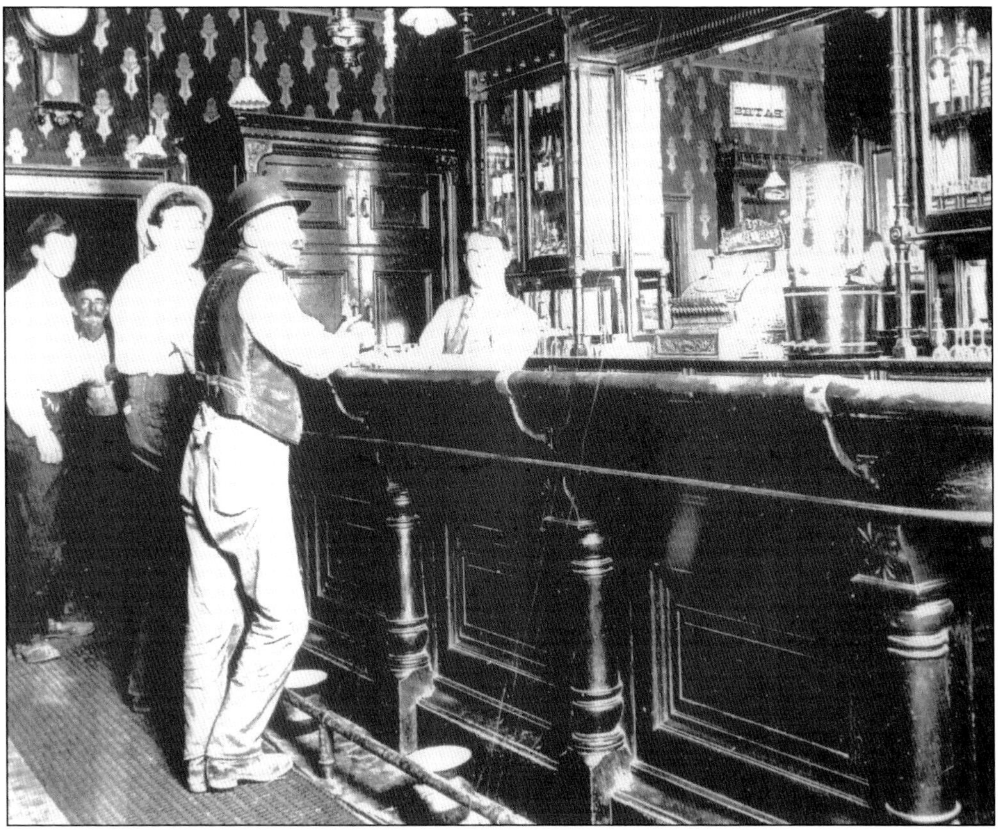

When this photograph was taken, the Willow had a gleaming new bar (purchased in San Francisco by new owner Frank Mayer and installed in 1898), complete with modern back bar, mirror, and liquors behind glass. The brass rail was still in evidence, and spittoons were regularly spaced for the use of those who chewed tobacco, but modern electric lighting had been installed, and towels were no longer provided. (Courtesy Gary Wilson.)

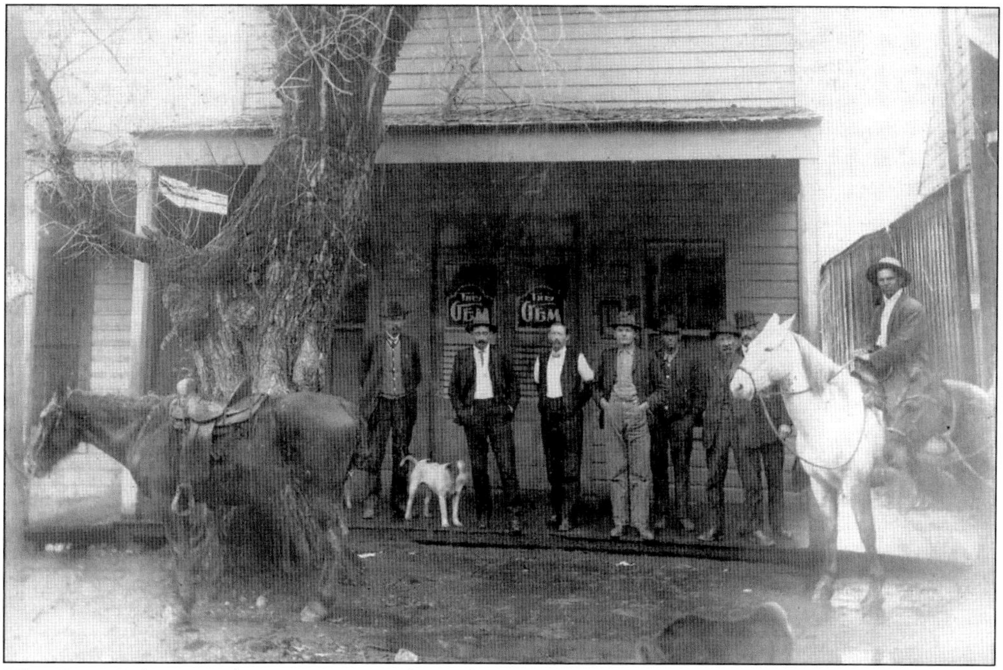

The Gem Saloon, with its swinging saloon doors, is depicted here in the 1890s. The bartender (third from left, in vest) and several of his patrons posed, along with a couple of horses and the town dog. The large cottonwood tree in front attests to the age of the false-fronted frame building. (Courtesy Wally Motloch.)

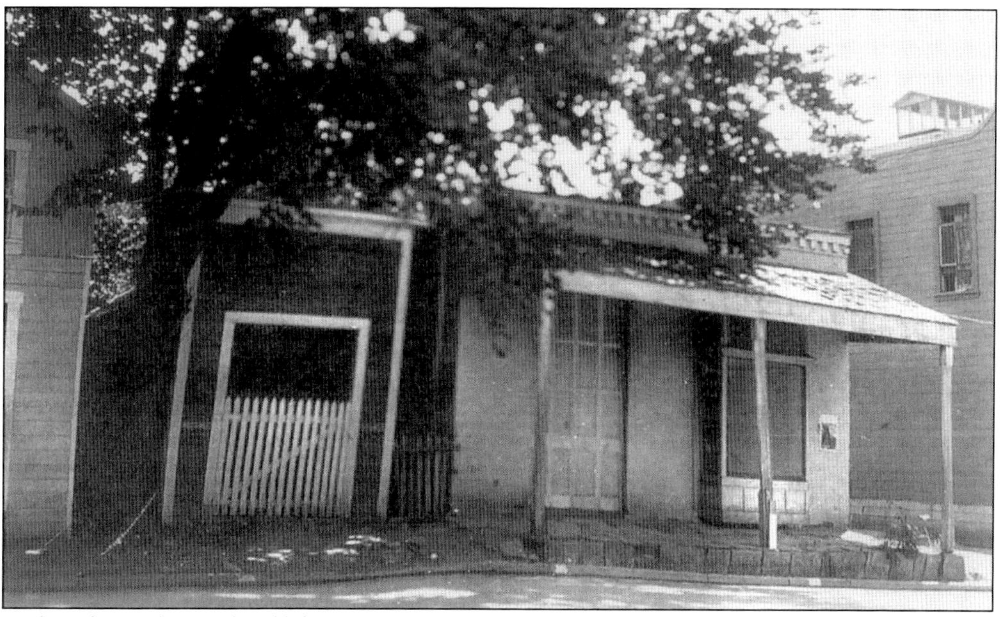

As bread was the staple of life in the early years for miners and families alike, bakeries were an important component of the community. The Leland Bakery, erected in the early 1850s, was one such establishment that supplied the needs of the town for many years. Photographed in 1928, the present Jamestown Hotel is to the far right. (Photograph by Jesse Brown Cook; courtesy Bancroft Library.)

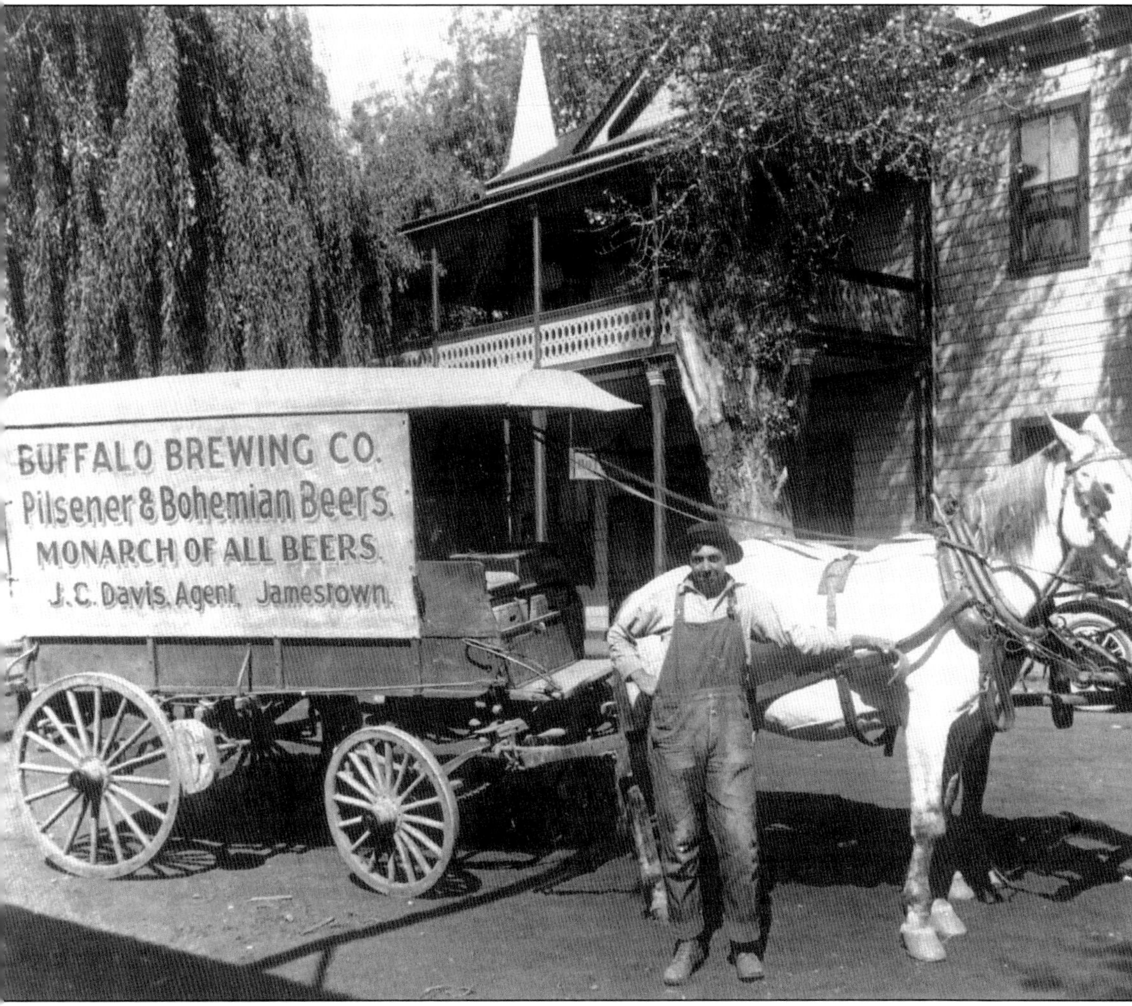

The Buffalo Brewing Company delivery wagon is pictured around 1918 in front of Hotel Willow. In the latter half of the 19th century and the early years of the 20th century, virtually every gold country town possessed a brewery. Hops were grown in fields, dried in kilns, and brewed in large copper vats. Without refrigeration, the product could not be kept for long, so much of it was preserved in ceramic bottles, with ceramic stoppers, for transport to distant camps and communities. This gentleman, however, was evidently delivering for the Buffalo Brewing Company of Sacramento, founded by Henry Grau in 1889. Grau, a native of Buffalo, New York, known for having over 19 breweries, reused the name in his Sacramento operation. The company sold lager, bock, and ale on draft and in bottles, but shut down in 1942. (Courtesy Stephen Willey.)

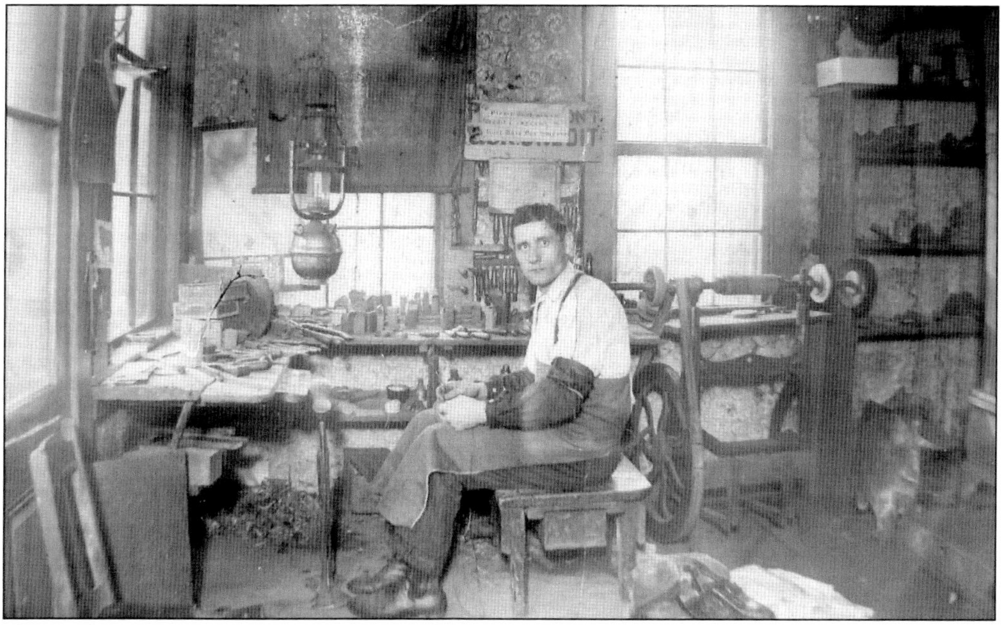

Shoemaker Luigi Marliani is pictured in his shop on Main Street about 1910. Born in 1882, he emigrated from Italy in 1905. His wife, Maria, joined him from Italy in 1907, and they became U.S. citizens in 1919. Maria took in boarders to help make ends meet, and they were successful enough to buy their building, which remains on Main Street, by 1920. (Courtesy Lewis "Butch" Marliani.)

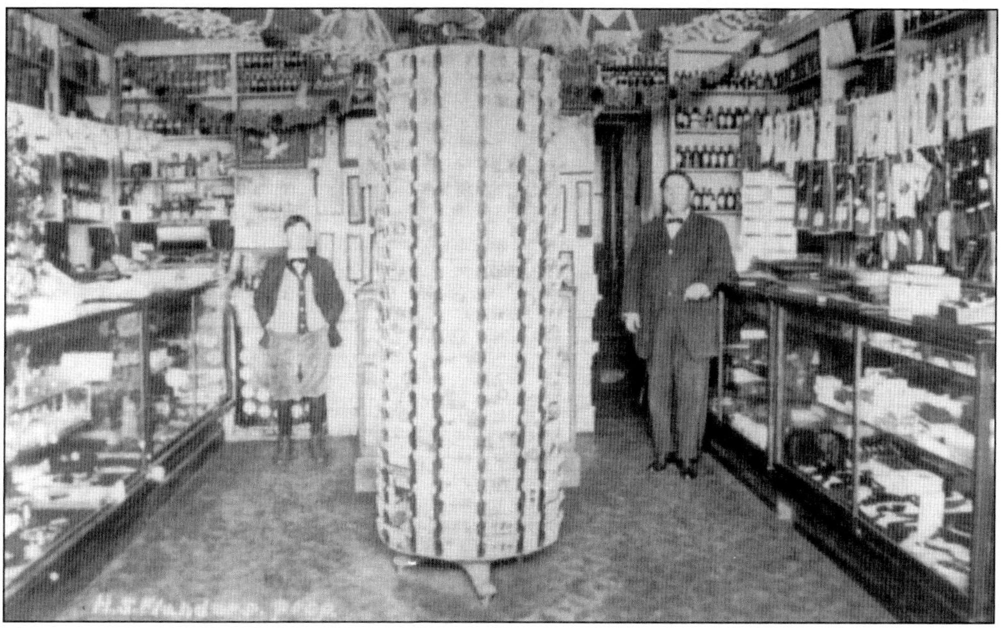

Pharmacist Harry Flanders (right) stands proudly with his unidentified clerk and their stock in trade in 1910. Flanders was noted in *Tuolumne County, California* (issued by the *Union Democrat* newspaper in 1909) as "providing the purest of drugs and the best of every other line carried," while the "popularity of his wife Mrs. Flanders [Olive] added to the flattering standing with physicians and residents." She was evidently quite popular with Dr. Percy Telford, whom she married after Harry's death. (Courtesy Gary Wilson.)

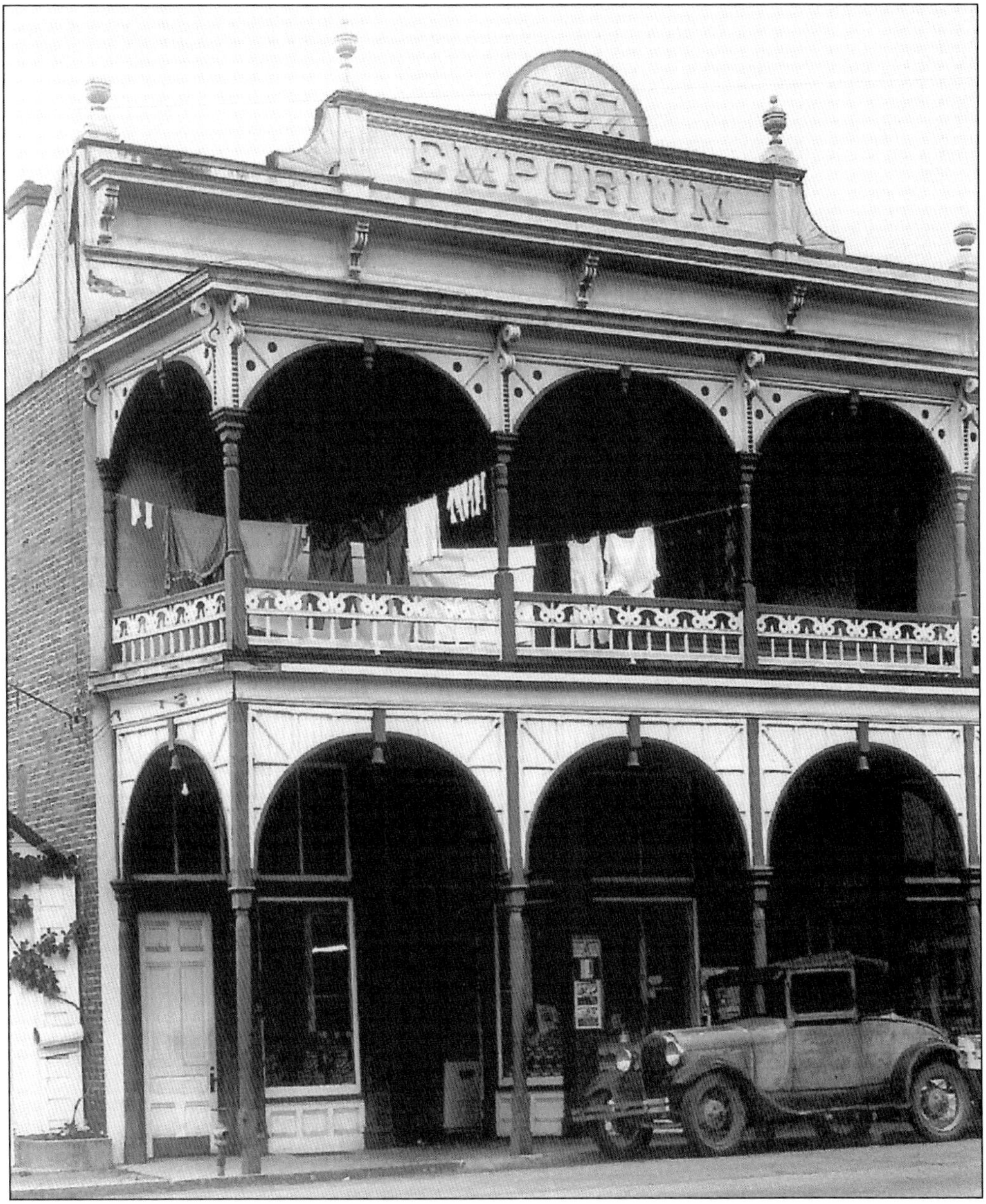

The most impressive commercial building in Jamestown, the Emporium, was constructed as a department store for J. W. Witney and Sons in 1897 and was noted as being the most imposing business structure in Tuolumne County, next to the Hotel Victoria in Sonora. The store was acquired by merchant Moses Arendt within a year and operated as a general merchandise store and telephone exchange. The first floor was a department store, carrying yard goods, linens, household items, clothing, gadgets, and toys. In 1909, the Emporium was described in *Tuolumne County, California* (issued by the *Union Democrat* newspaper) as "one of the finest clothing and furnishing goods houses in the county," with a large, varied, and up-to-date stock. It served as the county's telephone exchange from 1906 to 1923 and, from 1936 to 1967, as a grocery store owned by Jake Barendregt Sr. The Queen Anne building was listed on the National Register of Historic Places in 1978. (Courtesy Bancroft Library.)

Barendregt's Grocery is pictured in the 1930s with Jake Barendregt Sr. on the left and longtime clerk Jim Bristol on the right. Originally operated as Overholtzer and Porter, the business was purchased by Peter Barendregt in 1918, when it became Porter and Barendregt. After Porter's death in 1936, Barendregt's son Jake bought out the Porter estate's interest. (Courtesy Tuolumne County Museum.)

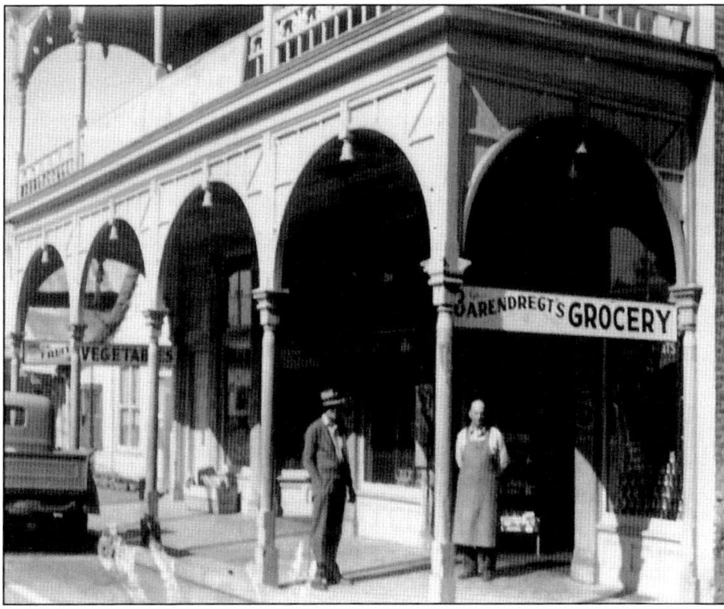

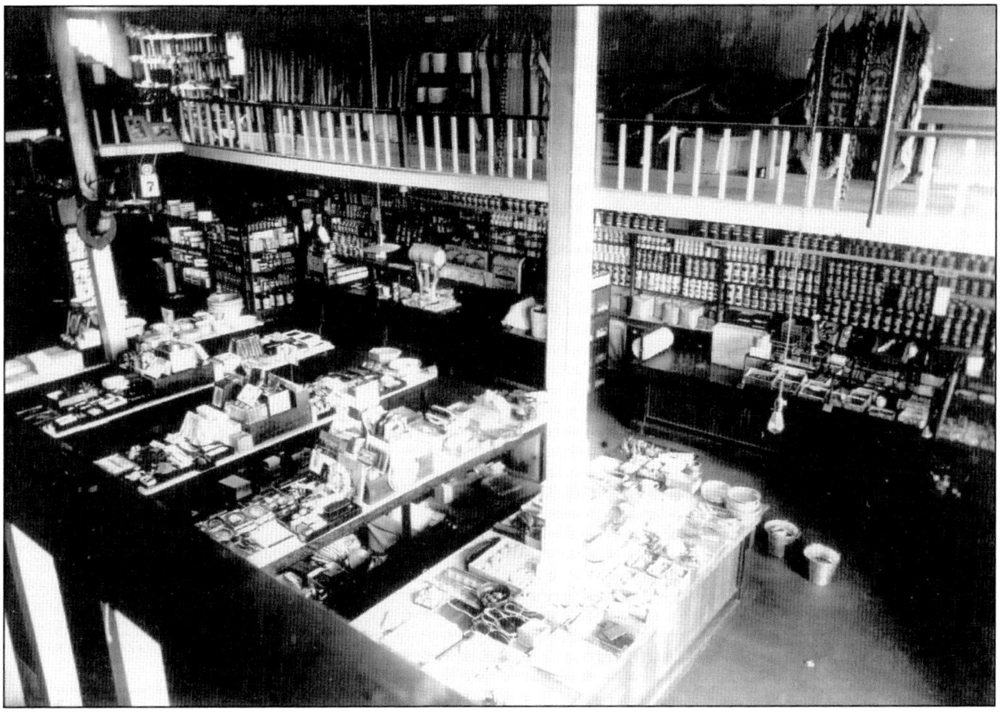

A Barendregt's Grocery clerk poses beside the impressive stock of wares. In addition to groceries and canned goods, they sold tobacco, thread, dog food, and all manner of comestibles. During the mining years, five or six trucks departed from Jamestown to surrounding communities, including Quartz, Stent, Melones, Moccasin, Jacksonville, and Shawmut, to take grocery orders. (Courtesy Gary Wilson.)

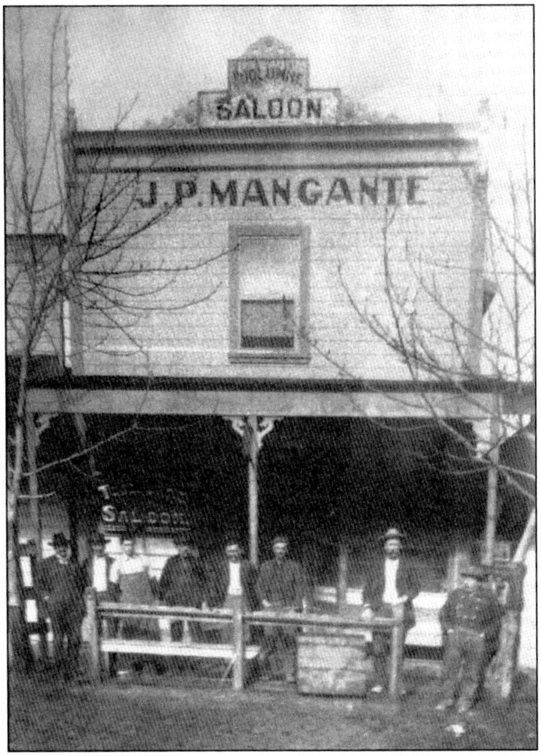

Jesse P. Mangante's Tuolumne Saloon was flanked by watering troughs and hitching racks. In *Sierra Railway* (1960), Dorothy Newell Deane provides the following description of the scene: "On hot summer afternoons, cottonwood seeds watered down like gentle snow upon gamblers and drifters dozing in barroom chairs, tilted against saloon fronts, until the evening's excitement began." Mangante was also the owner of the Mangante Mine. (Courtesy Stephen Willey.)

A crowd turned out to have their picture taken at John Rocca's Saloon and Jamestown Hotel sometime in the early 1890s. Prior to 1890, it was known as Whyte's Restaurant and Rooming House. It burned on December 17, 1896, and was replaced with the two-story J. Rocca Building, which burned in the mid-1960s. The hotel's name was adopted by the 1919 Jamestown Hotel at the south end of town. (Courtesy Tuolumne County Museum.)

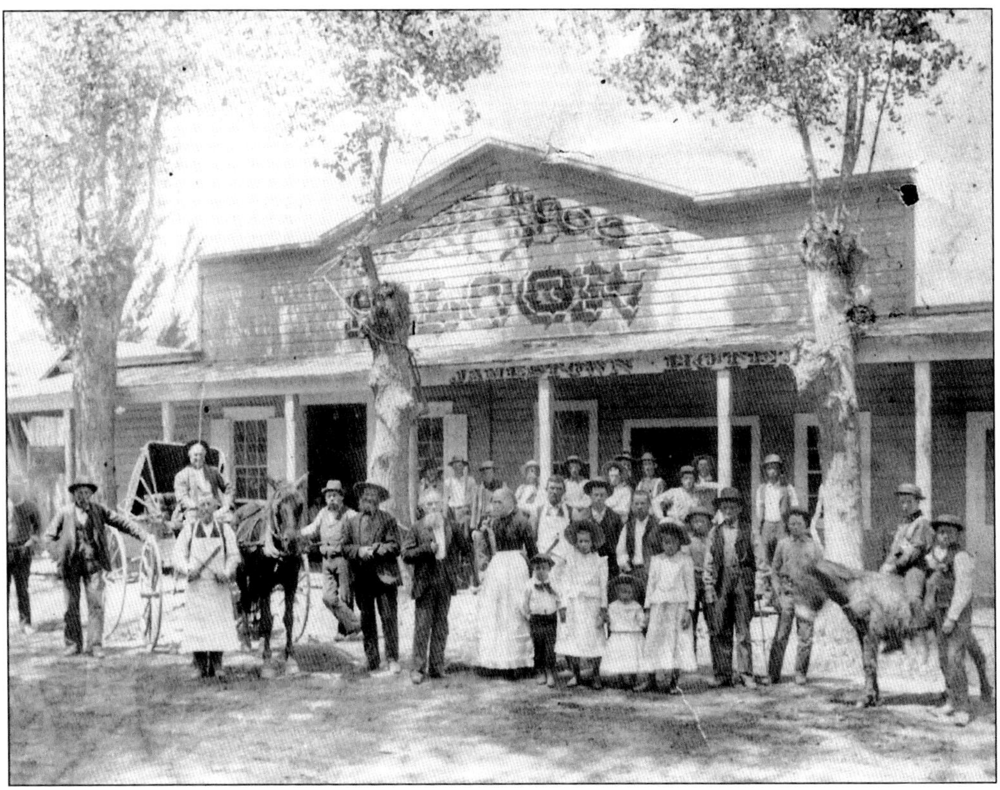

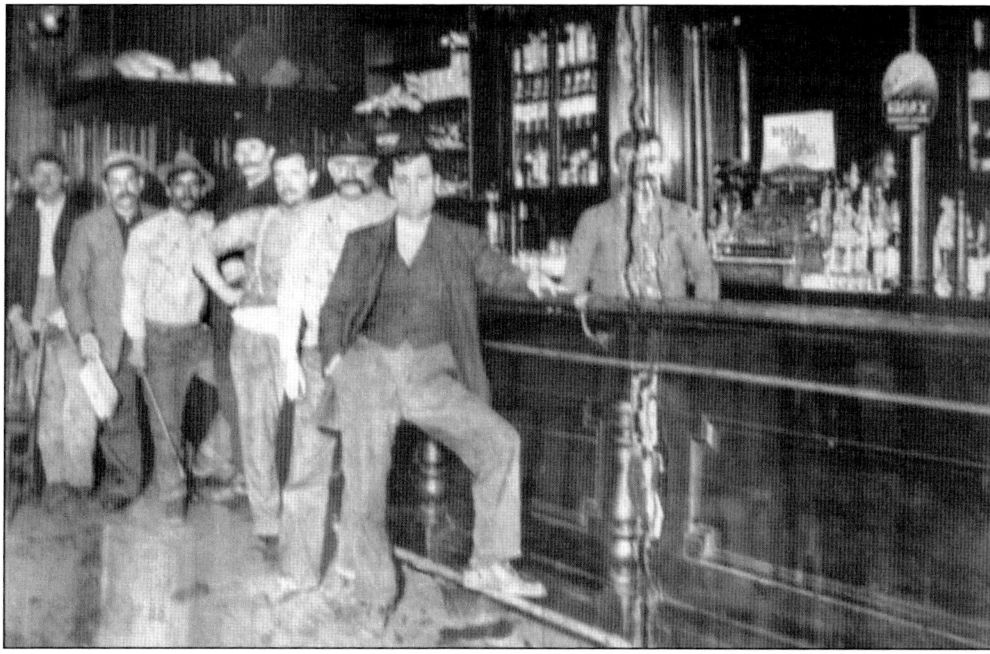

Saloons were the most prolific of all the enterprises in Jamestown, as they were in all of the mining communities. They were not only a place to drink, but also a spot for men to meet, exchange news, and enjoy the camaraderie of others after the long working day. In this 1895 view of the National Hotel bar, bartender Angelo Campari is serving the customers. (Courtesy Stephen Willey.)

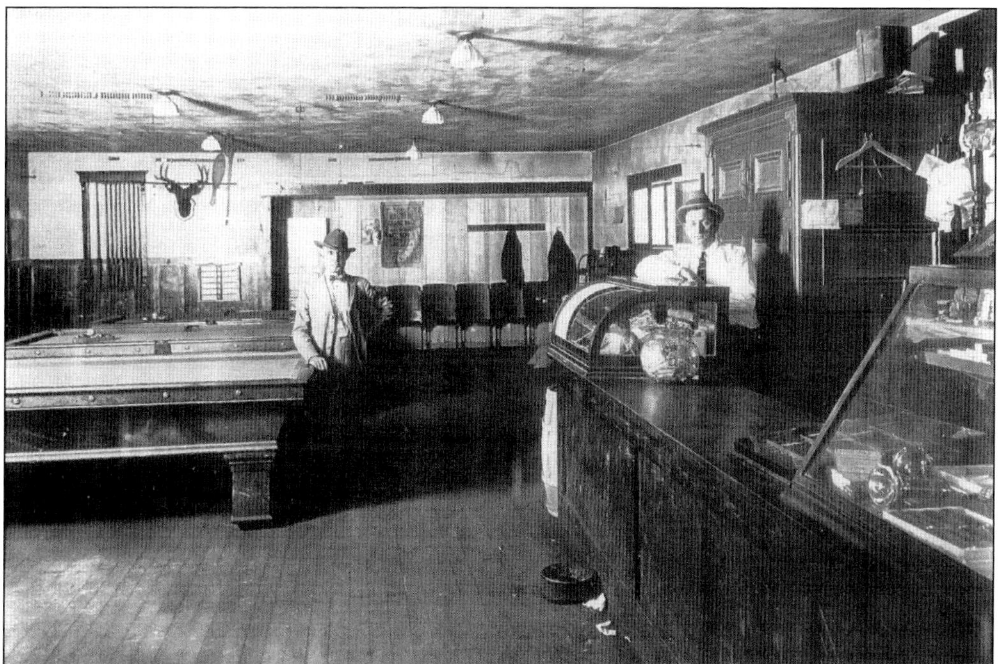

Pool halls, where these rather dapper gentlemen socialize near the magnificent billiard table sometime in the 1920s, were another staple of the local economy in Jamestown. An oak icebox, spittoon, and cigars complete the accoutrements. (Courtesy Jim Yeisley.)

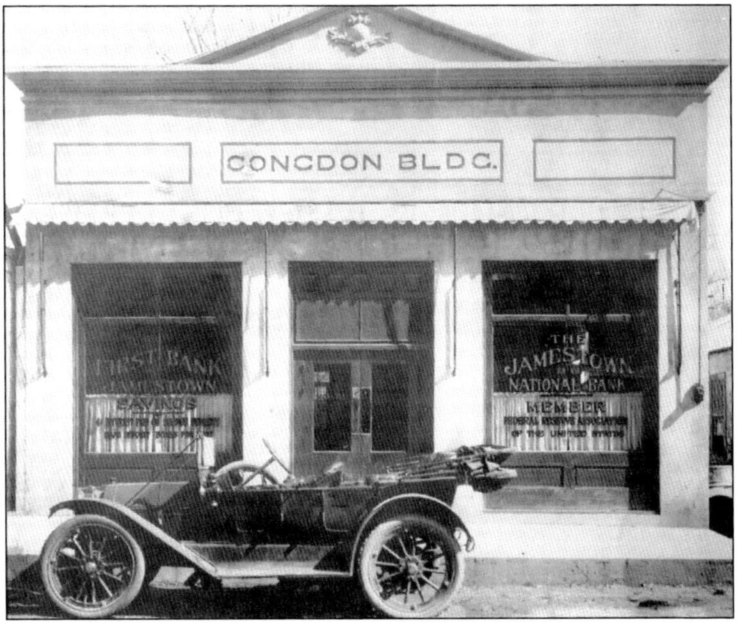

The First National Bank in Jamestown opened in 1916, with Joseph Ryan as manager, Charles F. Butterfield as cashier, and Edna Rocca as bookkeeper. Promoters included many of the local businessmen; the building was erected by Jamestown physician Dr. Charles Congdon and occupied by the bank until it sold to the Bank of America in 1929 and moved to Sonora. (Courtesy Gary Wilson.)

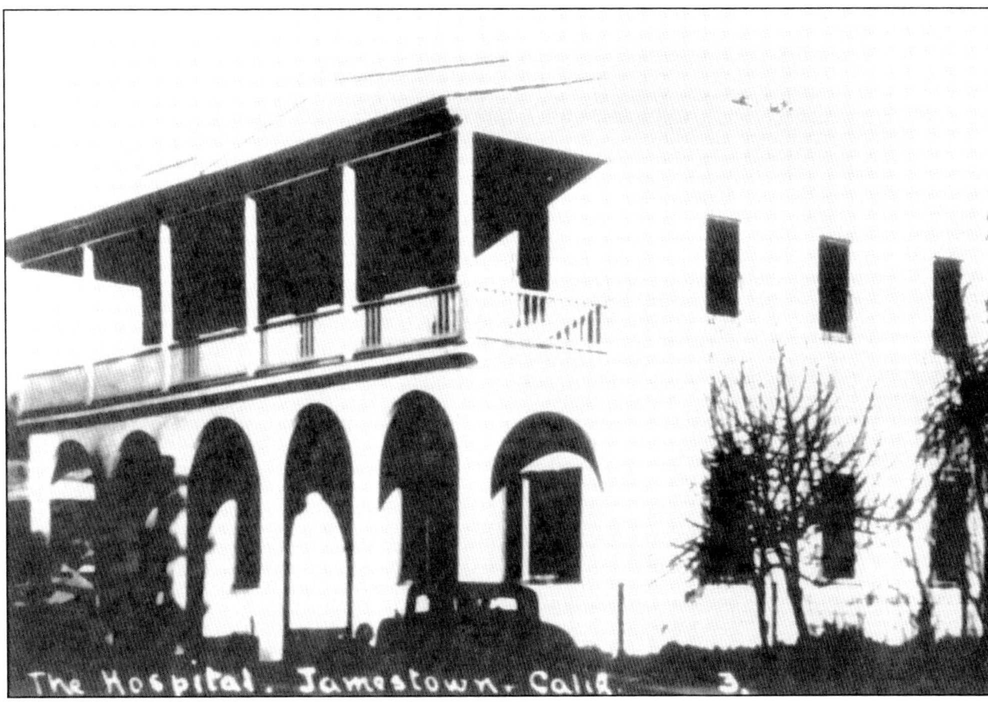

In 1938, Dr. D. L. Farrell converted the Jamestown Hotel into the Mother Lode Hospital, which operated until at least 1949. The building was erected by David Martinez in 1919 and was prosperous enough to expand to an additional structure in the 1920s, but business declined during the Depression. Crocker Associates purchased it in the 1970s and renovated it in the 1890s style as the Jamestown Hotel and Restaurant. (Courtesy Gary Wilson.)

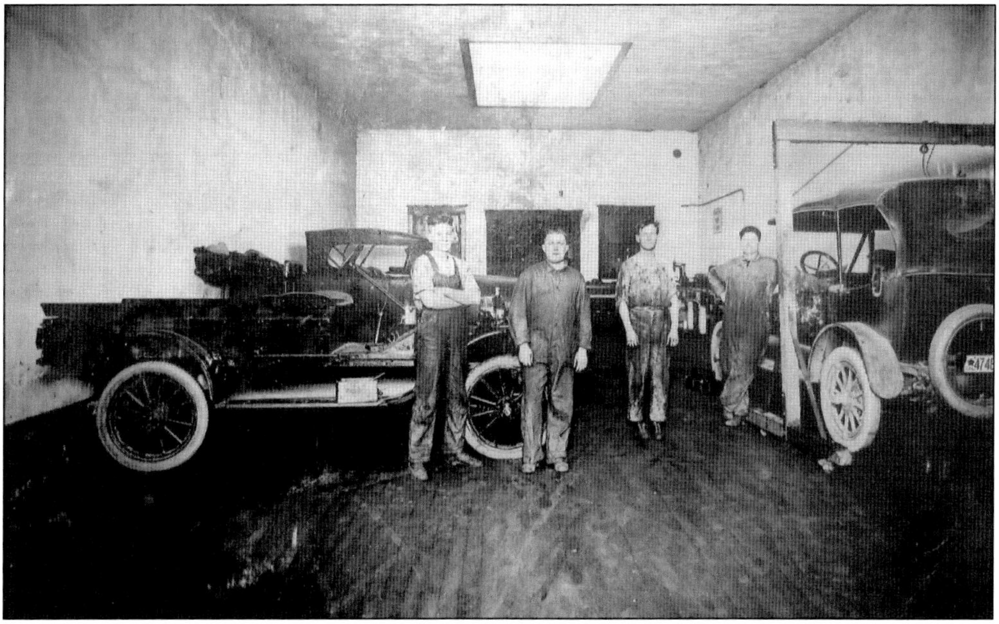

Booker's Garage was erected in 1922 by E. Booker on the site of the Jamestown Garage. This concrete building opened shortly after automobiles supplanted horses as the means of transportation. In this 1920s view, the mechanics pose with their repair projects. The garage operated through the 1940s, when it was converted to Barendregt's Grocery Store, but until 2009, the sidewalk still featured the concrete garage ramp. (Courtesy Donn Blount.)

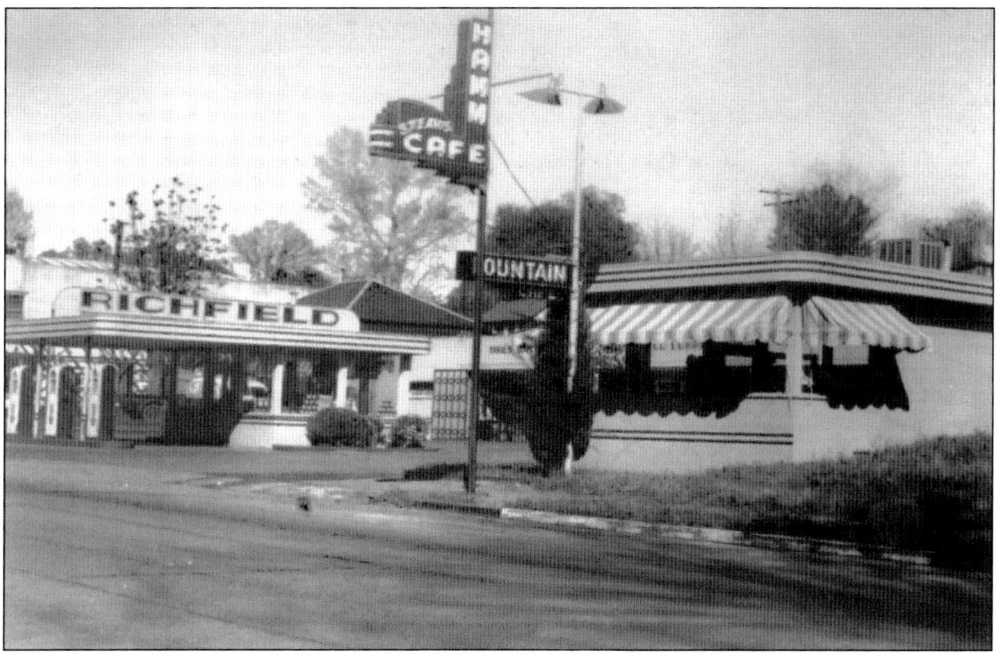

Pictured is the site of the present Mother Lode Coffee Shop in the late 1940s or early 1950s, when it was Hamm's Café and Fountain. The building was built by R. Booker in 1933 and adjoined the Richfield Service Station; both were constructed to serve the motoring public. (Courtesy Stephen Willey.)

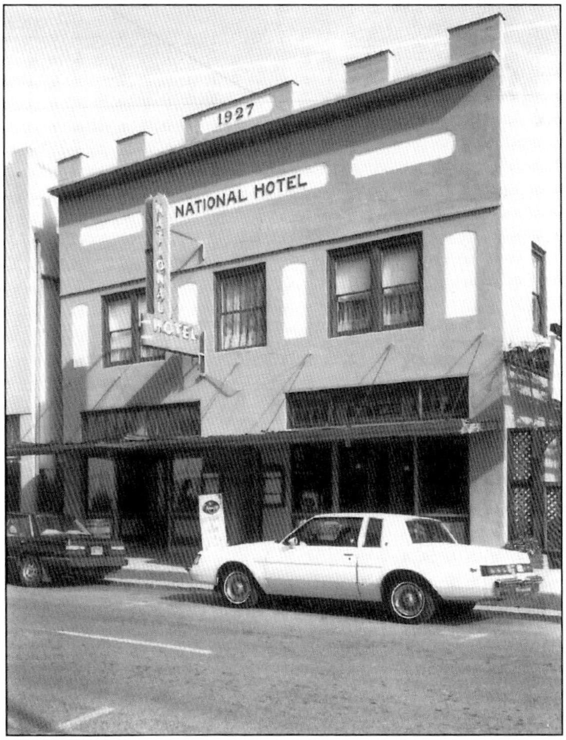

The wood-frame National Hotel was erected here in 1859, but gutted in 1927, when the adjoining Odd Fellows Hall was consumed by fire. Rebuilt in concrete, the hotel was operated by Angelina Carboni and Joe Graziano until it was sold to Charles and Olive Esgar in 1941. The National El Dorado Company, Inc., added a two-story porch and facade in 1974 as a reproduction of the 19th-century hotel. (Courtesy Scott Weber.)

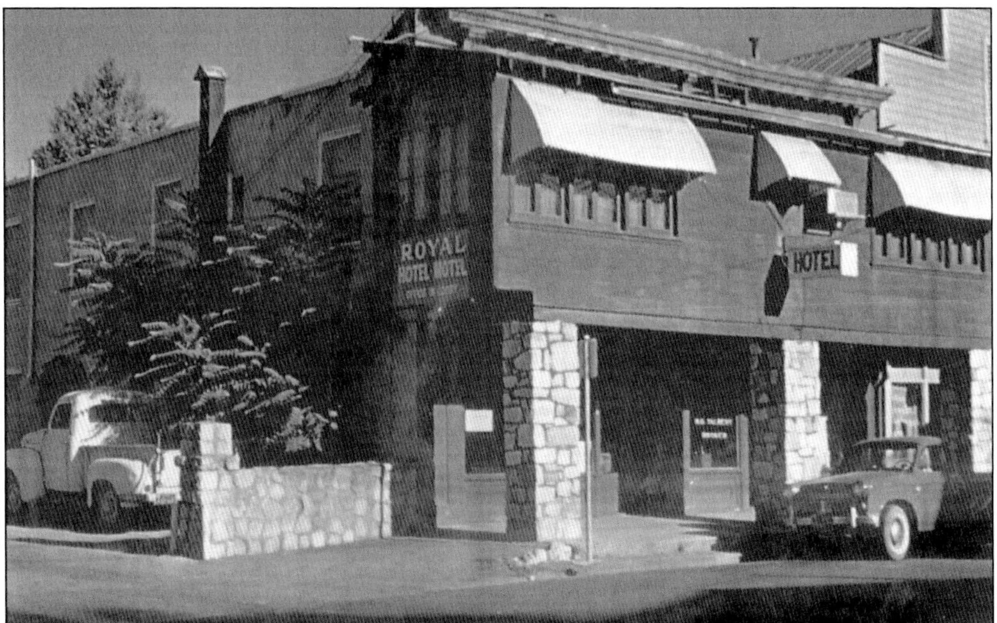

The Royal Hotel was built in 1925 by R. W. and Rae Rushing as a two-story concrete building and has operated nearly continuously since that time. In the 1950s, the original facade was altered with the addition of sandstone pillars from William Yeisley's quarry near Cooperstown and awnings over the windows. The facade was altered again in the 1970s, when the 1890s-style two-story porch was added. (Courtesy Jim Yeisley.)

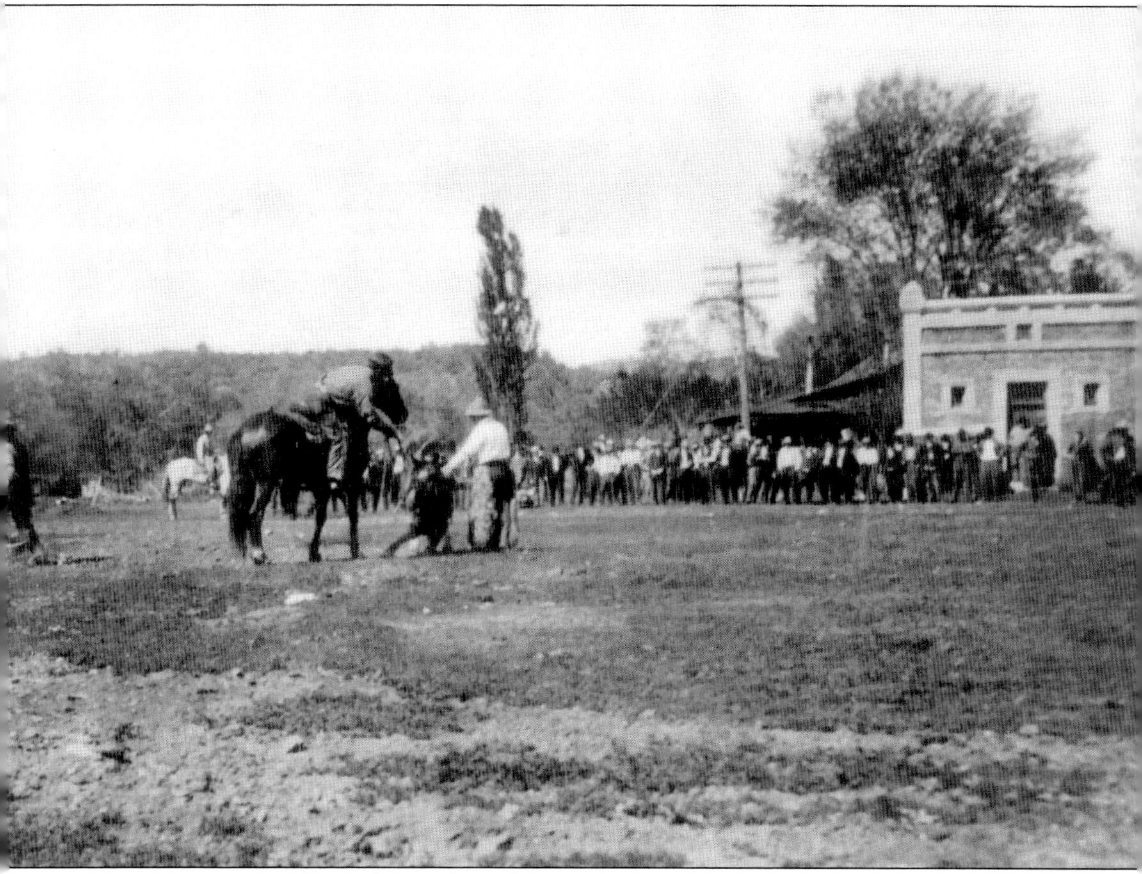

Between Main Street and Wood's Creek, with room for the men's horses to be inconspicuously hitched, was the location of the largest red-light district in the Mother Lode, known as "Back-of-Town." Although some "cribs" were built on site, others were moved there in the early 1920s, when the mines reopened after World War I and the Hetch Hetchy and Don Pedro Dam projects injected new life into the town. The Jamestown Jail, designed by architect C. W. Ayres, was built in this location in 1897, with the coming of the railroad, and is seen here as the backdrop to a rodeo. In 1964, it was taken down and moved to Pollardville, a Western-themed attraction near Lodi, and then moved back to Jamestown in 2007 and reconstructed nearby on a site behind Rocca Park. (Courtesy Tuolumne County Museum.)

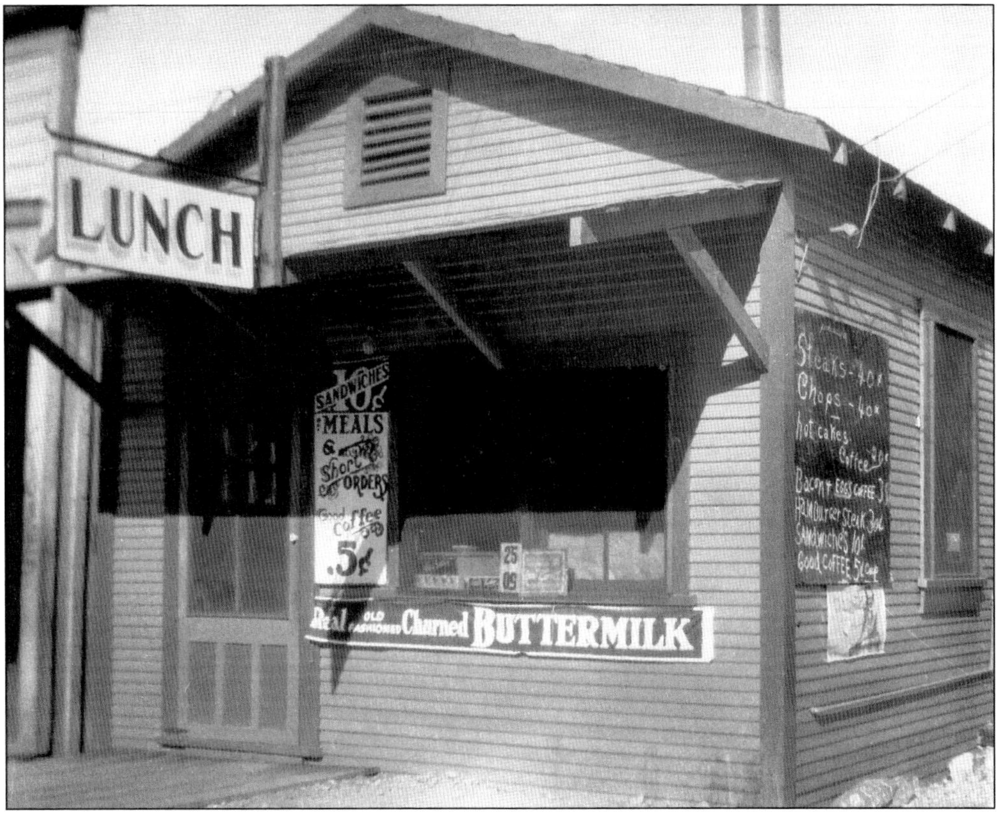

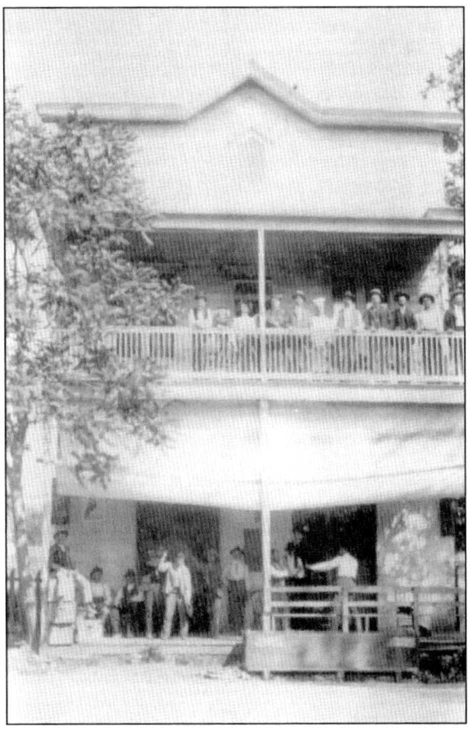

Verba's Lunch, originally the home of Edna Rocca but converted into a popular local dining spot, is pictured in 1933. At this time, the simple craftsman building served sandwiches for 10¢, coffee for 5¢, steaks and chops for 40¢, hamburger steak for 30¢, and a breakfast of hotcakes and coffee for 35¢. The building is still located on the west side of Main Street. (Courtesy Jim Yeisley.)

This building is thought to date to the Gold Rush. In 1898, a jeweler and the post office occupied the first floor, with lodgings on the second. Operated variously over subsequent years as the Europa Hotel and the Marengo Hotel, an explosion and fire in 1937 destroyed the Marengo's frame second story. The single-story brick building remains, its iron doors intact, at the south end of Main Street. (Courtesy Tuolumne County Museum.)

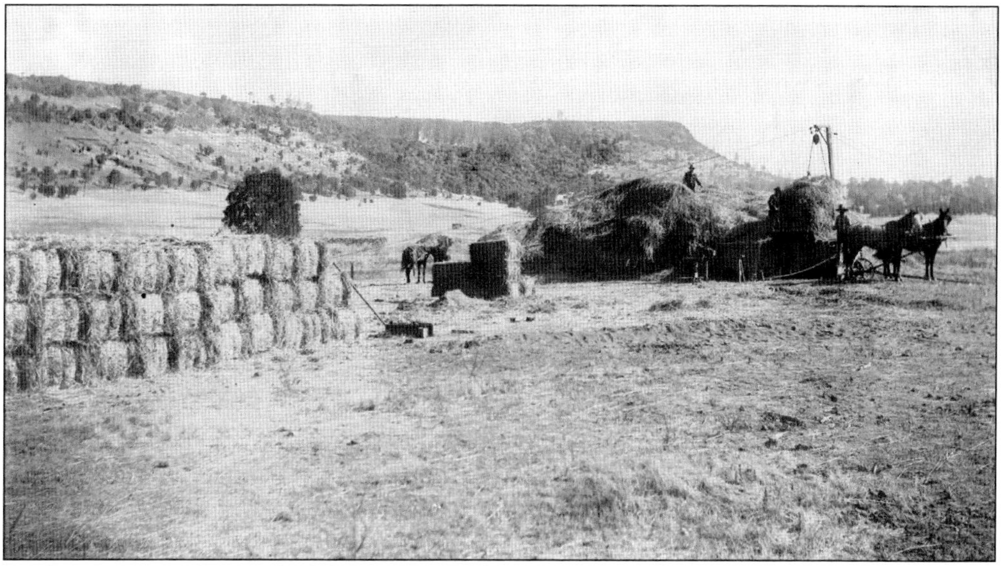

By the 1870s, ranching, which began as an adjunct to the production of hay and grain for the horses and oxen, had settled into an important agricultural base with the livestock operations on the grasslands in southwest Tuolumne County. Augustino, the patriarch of the Rosasco family, came to California from Italy in the 1860s to raise cattle. Above, a hay baler is working on Turner Flat, which was purchased by Ed Rosasco in 1919 to build the fine craftsman home below for his bride, Vandalia, in 1920. The family still resides in the home, a landmark along Highway 108, with its threshold palm trees. (Above, courtesy Tuolumne County Museum; below, courtesy Judith Marvin.)

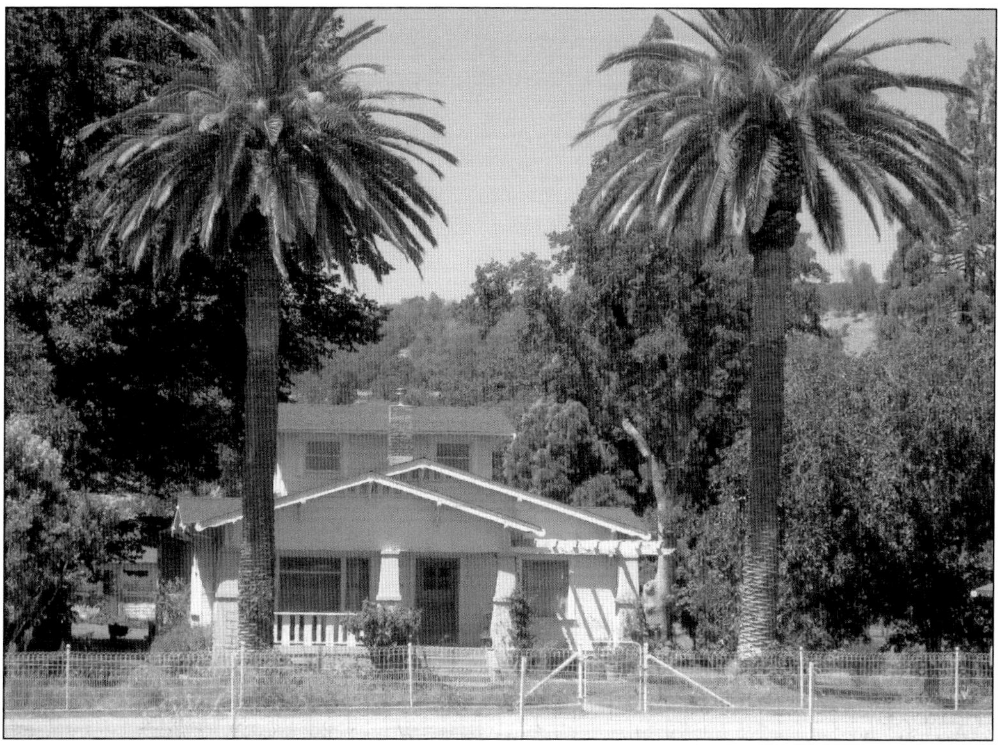

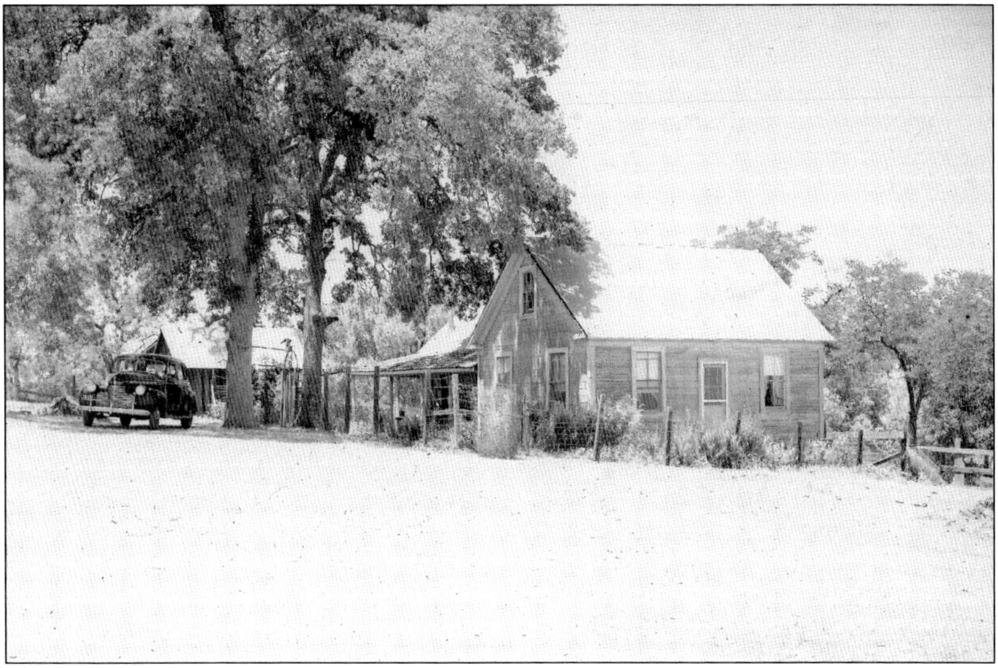

In the 1870s, Irishman James McFadden settled on what became known as the Wagner Ranch on O'Byrnes Ferry Road, a popular Western movie location during the 1930s and 1940s. McFadden came to California during the Gold Rush and gained U.S. citizenship in 1858. He acquired this land about 1870, constructing this house and other ranch buildings. Charles Wagner, a prominent cattleman, purchased the ranch from McFadden's widow, Mary, in 1907. (Courtesy Tuolumne County Museum.)

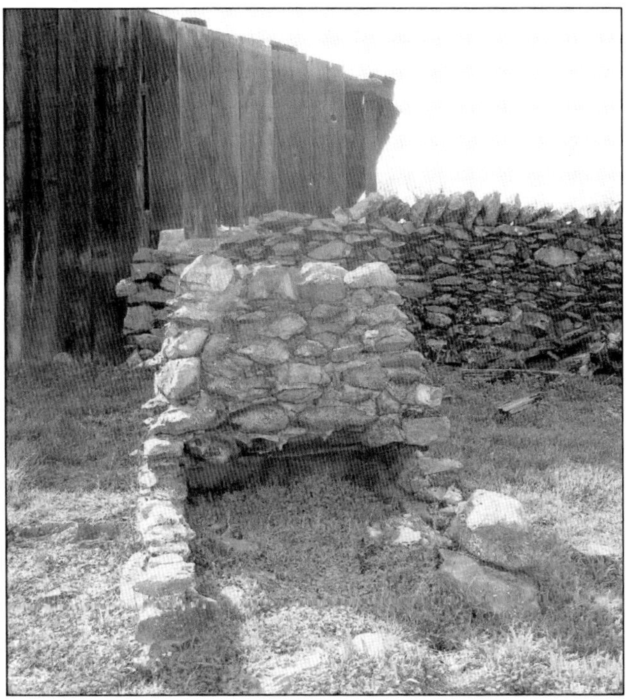

McFadden built an unusual square stone corral; many stone corrals were found on foothill ranches, used to contain horses during training and livestock during branding, vaccinating, and ear notching. Using the readily available material served two purposes: It cleared the land and corralled the herds. An interesting associated feature was this branding fireplace, where the irons were heated. (Courtesy Terry Brejla.)

Eight

Wealth from Water

Jamestown was ideally situated on Wood's Creek, which was dry during the summer months when first settled, but soon augmented with water brought through various ditch systems to work the placers. What would become the most important water system for Jamestown and its mines had its inception with the Tuolumne County Water Company, formed in Columbia in 1850. Tapping the headwaters of the South and Clark Fork Stanislaus and North Fork Tuolumne Rivers, over the years the system was expanded and lengthened to provide water to the entire area between the two rivers, with some 400 miles of main and branch ditches serving mining, agriculture, and residential users.

By the 1860s, the era of prosperity and development attendant upon the placer mining activities was over, and the company absorbed and purchased facilities from a large number of smaller companies. The purchase of the Phoenix Reservoir allowed the company to transfer water to Sonora and Jamestown, and by the early 1870s, Jamestown and Campo Seco were served by the Tuolumne County Water Company Ditch and the South Ditch. The company limped along for several decades, however, until the new power source of hydroelectricity was developed locally and mining technology improved, providing a resurgence in the industry.

Jamestown was at the center of these developments, as William Nevills, owner of the App and Rawhide Mines, provided capital to the water company to improve their conveyance and storage facilities, thereby providing his mines with electricity in repayment. As early as October 1896, the Tuolumne Electric Power and Light Company, a precursor to the Pacific Gas and Electric Company, provided power from the Phoenix Powerhouse to the mines.

South of Jamestown, the Old Don Pedro Dam and Reservoir, completed in 1923 and eventually replaced by the New Don Pedro Dam and Reservoir in 1971, are the largest water and power projects in Tuolumne County. The system provides water to the Modesto and Turlock Irrigation Districts for agricultural irrigation over several hundred square miles of Central Valley farmland.

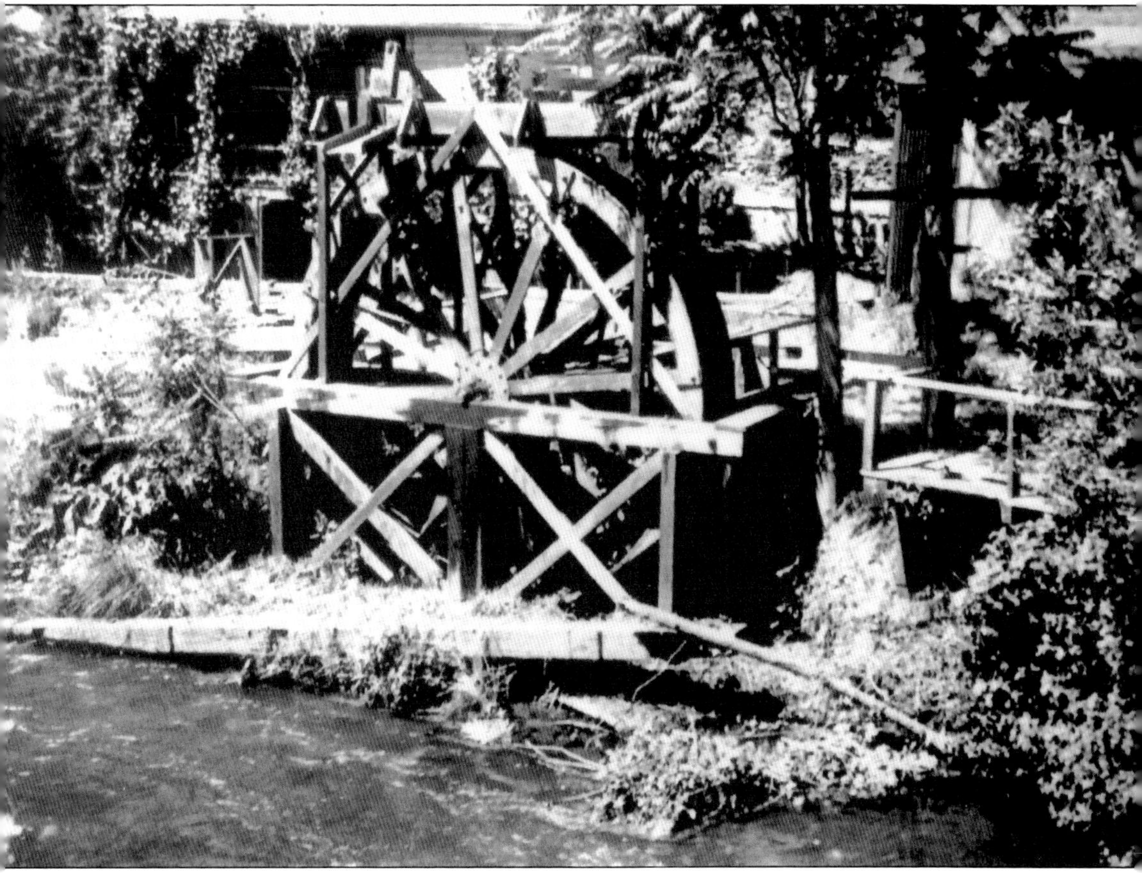

This old undershot waterwheel and mill at Jamestown was powered by one of the early Jamestown ditches, with the overflow dumped into Wood's Creek. The wheel is visible in the foreground, and the mill is to the rear. Flumes and ditches brought mountain water to the gold fields in the foothills. Two of the earliest ditches in Jamestown were Johnson's and Gleason's, with other ditches along the face of Table Mountain, including the Columbia and Stanislaus, Dockendorf, Pine, Ratcliff, Peppermint Creek, Brunton's, and Yorktown Ditches to the southeast. Surplus water from these ditches was conveyed from a dam below town to Chinese Camp, where it was reused in their diggings. (Courtesy California State Library.)

Two ditches noted in Jamestown in 1857 were the 2-mile-long Jamestown Ditch and the 10-mile-long Jamestown Camp Ditch. Ditches were dug by hand or with scrapers drawn by horse or mule, while wooden flumes, which used thousands of board feet of lumber, were required to carry the water around the steep cliffs and over the canyons, as in this image. (*Hutchings' California Magazine*.)

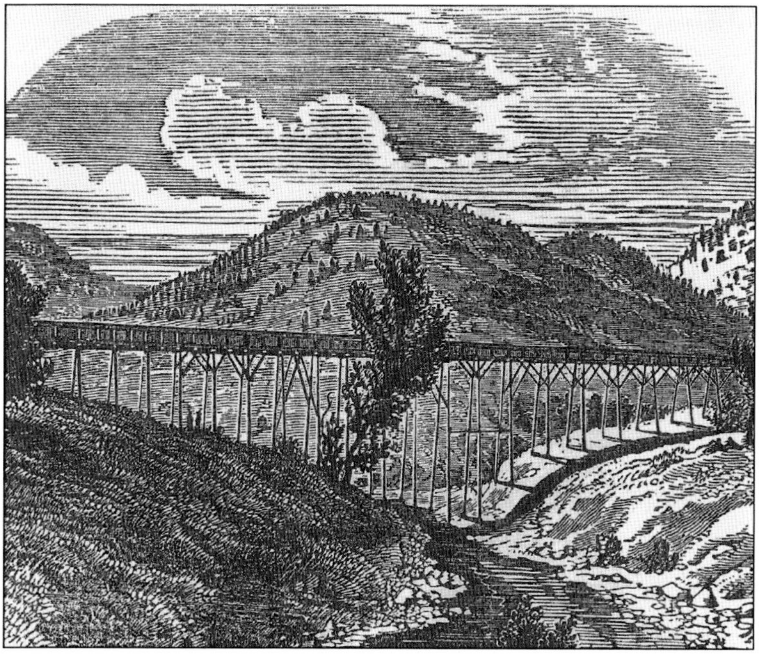

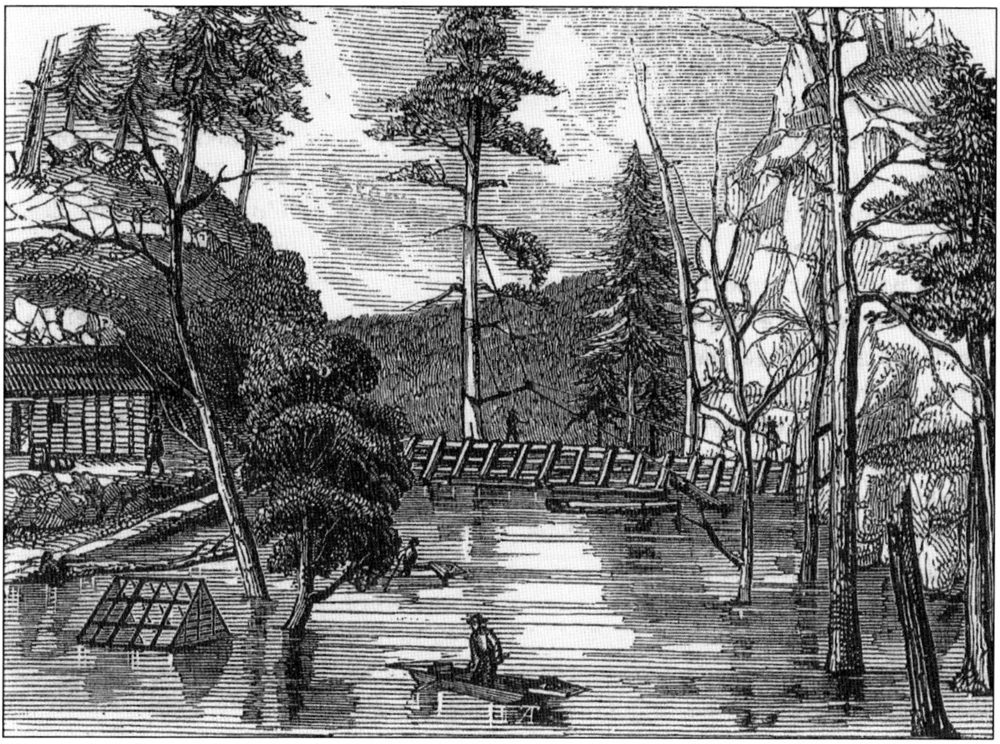

This early lithograph depicts the Tuolumne County Water Company's 1859 reservoir located at Strawberry Flat (now Pinecrest Lake) on the South Fork of the Stanislaus River. About a mile long by one-third to one-half of a mile wide, with a depth of 30 feet, the timber crib dam was 60 feet high with a span of 250 feet and constructed of heavy barked timber, platted and graveled. (*Hutchings' California Magazine*.)

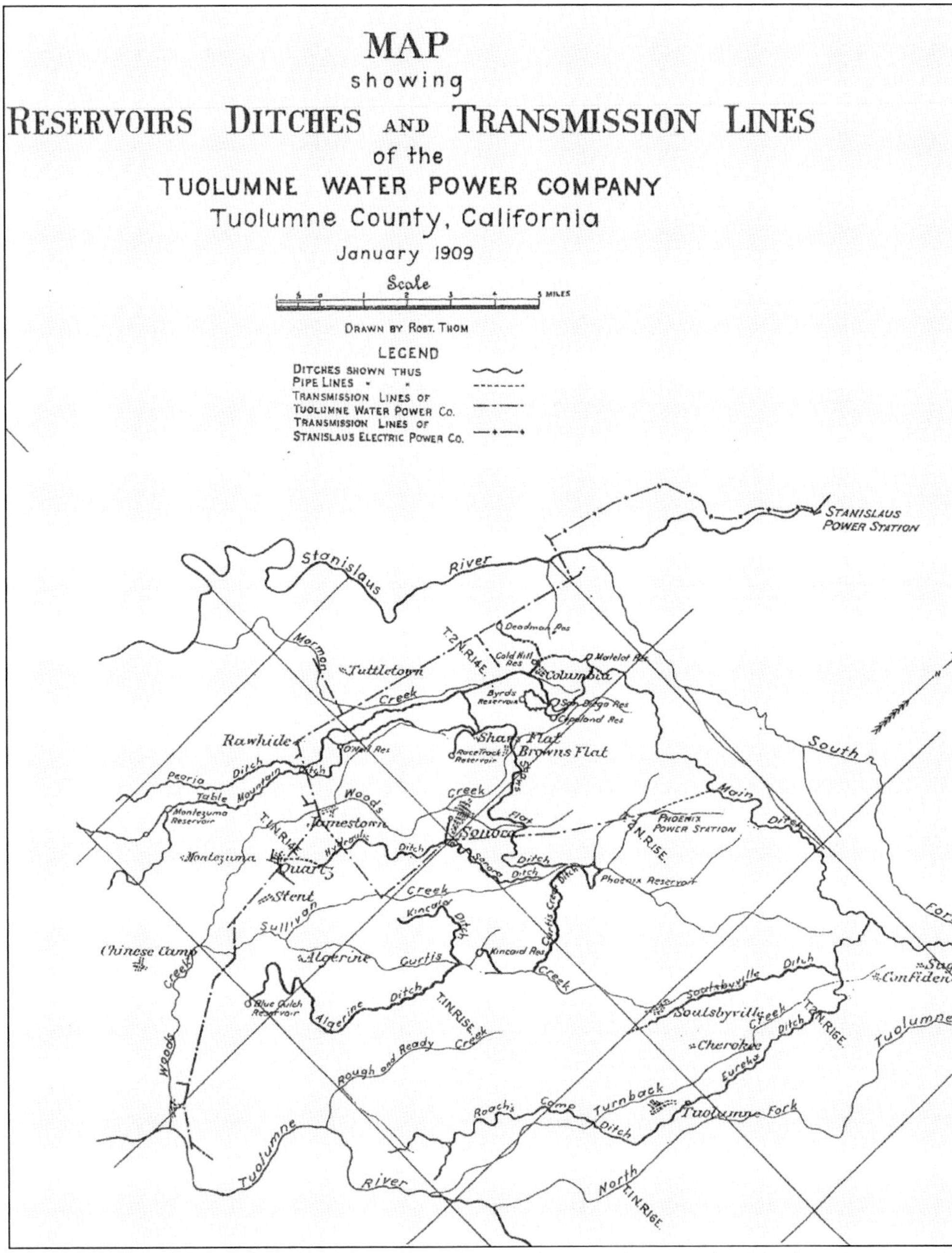

This 1909 map depicts the Tuolumne Water Power Company's network of ditches that brought water from the high country to the dry western county for mining and agriculture. (*Tuolumne County, California.*)

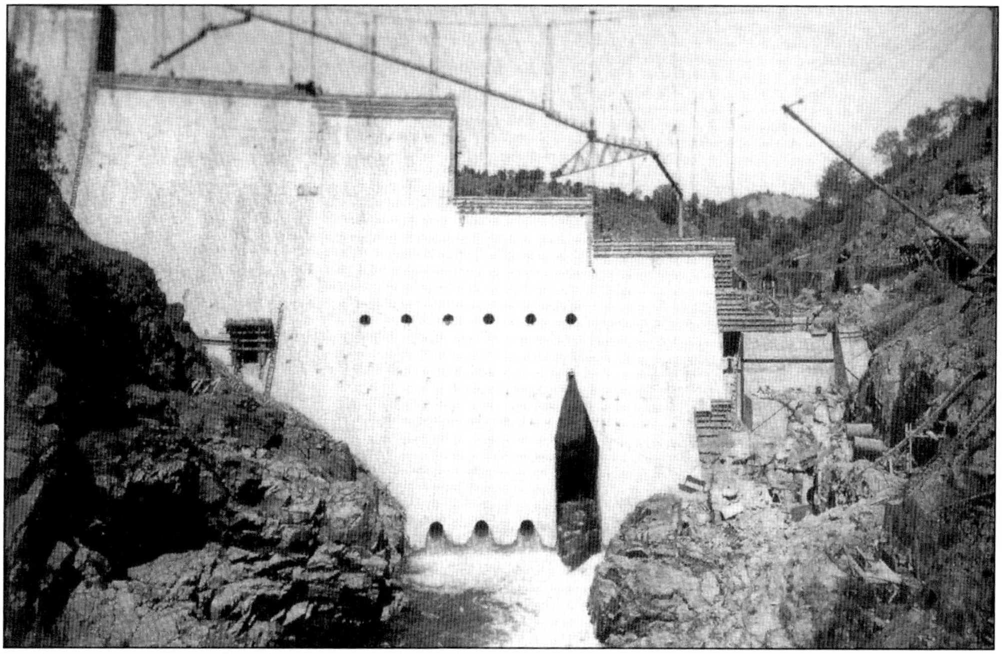

With San Francisco firmly ensconced on the Tuolumne River Watershed in 1921, and fearing that any additional water would be lost to them, the cities of Modesto and Turlock set about establishing a new storage reservoir to augment the waters of their 1893 La Grange Dam and Reservoir. (Courtesy Modesto Irrigation District.)

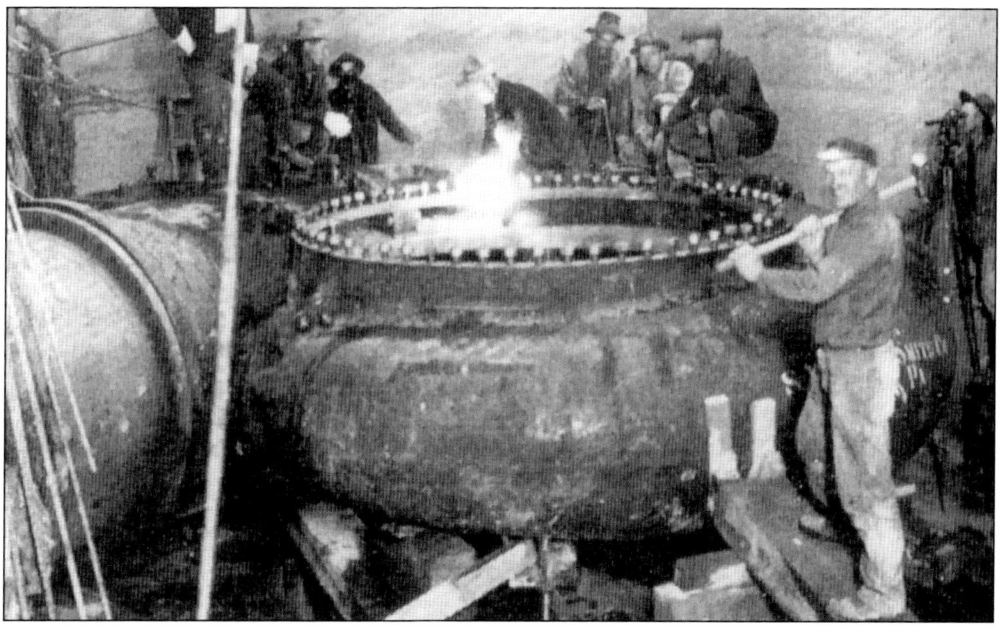

In addition to irrigation water, Turlock voters overwhelmingly approved construction of a powerhouse. Total cost of the dam was $3.7 million, not including the powerhouse, which cost an additional $1.1 million. Both the dam and the powerhouse were completed by the two irrigation districts, serving as their own contractors. The men shown here were setting the scroll case for the powerhouse turbines. (Courtesy Modesto Irrigation District.)

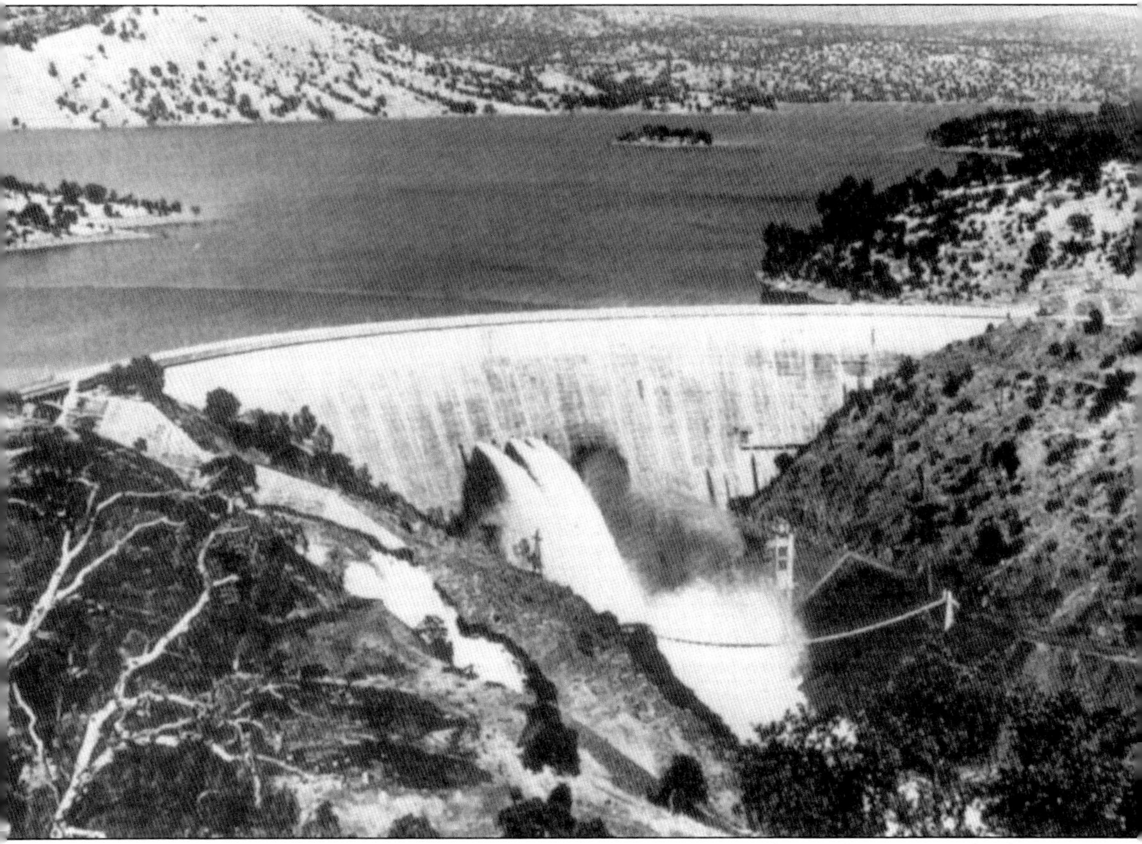

An 8.5-mile railroad branch was built from the dam site to Hetch Hetchy Junction by the Sierra Railroad, which carried gravels from the Stanislaus River. Other tasks included building barracks, family housing, a mess hall, hospital, and schoolhouse. Work began on June 25, 1921, and the official dedication took place two years to the day from the start of the project. The dam had a storage capacity of 300,000 acre-feet of water, giving the Modesto and Turlock Irrigation Districts the "greatest supply of water for irrigation purposes of any district in the world," according to Dwight H. Barnes in *The Greening of Paradise Valley* (published by the Modesto Irrigation District in 1987). Additional improvements to the canals were accomplished by the Public Works Administration in the 1930s. A larger New Don Pedro Dam was completed in 1971, enlarging the capacity of the reservoir by seven times; hydroelectric generation was increased by nearly the same amount with the new powerhouse. (Courtesy Modesto and Turlock Irrigation Districts.)

Nine

CAMPS AND COMMUNITIES

With Jamestown as the transportation hub, several smaller communities developed around the placer diggings on the Tuolumne River and its tributaries, the Table Mountain drift mines, and the hard rock mines on the Mother Lode vein, as well as at the outlying stage stops, ranches, and railroad stations.

Two of the most important Gold Rush–era camps in southwestern Tuolumne County were named for their ethnic makeup: Campo Seco (Dry Camp) and Chinese Camp, as were Algerine (Algiers Camp), French Flat, Indian Bar, Camp Salvado, and Montezuma (the Aztec king). Others were named for persons: Wood's Crossing, Jacksonville, Stent, Stevens Bar, Don Pedro Bar, Hawkins Bar, Swett's Bar, and Frazier's Flat. The names of several camps denigrated their findings: Poverty Hill, Hungry Hill, Six-Bit Gulch, Poor Man's Gulch; some were descriptive: Green Springs, Quartz Mountain, Red Mountain Bar, Minnow Gulch; and others celebrated places or events: Peoria Bar and Basin, Crimea House, Belvedere Flat, Camp Washington, Yorktown, and Blanket Creek. Rough and Ready obviously denoted the demeanor of the miners in its camp, while the Sierra Railway was responsible for several names on the land: Keystone, Rosasco, and Chinese Stations, as well as Hetch Hetchy Junction, Quinn's Spur, and Jack's Siding.

Many mining camps were located along the Tuolumne River and its tributaries: Wood's, Blanket, Rough and Ready, Kanaka, Curtis, and Sullivan Creeks. Those located at Jacksonville and downstream were inundated when the irrigation districts of Modesto and Turlock created the Don Pedro Dam and Reservoir in 1923. Most of the other camps that were settled in the early 1850s were abandoned by the 1860s and 1870s, when the gold played out, leaving only their names on maps and in the histories of their prospectors, miners, and settlers.

The camps or communities that remain today are mere remnants of those resurrected during the second gold rush (Campo Seco, Stent, Quartz), that were depots for stagecoaches and freight runs and those from the surrounding area dependent on their services (Chinese Camp), or were locations along important roads and the larger ranches (Crimea House, Keystone, Rosasco, Montezuma).

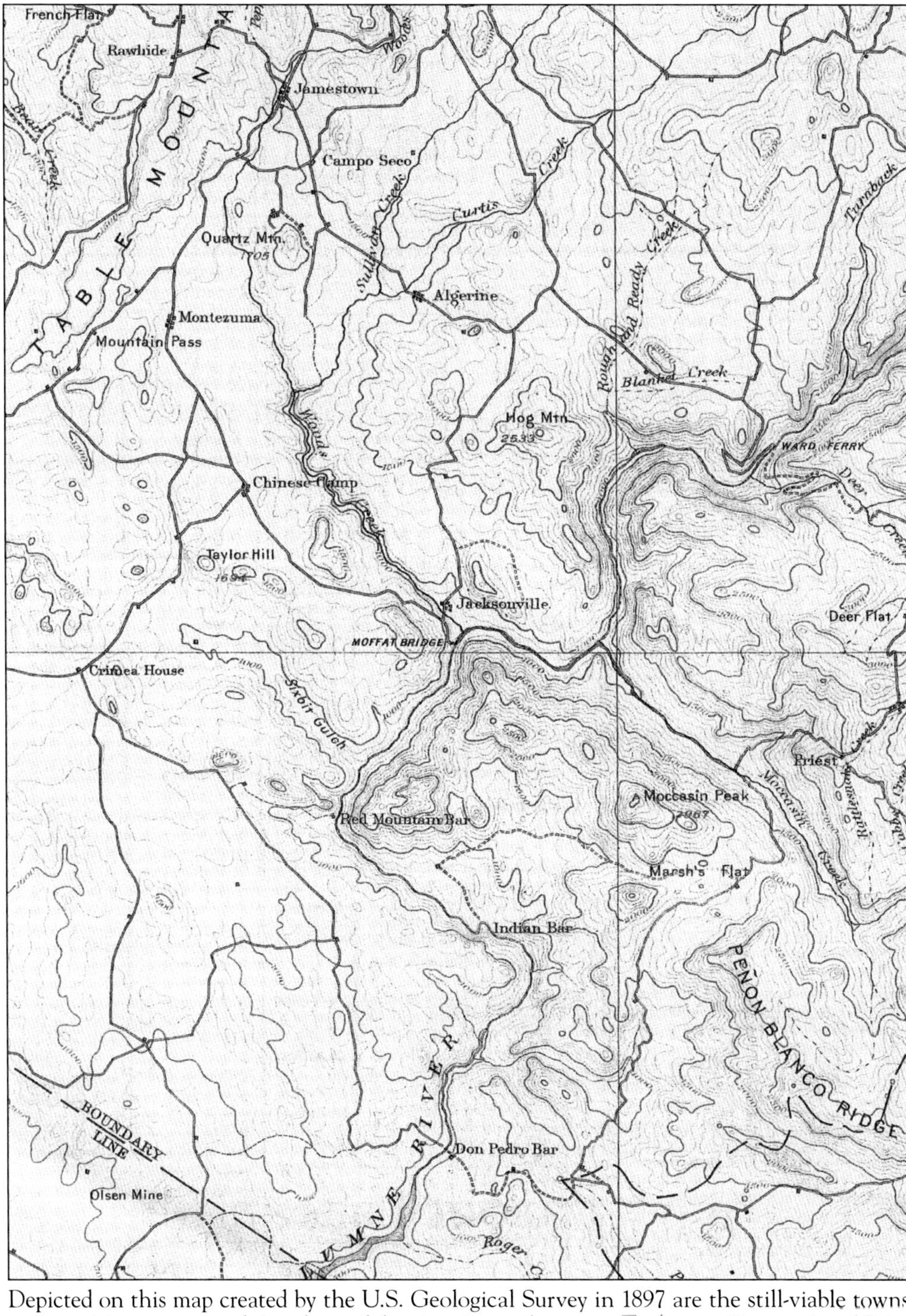

Depicted on this map created by the U.S. Geological Survey in 1897 are the still-viable towns, communities, camps, and river bars of the time in southwestern Tuolumne County, in addition to the Tuolumne River and the important creeks. (Authors' collection.)

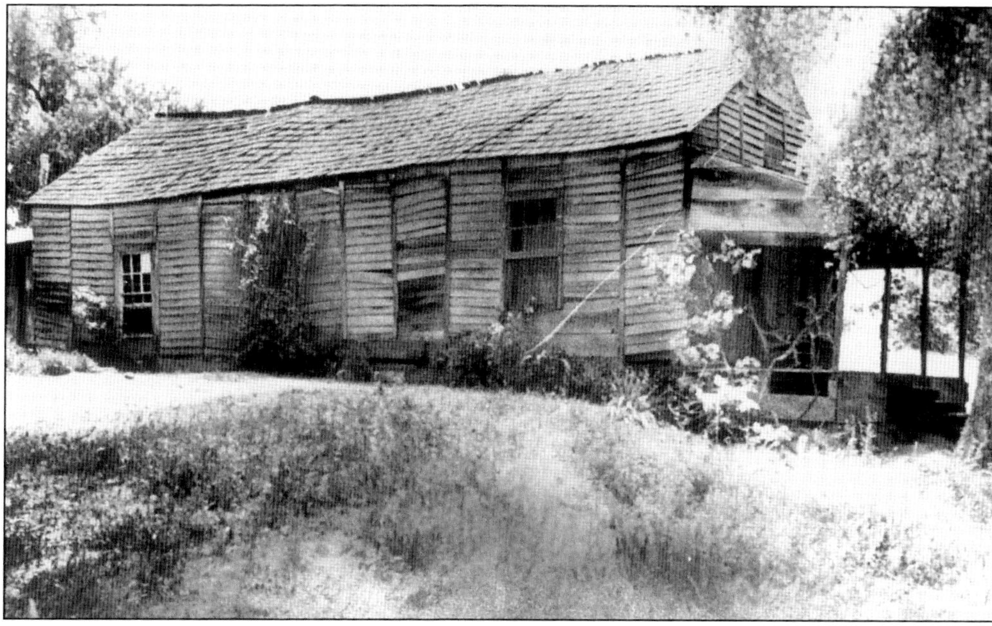

Settled in August 1848 and named for the Benjamin Wood, an early miner, Wood's Crossing was the earliest mining camp established in the area, about a mile south of Jamestown. The longest-lasting remnant of the boom years, Bellingham's Store was an adobe structure located on the west side of the creek, later covered with hand-split cedar slabs. It endured until 1946. (Courtesy California State Library.)

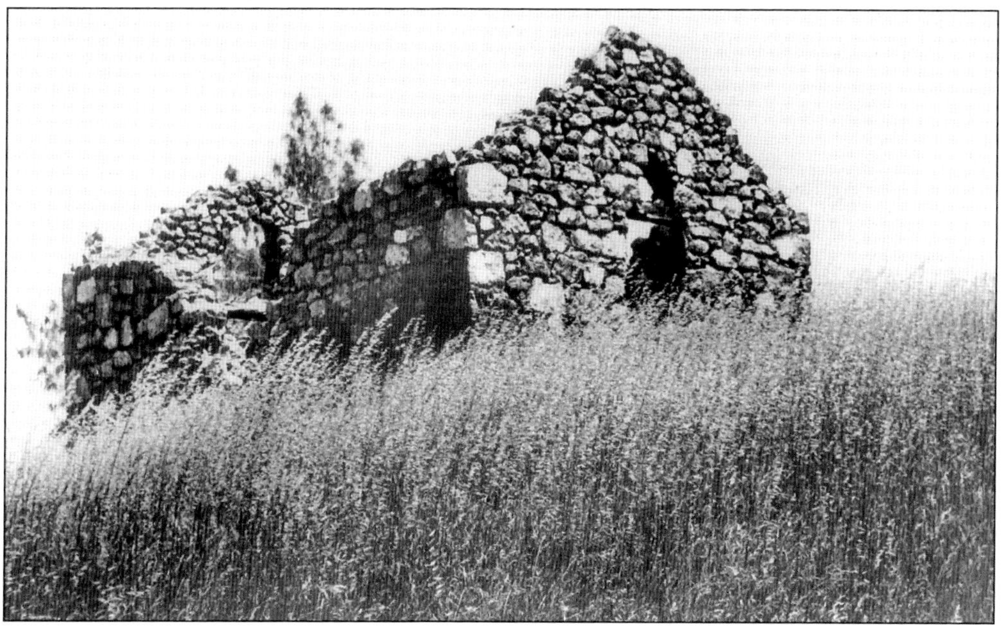

This stone ruin stood for many years on the hillside above Yosemite Junction. All that remains of the sites of many early gold camps and settlements are the remnants of stone buildings, structures, foundations, and walls. Contrary to popular lore, very few stone walls were built by Chinese, but by people from every country in Europe and South America, as well as the eastern United States. (Courtesy California State Library.)

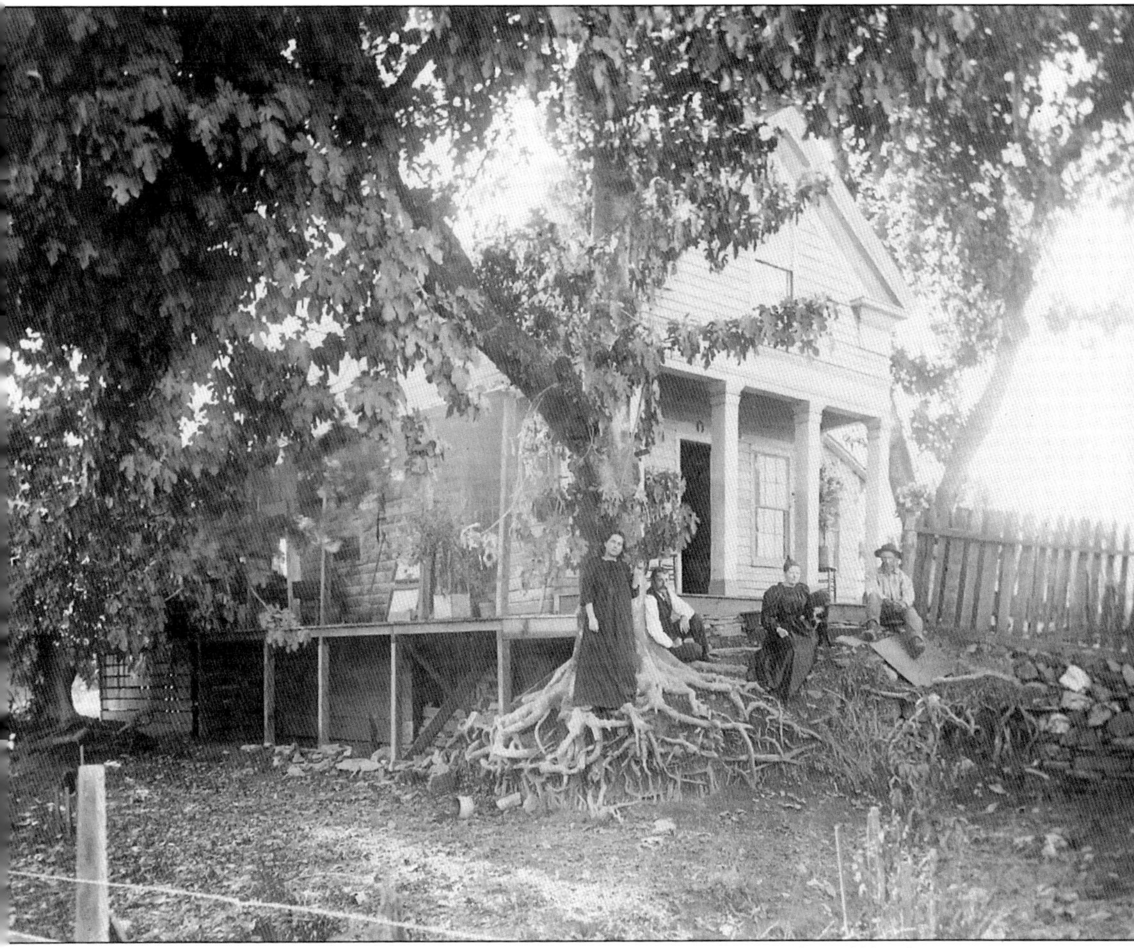

By 1855, there were still several miners, a teamster, a merchant, and a toll bridge operator among the population of Wood's Crossing, but most prospectors and miners had moved upstream to Jamestown. One who remained was John Mooney, operator of the Mooney Mine, later part of the Harvard Mine. His lovely Greek Revival home at Wood's Crossing was a popular stopping place for many years. (Courtesy California State Library.)

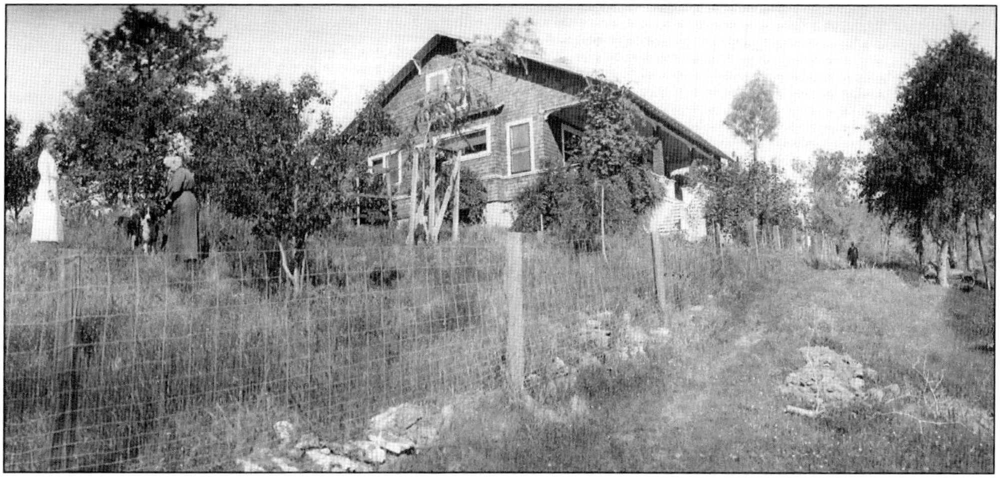

Belle Mooney (also known as Bell, Isabella, or Arabella), the daughter of John and Ellen, built this fine craftsman home on the west bank of Wood's Creek in 1905. Born in neighboring Stent in 1857, she resided on the family property, except for a stint as a cook in the 1880s, boarding miners and operating a dairy farm after the death of her parents. She died at age 89 in December 1939. (Courtesy California State Library.)

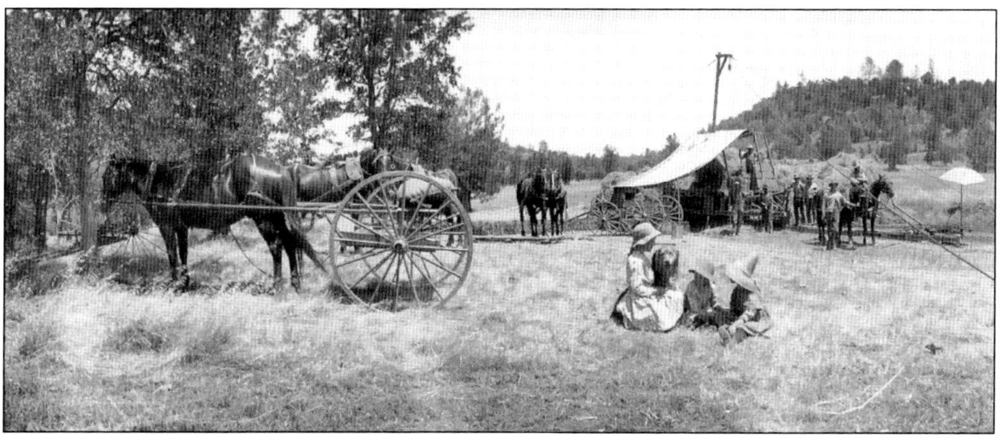

In this view of Belle Mooney's farm, three young children play with a dog, while the carts and horses of other visitors stand ready. Table Mountain and Mountain Pass are seen in the background. Belle's name has been preserved in Bell Mooney Road, south of Jamestown. (Courtesy California State Library.)

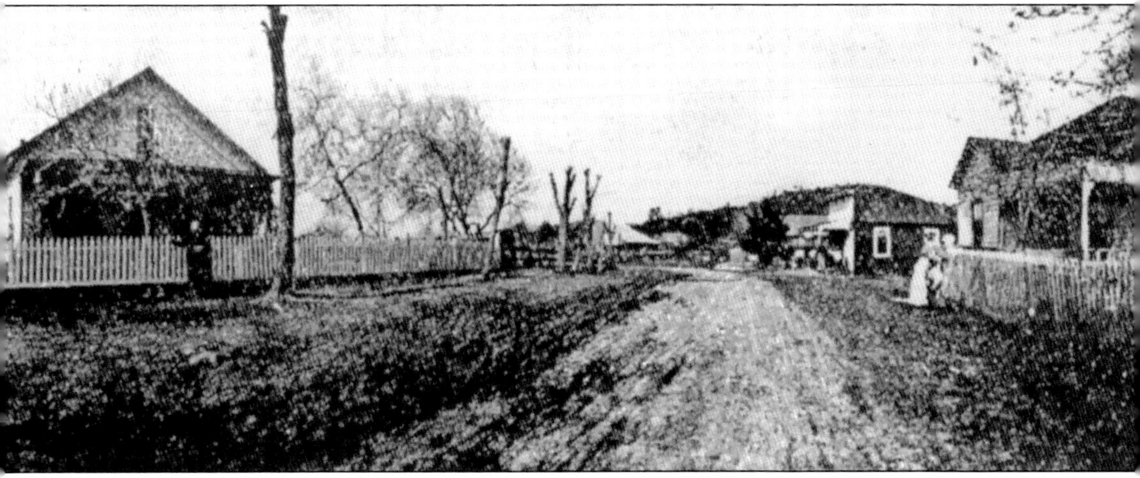

Campo Seco (Dry Camp) was described in the journal of Charles L. Scott, Esq. during its heyday in the early 1850s as "a lively place possessing all the allurements, amusements and attractions of a mining town in those days. Almost every store or tent had one or more crude tables where card playing was indulged in for drinks, or where monte, the favorite gambling game, was played for dust, and at night these places were alive with miners purchasing supplies or trying their luck at the tables." A Mr. Richardson and a Mr. Imbrie erected one of the earliest theater structures; constructed of wood, boarded up at the sides, and covered with canvas, it was hardly more than a tent, but its El Dorado saloon was recounted as the "finest house," with a commodious main room, decorated with paint and brush, and a well-furnished and tasteful bar, dispensing liquors at $1 a drink. (Courtesy Tuolumne County Museum.)

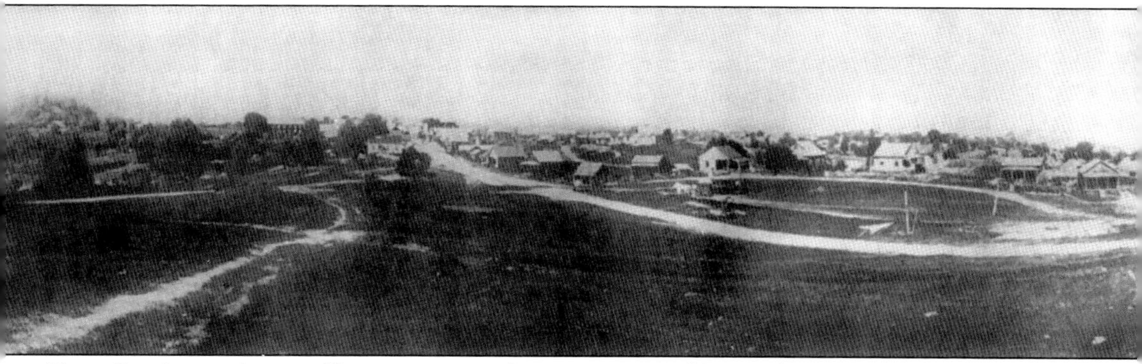

About 2 miles southwest of Jamestown was the community of Stent, the "Poverty Hill" of Bret Harte's stories. After the placer diggings played out, the town slumbered, but by 1900, with the hard rock mining boom on the Mother Lode, the population of the town reached its peak, with the Jumper Mine and others operating around the clock. In 1902, the town had one main street, several stores, hotels, saloons, a post office, a church used by all denominations, a public school with two teachers, an attorney, the finest opera hall in the county, and "many neat and comfortable family residences," as noted in *Tuolumne County, Califorina* (issued by the Progressive Association, Sonora, Tuolumne County). (Courtesy Jim Yeisley.)

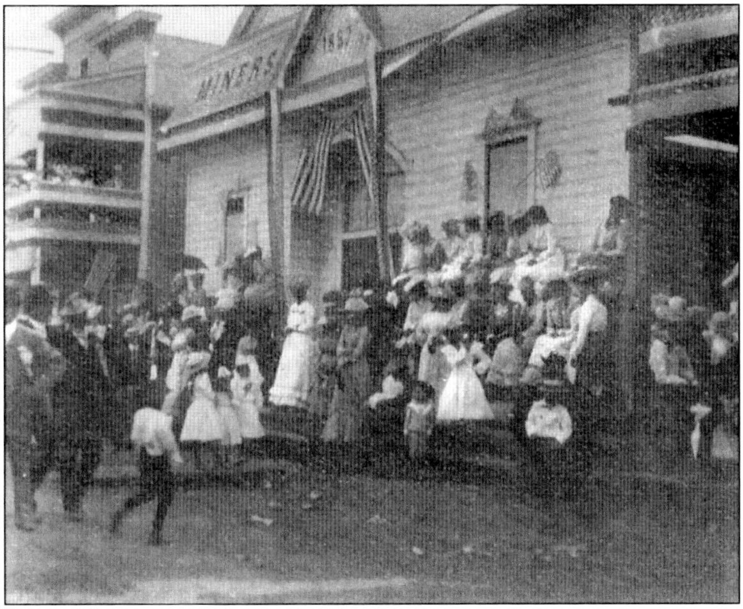

The townspeople of Stent turned out to celebrate Labor Day in 1903, the ladies and girls in fine white dresses, the boys in white shirts and hats, and the gentlemen in jackets and bowlers. This view was taken in front of the Miners' Union Hall, the former Opera Hall, erected in 1887. One of the ubiquitous saloons and boardinghouses is located to the left. (Courtesy Jim Yeisley.)

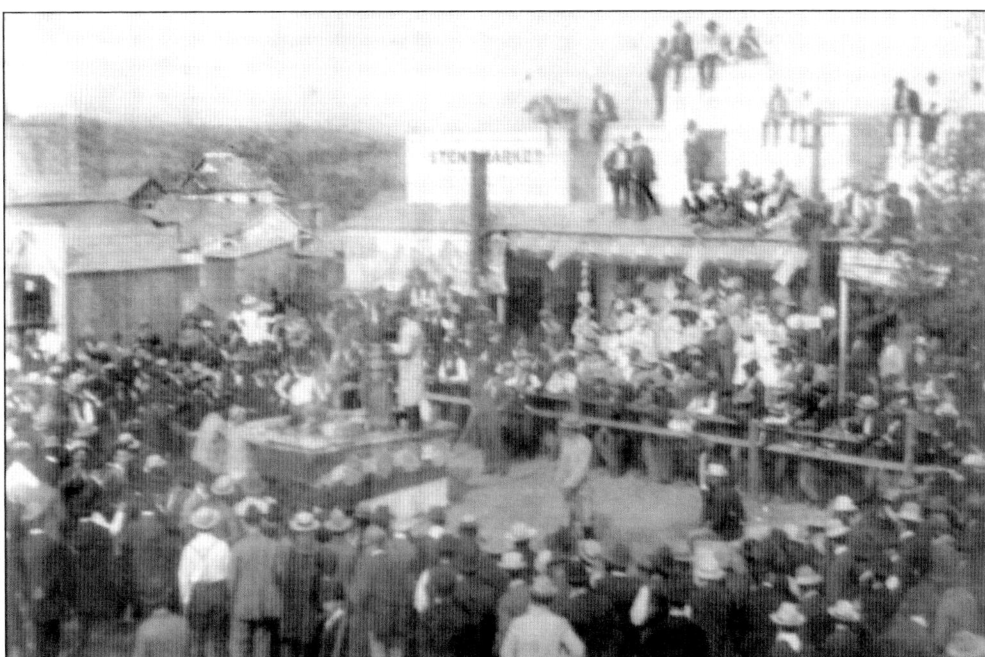

In this view, a large crowd had gathered on Broadway Street in the center of Stent to watch the drilling contest. These contests were popular events in mining communities, with miners competing in a timed drilling of a granite rock to a particular depth. (Courtesy Dan and Georgia Vuyovich.)

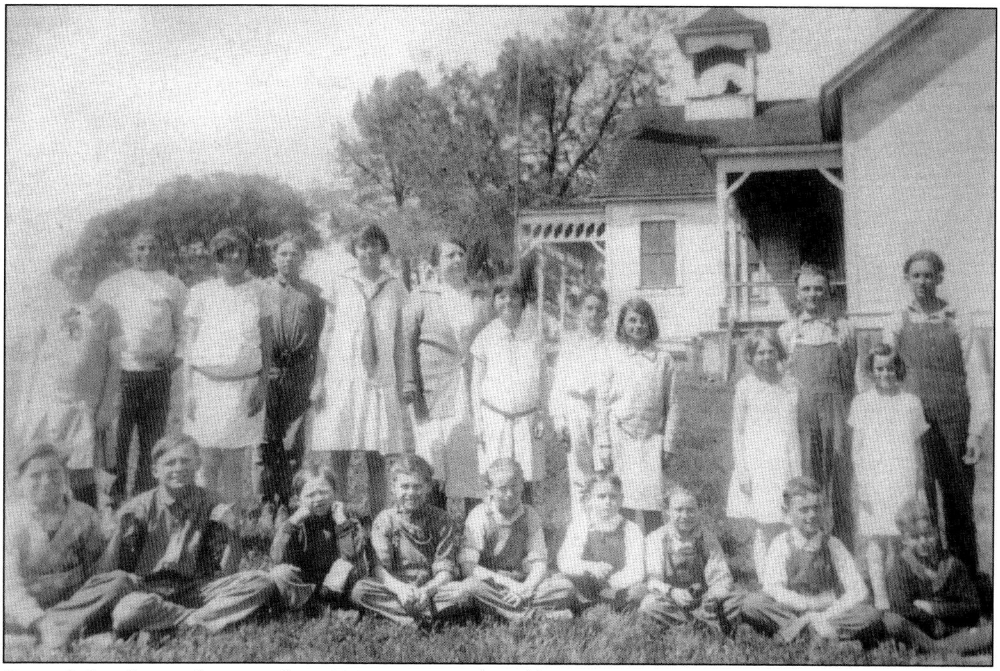

Stent School, seen here in the 1920s, was populated by several students whose families came from Serbia, with the men employed in the area's quartz mines. Immigrating to California during the Great Migration of the late 19th century, many Eastern Europeans came to the gold country to work in the hard rock mines of Amador, Calaveras, and Tuolumne Counties. (Courtesy Dan and Georgia Vuyovich.)

Green Springs, located near the head of Green Springs Run, a tributary to the Stanislaus River, was another placer mining community with a sizeable population in 1849. By the time this photograph was taken in 1894, the area had been taken up by farmers, and the class was made up of members of the Brunson, de Bernardi, Adams, Carlon, Evans, Graham, and Wight families. (Courtesy Gary Wilson.)

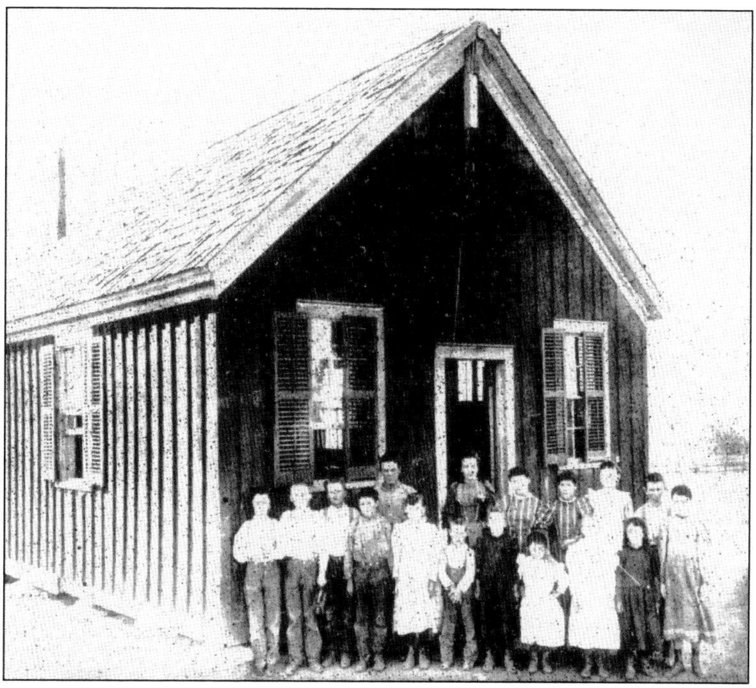

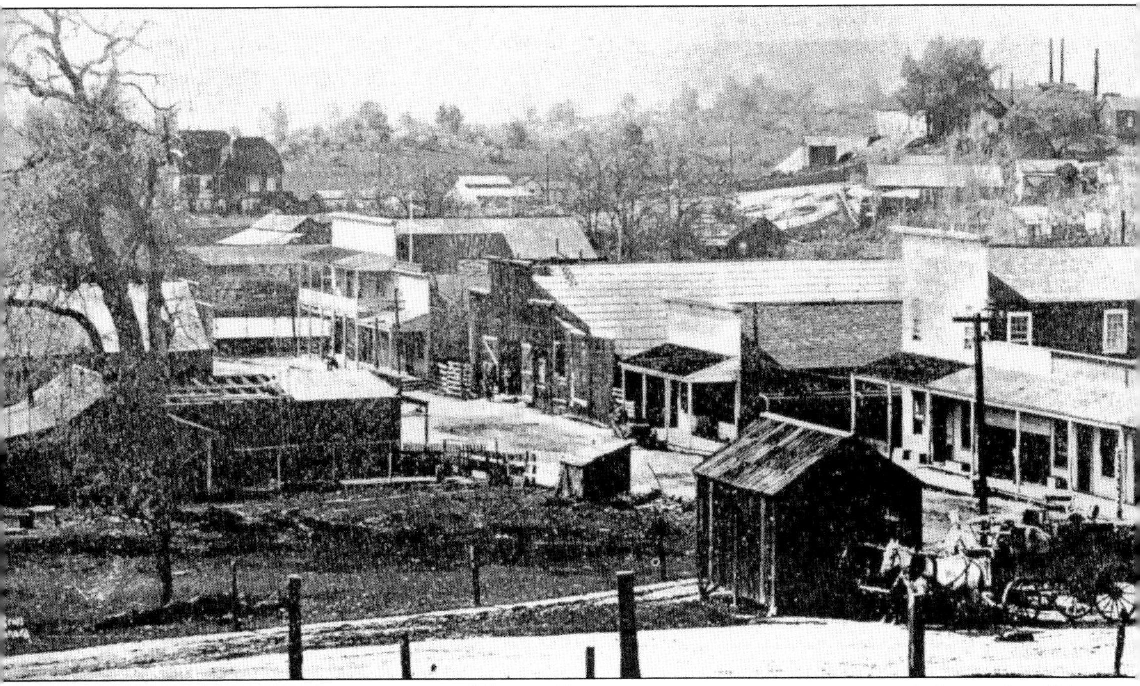

Quartz Mountain, the nearest neighbor to Stent, was an important quartz mining and milling center as early as the 1850s, with four water-driven stamp mills and four arrastras operating in those years. The mountain was included within the town limits. Located on the Mother Lode, it was the site of the Dutch, App, and Santa Ysabel Mines, which were very productive in the hard rock mining era and notorious as some of the most prolific gold producers in the West. In the early 1900s, the town had two hotels, boardinghouses, a church, a post office, and "several different lines of business," as noted in *Tuolumne County, Califorina* (issued by the Progressive Association, Sonora, Tuolumne County). (Courtesy Tuolumne County Museum.)

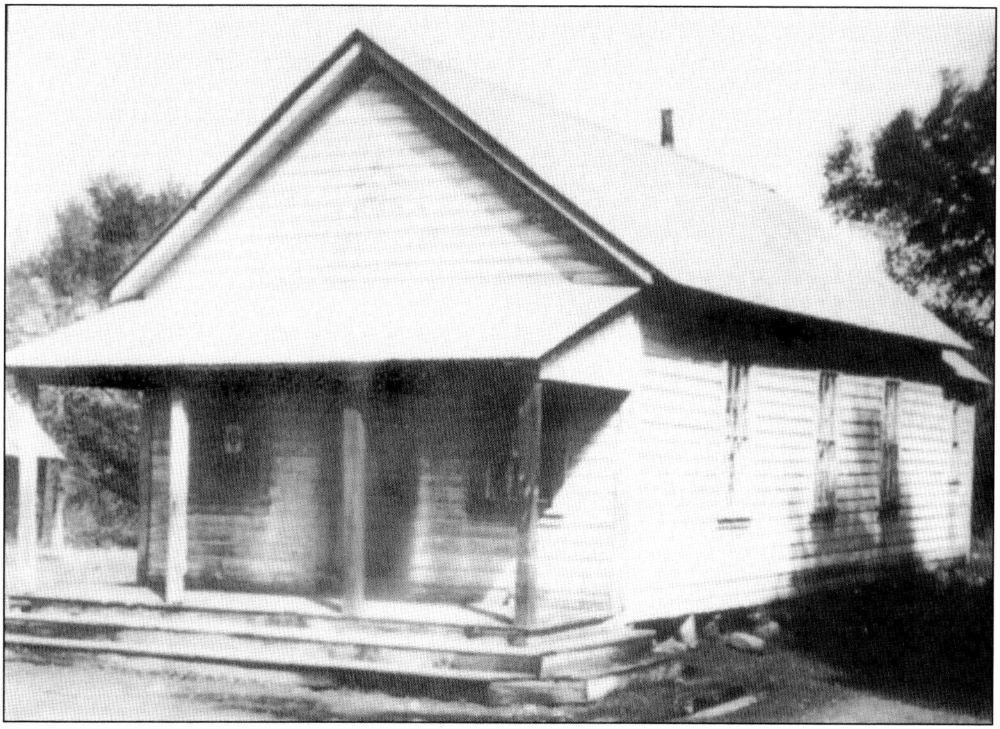

Diggings were located at Algerine Camp in May 1852, after Frenchman Ramon Germain and two others discovered rich diggings there. Originally known as Providence Camp, the name was soon changed to Algiers and subsequently broadened to Algerine. Large amounts of gold were soon taken out, aided by the Algerine Ditch, and a wide street was laid out, tents were erected, and 15 or 20 homes and a hotel were built. When the diggings were exhausted, farmers took up homesteads, and the area became agricultural, with Algerine School (above) at its center. The school served from 1877 to 1909; these pupils below are pictured with their teacher about 1899. (Courtesy Tuolumne County Museum.)

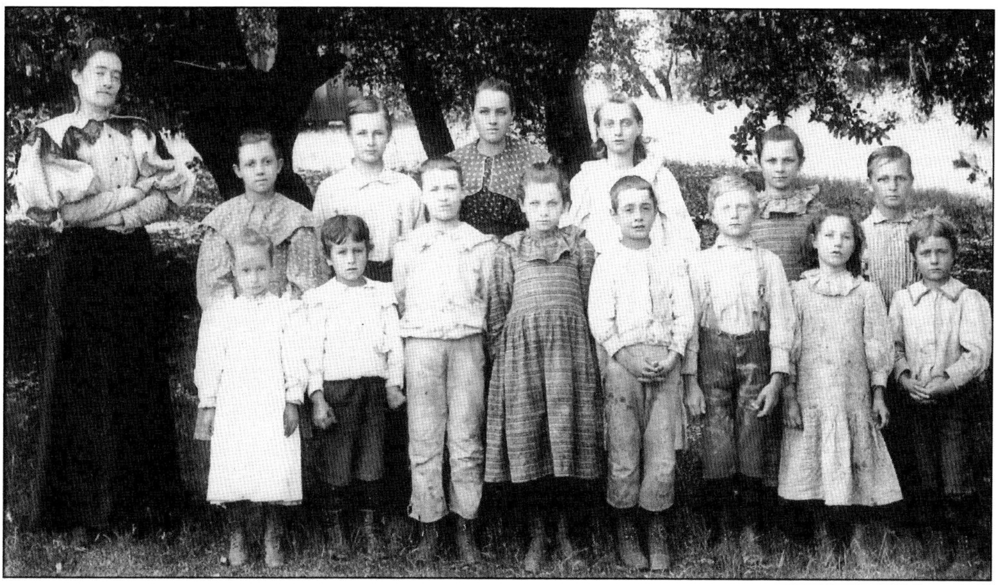

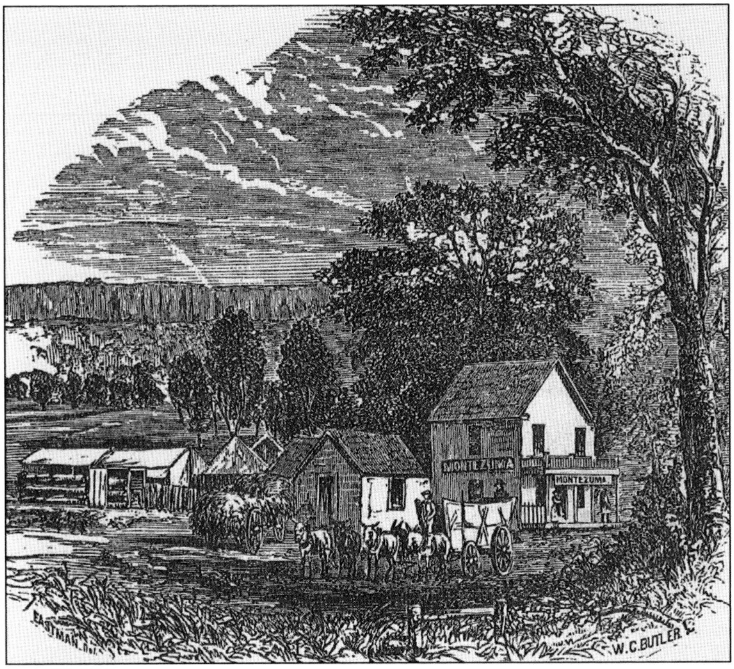

Mining started at "Montezuma's Tent" in 1852, and the camp was quite a town by 1856, even boasting a "doctor's shop" in 1862, but by the late 1860s, the diggings had petered out, and it was virtually abandoned. One of the primary enterprises was the Montezuma House, a popular hostelry on the road from Stockton, which outlasted the vicissitudes of mining. (*Hutchings' California Magazine.*)

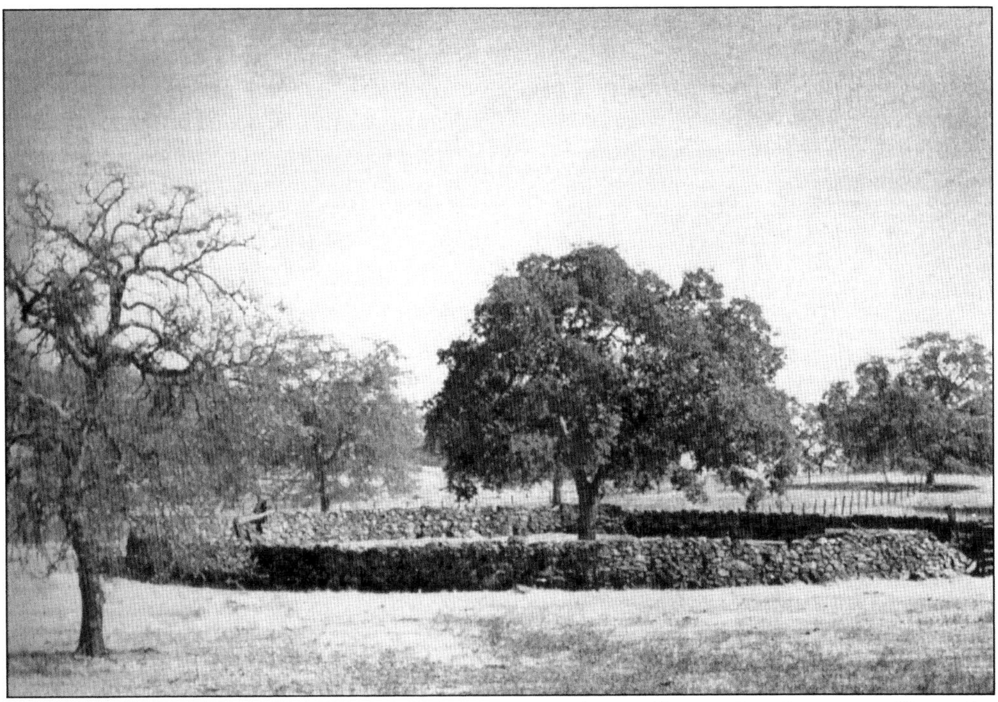

This 1850s stone corral marks the site of a once popular roadhouse first known as Kentucky House (on the road from Stockton where it branched to Sonora, Chinese Camp, and Mariposa) until a nearby tong, or gang, war fought by competing Chinese associations in 1856 reminded the locals of the Crimean War being fought about the same time, and thereafter it became known as Crimea House. The near-perfect circle was scribed using an oak tree as its center. (Courtesy California State Library.)

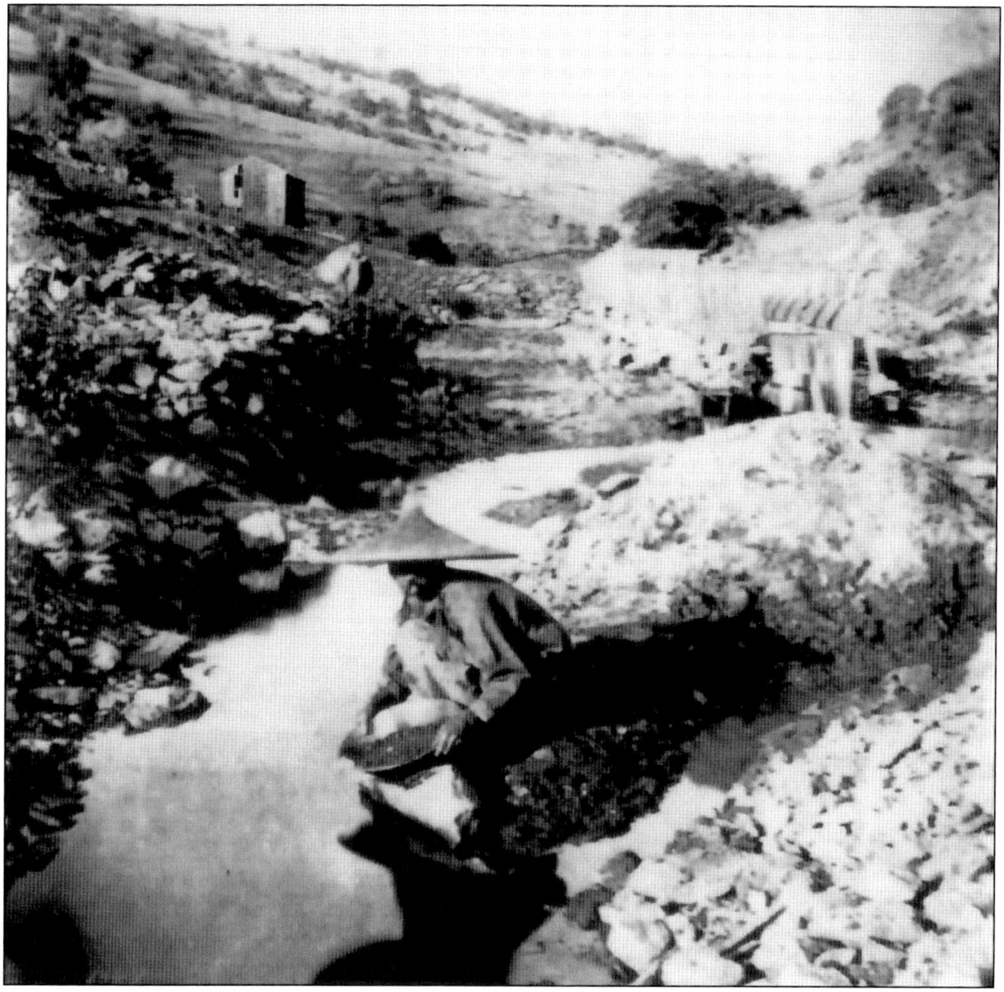

The lure of gold drew single Chinese men to California. Coming from Guandong (Canton) Province to the "Gold Mountain," they emigrated in increasingly large numbers. In 1848, there were only 781 Chinese in San Francisco and the gold fields. Just two years later, in 1850, the number had grown to 4,025 and continued to increase exponentially, reaching 12,000 in 1851 and an astonishing 40,000 in 1854. By 1860, one in every 16 people in California was Chinese. The majority worked in companies ranging from a handful of men to 25 or 30 and were noted as expeditious, practical, and industrious. By 1852, however, reaction had set in, and agitation against them commenced so that they were only allowed to purchase second-hand surface claims considered worthless by white miners. After the Chinese Exclusion Act of 1882, many returned home, and only a trickle entered California. This Chinese miner near Jacksonville in 1852 is one of the earliest known photographs of Chinese in the diggings. (Photograph by Edward Muybridge; courtesy Bancroft Library.)

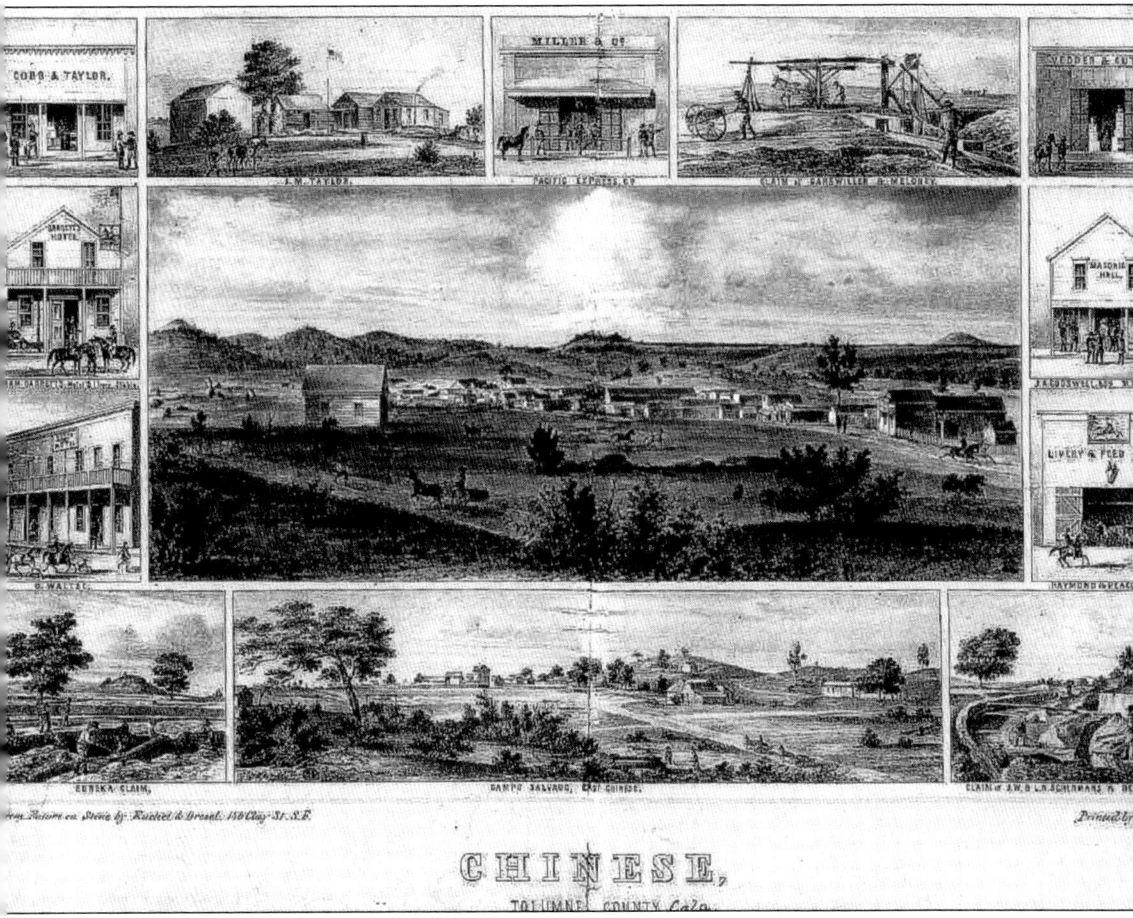

Chinese Camp was already a thriving community when lithographers Kuchel and Dresel depicted it in 1856–1858. It had two-story buildings, a prominent Main Street, and various placer mining activities. Known also as "Chinee," it was mentioned as Chinese Diggings as early as December 1849, when Chinese miners, forced out of the nearby Mexican Camp Salvado, came over the hill to the American Camp Washington (Chinese Camp). In the early 1850s, four of San Francisco's Chinese Six Companies placed agents in town. In 1856, at nearby Six Bit Gulch, 1,000 Sze Yups fought 1,000 Yeong Woos in the most deadly tong war in California. (Courtesy Bancroft Library.)

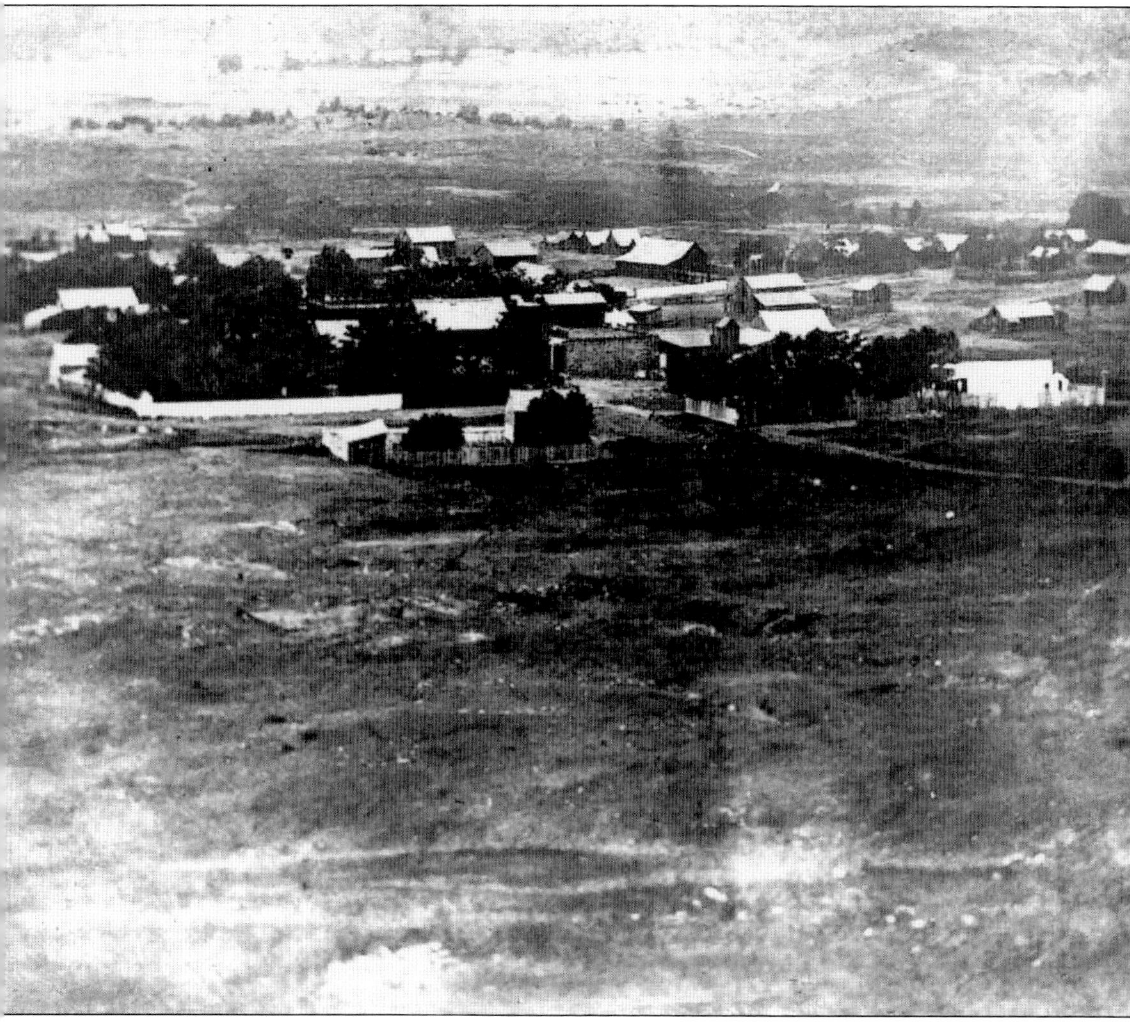

By 1870, the town of Chinese Camp appeared little changed from its 1850s appearance, due to its continuance as a center of placer mining activity and staging. As a locus of management, a changing station, and overnight stop for the local transportation industry, Chinese Camp was able to weather the vicissitudes of placer and hard rock mining and maintain its viability into the 20th century. (Courtesy California Historical Society.)

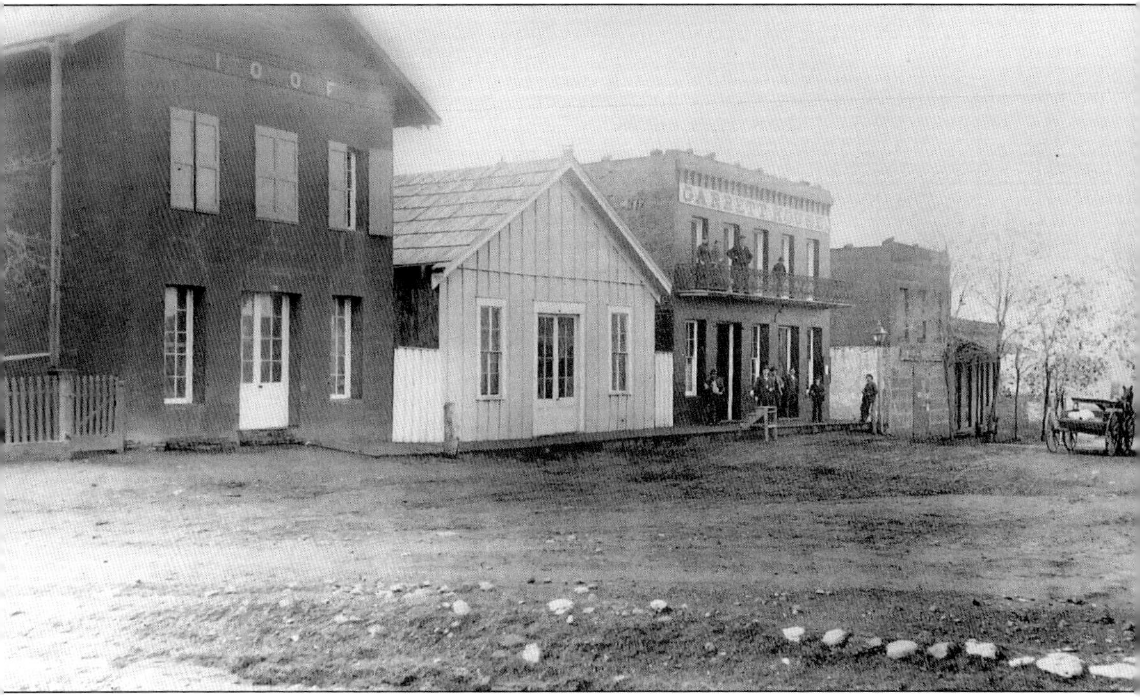

The south side of Main Street in Chinese Camp is pictured here in about 1900. The two-story brick Odd Fellows Hall anchors the west of the street, followed by the frame Garrett House Annex, the two-story brick 1850s Garrett House Hotel, the Masonic Hall, and the one-story Myers Brewery and Saloon/Lafayette Restaurant running east. The 10-room Garrett House Hotel retained a reputation for gracious hospitality and clean beds, catering principally to Yosemite tourists. The most prominent proprietor was the European count C. W. Solinsky, who was a banker, storekeeper, and Wells Fargo agent. The population was about 600, with many employed in the staging industry and its supporting hotels and restaurants. (Courtesy California State Library.)

One of the few remaining Chinese, identified as "Dick, the Mayor of Chinese Camp," is seen on Main Street in 1914. He was evidently the man identified as "Ah Dick" in the 1910 census, age 72, who emigrated from China in 1864. At that time, he was residing with six other Chinese, ages 56 to 72, all working as gold miners. (Courtesy California Historical Society.)

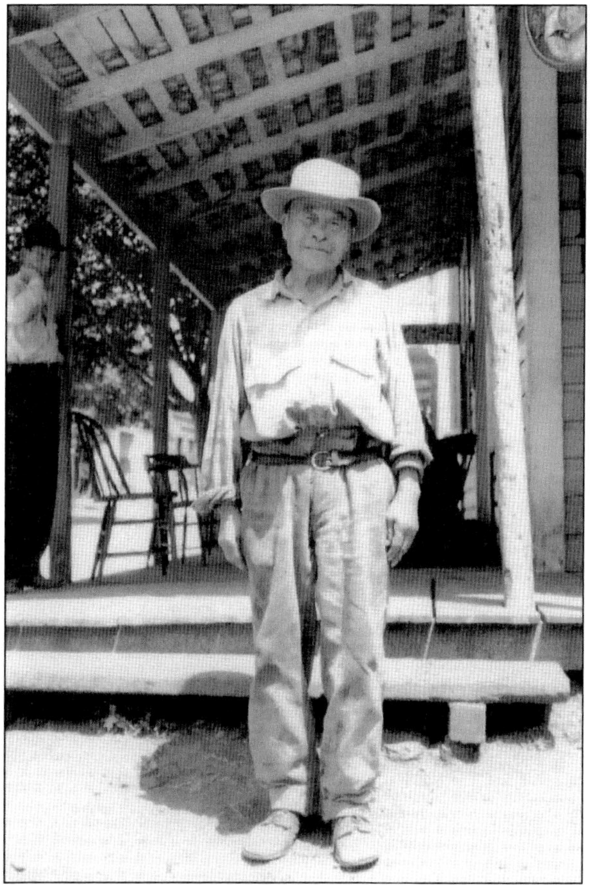

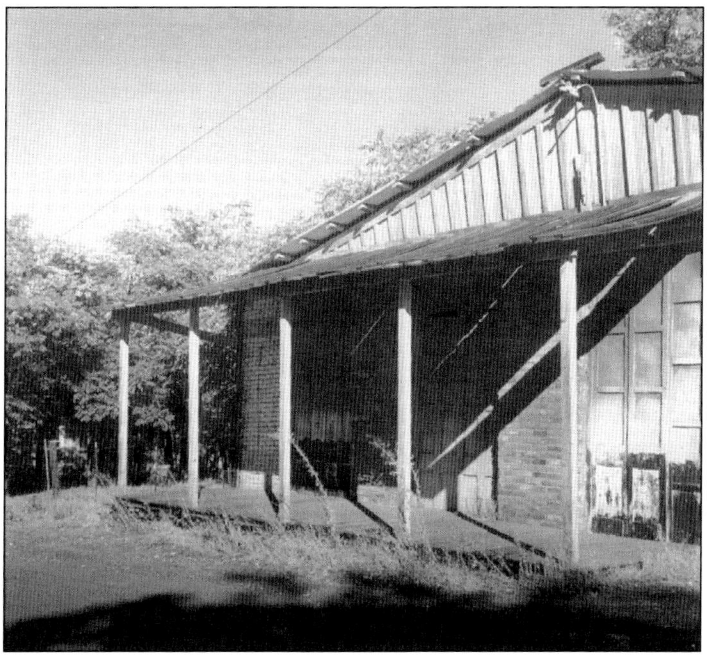

The Cohn-Morris Store, shown in the 1950s, was built sometime before 1860, when $500 of its value was assessed to Joseph Cohn, a Jewish merchant from Poland and the remaining $1,500 to American mortgage holders. (Photograph by Alma Lavenson; courtesy Bancroft Library.)

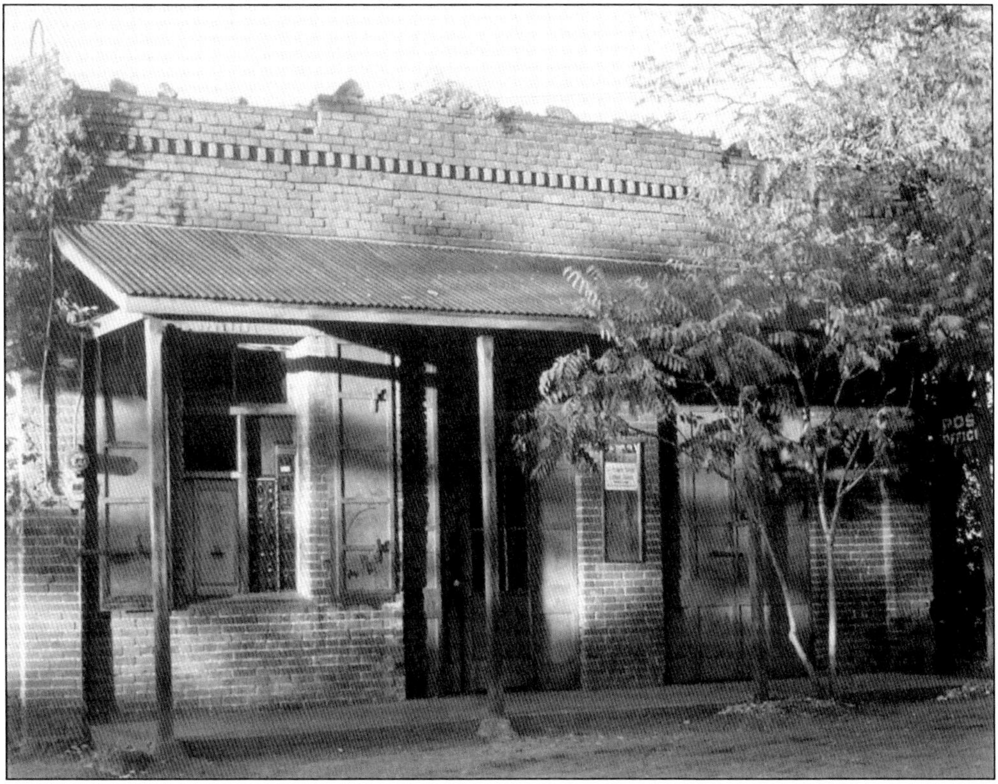

Another brick building in Chinese Camp was photographed in 1950 with its iron doors intact. Iron doors and shutters were ubiquitous in the gold country, affixed to brick and stone buildings to provide protection from the fires that engulfed many early communities. (Photograph by Alma Lavenson; courtesy Bancroft Library.)

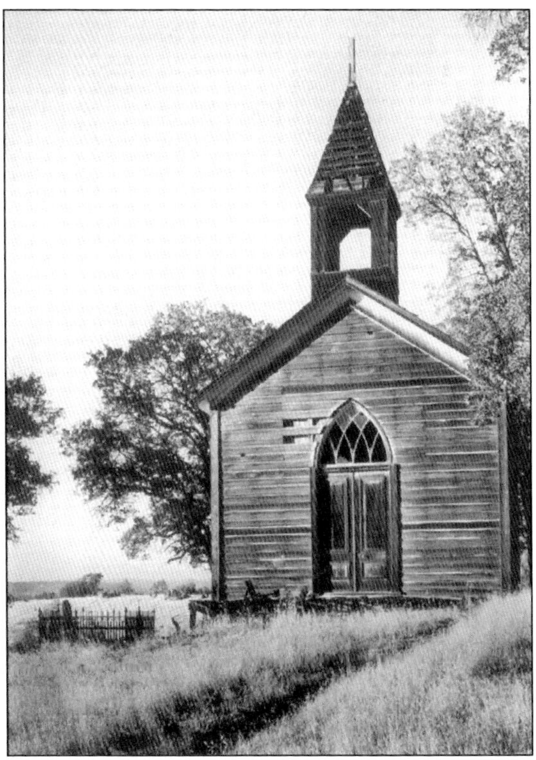

St. Francis Xavier Roman Catholic Church, erected sometime prior to 1855, is one of the oldest churches in Tuolumne County. Its rectangular mass, Gothic arched windows, horizontal board siding, and surrounding graveyard make it one of the most photographed buildings in the Mother Lode. (Photograph by Alma Lavenson; courtesy Bancroft Library.)

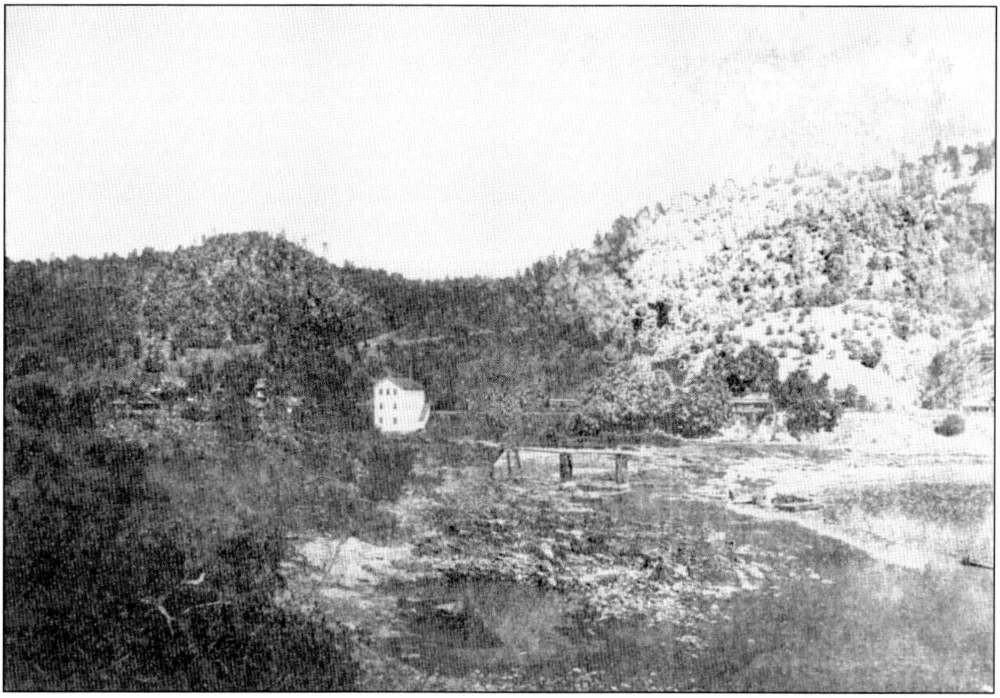

The Jacksonville Hotel stands proudly beside the river in 1900, before it was washed away in a flood. Residences are seen to the left, while the Eagle-Shawmut mine was downstream to the right, below the bridge. (Courtesy Jim Yeisley.)

Jacksonville, at the junction of Wood's Creek and the Tuolumne River at the south end of Tuolumne's Mother Lode belt, was one of the oldest towns in the Southern Mines. It was founded in the spring of 1849 by Col. Aldan Apollo Moore Jackson, who discovered gold and erected the first store that June to supply the demands of the miners whom he knew would soon stampede the diggings. Jacksonville became a small trading center for the river bars and camps, including Indian Bar, Red Mountain Bar, and Don Pedro Bar, named for Pierre "Don Pedro" Sansevain (right), an early pioneer of California who mined there (Courtesy Modesto Irrigation District).

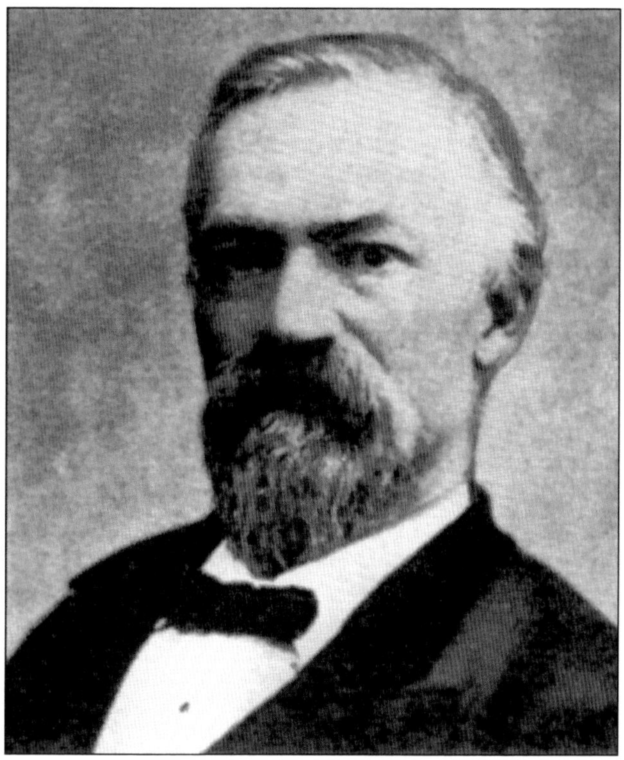

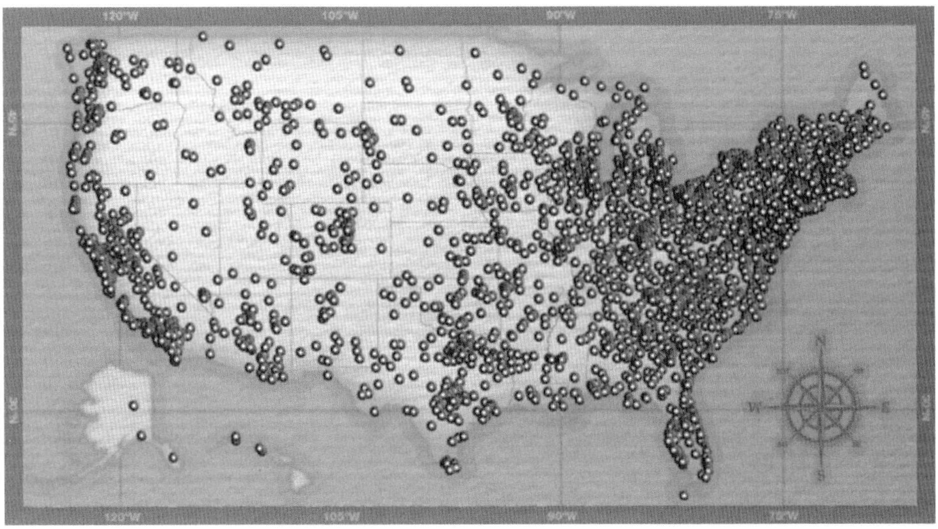